0 500 1000 1500 2000 kilometres

0 250 500 750 1000 1250 miles

R U S S I A N F E D E R A T I O N

Krasnoyarsk

Lake Baykal

Irkutsk

Amur

M O N G O L I A

Ulaanbaatar

Harbin

G O B I D E S E R T

Urumqi

Shenyang

NORTH KOREA

Beijing
Tianjin
Dalian
Pyongyang

TAKLAMAKAN DESERT

C H I N A

Huang He Yellow River

Taiyuan

Jinan

Seoul
SOUTH KOREA

Hotan

Lanzhou

Qingdao

Yellow Sea

Zhengzhou

Xi'an

Wuxi
Suzhou
Nanjing
Hangzhou
Shanghai

Chengdu

Chang Jiang Yangtze River

Wuhan
Chongqing
Nanchang
Yiwu
Wenzhou

East China Sea

Lhasa

Brahmaputra

Saluween

NEPAL

BHUTAN

Fuzhou
Quanzhou
Taipei

New Delhi

Kathmandu
Lucknow
Kanpur

Doklam
Thimphu

Kunming

Dongguan
Guangzhou
Xiamen
Shantou
Shenzhen

TAIWAN

Ganges
Yamuna

Dhaka

Hong Kong

Kolkata

I N D I A

BANGLADESH

MYANMAR

Irrawaddy

LAOS

Hanoi

Mekong

VIETNAM

South China Sea

Hyderabad

Bay of Bengal

Yangon (Rangoon)

Vientiane

THAILAND

Bangkok

CAMBODIA

Manila

PHILIPPINES

Chennai

Bangalore

Phnom Penh

Ho Chi Minh

Kochi

SRI LANKA

Colombo

Hambantota

BRUNEI
Bandar Seri Begawan

Cebu

Medan

M A L A Y S I A

Kuala Lumpur

Padang

Singapore

I N D O N E S I A

Indian Ocean

Pelembang

THE NEW SILK ROADS

BLOOMSBURY PUBLISHING
Bloomsbury Publishing Plc
50 Bedford Square, London, WC1B 3DP, UK

BLOOMSBURY, BLOOMSBURY PUBLISHING and the Diana logo are
trademarks of Bloomsbury Publishing Plc

First published in Great Britain 2018

A catalogue record for this book is available from the British Library

ISBN: HB: 978-1-5266-0742-3; TPB: 978-1-5266-0806-2;
HB Special Edition: 978-1-5266-1138-3; eBook: 978-1-5266-0743-0

4 6 8 10 9 7 5

Typeset by Newgen KnowledgeWorks Pvt. Ltd., Chennai, India
Printed and bound in Great Britain by CPI Group (UK) Ltd, Croydon CRO 4YY

To find out more about our authors and books visit www.bloomsbury.com
and sign up for our newsletters

THE NEW SILK ROADS

The Present and Future of
the World

PETER FRANKOPAN

BLOOMSBURY PUBLISHING
LONDON · OXFORD · NEW YORK · NEW DELHI · SYDNEY

To Louis Frankopan,
my glorious and beloved father
(1939–2018)

refine and improve their understanding of the past. This is what makes history such an invigorating and exciting subject: there is a thrill in being prompted to think about things in a different way, and also discover connections that link peoples, regions, ideas and themes together. The excitement of understanding how new discoveries, new tools and new techniques help illuminate the past is what made writing *The Silk Roads* such a joy in the first place.

This book is a sibling to the earlier one. Given how the world has changed in the last few years, I originally wanted to add a chapter to sharpen the conclusion and bring it up to date. I wanted to explain that however traumatic or comical political life appears to be in the age of Brexit, European politics or Trump, it is the countries of the Silk Roads that really matter in the twenty-first century. I wanted to show that the decisions being made in today's world that really matter are not being made in Paris, London, Berlin or Rome – as they were a hundred years ago – but in Beijing and Moscow, in Tehran and Riyadh, in Delhi and Islamabad, in Kabul and in Taliban-controlled areas of Afghanistan, in Ankara, Damascus and Jerusalem. I wanted to remind the reader that the world's past has been shaped by what happens along the Silk Roads. And I wanted to underline that so too will its future.

As I started to write, I realised that I wanted to say more than an epilogue could (and probably should) try to say. Rather, I thought that it was important to provide a detailed snapshot of contemporary affairs, but through a wide lens in the hope of providing context for what is going on around the world, and also to highlight some of the themes on which all our lives and livelihood depend. The Silk Roads lie at the heart of this picture – so central, in fact, that it is not possible to make sense of what today and tomorrow have in store without taking the region lying between the Eastern Mediterranean and the Pacific into account. This book is therefore intended to bring the story up to date and to interpret what has happened in the last few years at a time of profound transformation.

Since 2015, the world has changed dramatically. Life was becoming more difficult and more challenging for the west, I wrote at that time. It certainly seems that way following the Brexit vote and the uncertainty that surrounds the future of the European Union, which I discuss here. The United States too is on a new trajectory following the election of Donald Trump – one that is confusing to monitor and to assess. The problem is not so much the president's Twitter feed, which is a source of much mirth for commentators, but trying to understand if the White House wants to retreat from or reshape global affairs – and why. This too is discussed in this book.

Then there is Russia, where a new chapter of relations with the west has opened, despite the continued leadership of President Putin and an inner circle that has led the country for two decades. Military intervention in

Ukraine, alleged interference in elections in the US and the UK and accusations of the attempted assassination of a former intelligence officer have led to the worst moment in Russia's relations with the west since the fall of the Berlin Wall – and, as we shall see, have laid the basis for a reconfiguration of Moscow to the south and to the east.

In the heart of the world, the continued problems in Afghanistan, the breakdown of Syria as a result of years of civil war and the tortuous process of rebuilding Iraq fill few with confidence, despite the considerable financial, military and strategic expense that has gone into trying to improve the situation in each one. Antagonisms between Iran and Saudi Arabia and between India and Pakistan are rarely dampened down, with frequent angry recriminations threatening to develop into something more serious than words.

Times have been difficult in Turkey too, where a faltering economy and mass protests gave way to an attempted coup in 2016, when a faction in the armed forces tried to seize control. In the aftermath, tens of thousands of people were arrested and perhaps as many as 150,000 dismissed from their jobs because of their supposed links with the alleged mastermind, Fethullah Gülen. These include senior members of the judiciary, academics, teachers, police and journalists – as well as members of the military.[11] Pressure on prison space has become so acute as a result that in December 2017, the government announced that it would build an additional

228 prisons in the next five years – almost doubling the number of prison facilities in the country.[12]

*

And yet, all across Asia, these are also hopeful times. There is a strong sense of states trying to work more closely together and to elide their interests while putting differences behind them. As we shall see, a host of initiatives, organisations and forums have been established in recent years that aim to encourage collaboration, cooperation and discussion, and which provide a common narrative of solidarity and shared future.

This has been noted and acted on by those whose financial success depends on them identifying and setting trends. In 2015, for example, Nike introduced a new design to its range of trainers. The basketball player Kobe Bryant's experiences travelling in Italy and China established, 'connections to both the European and Asian continents', according to Nike, and the sports manufacturer's designers to think about 'the legendary Silk Road, the inspiration for the new KOBE X Silk shoe'.[13]

An ideal companion to these trainers is the Poivre Samarcande eau de toilette by Hermès, with its 'peppery, musky, slightly smoky scent of cut wood', where 'the soul of the old oak, mixed with pepper, lives on in this fragrance'. This too was inspired by the Silk Roads: 'the name Samarcande,' revealed master parfumier Jean-Claude

Ellena, 'is a homage to the city through which spice caravans once passed on their way from East to West.'[14]

Someone who was even quicker off the mark than Nike and Hermès to identify the potential of the Silk Roads was none other than Donald J. Trump, forty-fifth president of the United States, who in 2007 trademarked the Trump brand in Kazakhstan, Uzbekistan, Kyrgyzstan, Turkmenistan, Azerbaijan and Armenia with the intention of producing name-brand vodka. He did the same in 2012, seeking to trademark his name for hotels and real estate in all the countries lying across the spine of the Silk Roads – including Iran, a country he has tried to isolate since taking office in 2017. Trump also had dealings in Georgia, where plans were hatched to develop 'glitzy casinos', with the appropriately named Silk Road Group, which has subsequently become the focus of considerable media scrutiny.[15]

The Silk Roads are ubiquitous across Asia. There are, of course, the endless tourist companies that offer to reveal the glories of a mysterious past of the countries lying in the heart of the world that has been lost in the mists of time. But there are also many more up-to-date manifestations that show the power of the networks of the present and future as well as of the past. The Mega Silk Way shopping mall in Astana, Kazakhstan, provides one example, while the glossy *SilkRoad* inflight magazine aboard Cathay Pacific flights provides another. At Dubai airport, travellers are greeted by adverts for Standard Chartered Bank that declare: 'One Belt. One Road. One

Bank connects your business across Africa, Asia and Middle East.' Or there is gas-rich Turkmenistan nestled to the east of the Caspian Sea, where an official national slogan has been adopted for 2018: 'Turkmenistan – the Heart of the Great Silk Road.'[16]

One reason for the optimism across the heart of Asia is the immense natural resources of the region. For example, BP estimates that the Middle East, Russia and Central Asia account for almost 70 per cent of global total proven oil reserves, and nearly 65 per cent of proven natural gas reserves – a figure that does not include Turkmenistan, whose gas fields include Galkynysh, the second largest in the world.[17]

Or there is the agricultural wealth of the region that lies between the Mediterranean and the Pacific, where countries like Russia, Turkey, Ukraine, Kazakhstan, India, Pakistan and China account for more than half of all global wheat production – and, when added to countries of South East and East Asia like Myanmar, Vietnam, Thailand and Indonesia, account for nearly 85 per cent of global rice production.[18]

Then there are elements like silicon, which plays an important role in microelectronics and in the production of semiconductors, where Russia and China alone account for three-quarters of global production; or there are rare earths, like yttrium, dysprosium and terbium that are essential for everything from super-magnets to batteries, from actuators to laptops – of which China alone accounted for more than 80 per cent of global production in 2016.[19] While futurologists and networking pioneers often talk about how the exciting world of artificial intelligence, Big Earth Data and machine learning promise to change the way we live, work and think, few ever ask where the materials on which the digital new world come from – or what happens if supply either dries up or is used as a commercial or a political weapon by those who have a near-monopoly on global supply.

Other riches also abound that offer rewards to those who control them. These include heroin, which for more than a decade has been a vital financial resource for the Taliban in Afghanistan, who according to the United Nations long ago 'started to extract from the drug economy resources for arms, logistics, and militia pay'.[20] By 2015, a UN envoy reported, there were 'roughly 500,000 acres, or about 780 square miles, devoted to growing the opium poppy'. To put that in perspective, he added, 'that's equivalent to more than 400,000 US football fields – including the end zones'.[21] A hefty increase in the opium poppy cultivation in 2017 led to 800,000 acres producing opium – and a record harvest that accounts for 80 per cent of a global market that has a total value of more than $30 billion.[22]

Resources have always played a central role in shaping the world. The ability of states to provide food, water and energy for their citizens is obvious and important, as is providing protection from external threats. This makes control of the Silk Roads more important than ever, but also goes some way to explaining the pressure on human rights, press freedom and freedom of speech across all of Asia – something that has been noted recently by Andrew Gilmour, UN assistant secretary-general for human rights. 'Some governments feel threatened by any dissent,' he said, and label human rights concerns as 'illegal outside interference' in their internal affairs; or as an attempt to overthrow regimes; or to try to impose alien 'western' values. Decisions about whose voice should and whose should not be heard are closely linked to the consolidation and retention of power in a changing world and with fears about the consequences if alternative views are allowed to be expressed.[23]

We are living in the Asian century already, a time when the movement of global gross domestic product (GDP) from the developed economies of the west to those of the east is taking place on an astonishing scale – and at astonishing speed. Some projections anticipate that by 2050 the per capita income in Asia could rise sixfold in purchasing power parity (PPP) terms, making 3 billion additional Asians affluent by current standards. By nearly doubling its share of global GDP to 52 per cent, as one recent report put it, 'Asia would regain the dominant economic position it held some 300 years ago, before the Industrial Revolution.'[24] The transference of global economic power to Asia 'may occur somewhat more quickly or slowly', agreed another report, 'but the general direction of change and the historic nature of this shift is clear' – concluding similarly that we are living through a reversion to how the world looked before the rise of the west.[25]

The acute awareness of a new world being knitted together has helped prompt plans for the future that will capitalise on and accelerate the changing patterns of economic and political power. Chief among these is the 'Belt and Road Initiative', President Xi's signature economic and foreign policy, which uses the ancient Silk Roads – and their success – as a matrix for Chinese long-term plans for the future. Since the project was announced in 2013, nearly $1 trillion has been promised to infrastructure investments, mainly in the form of loans, to around 1,000 projects.

Some believe that the amount of money that will be ploughed into China's neighbours and countries that are part of the 'Belt and Road' over sea and land will eventually multiply several times over, to create an interlinked world of train lines, highways, deep-water ports and airports that will enable trade links to grow ever stronger and faster.

There are other challenges facing China too, not least what one leading economist has called a 'baby bust' that comes from a population that is getting older and not replacing itself.[26] Then there are the difficulties posed by the credit bubble, which is so large that the International Monetary Fund issued a warning in 2017 that debt levels were not so much a concern as 'dangerous'.[27]

But then there are other ways, too, of understanding what is going on in the world of today – and that of tomorrow. At the start of the twentieth century, Rudyard Kipling helped popularise the idea of a 'Great Game', where the British and Russian empires competed politically, diplomatically and militarily for position and dominance in the heart of Asia. Today, there is a series of 'Great Games' taking place, over competition for influence, for energy and natural resources, for food, water and clean air, for strategic position, even for data. The outcomes will have a profound effect on the world we live in in decades to come.

This book follows on from where *The Silk Roads* ended. The Silk Roads, I wrote in 2015, are rising. They have continued to do so. It is worth following carefully how and why this will affect us all.

The Roads to the East

Twenty-five years ago, when I was about to leave university, the world seemed a different place. The Cold War was over, leading to hopes for peace and prosperity. 'The heroic deeds of Boris Yeltsin and the Russian people' had steered Russia onto a course of reform and democracy, said President Bill Clinton at a meeting with the Russian president in Vancouver in 1993. The prospect of a 'newly productive and prosperous Russia' was good for everyone, he noted.[1]

Hopeful times lay ahead too in South Africa, where fraught negotiations to end apartheid had advanced sufficiently for the Nobel committee to award the Peace Prize for 1993 to F. W. de Klerk and Nelson Mandela for their 'their work for the peaceful termination of the apartheid regime, and for laying the foundations for a new democratic South Africa'.[2] The award of the prestigious prize was a moment of hope for South Africa, for Africa and for the world – even if it later emerged that many of Mandela's closest confidants urged him not to accept the prize if it meant having to share it with a man they referred to as 'his oppressor'. Mandela insisted, however, that forgiveness was a vital part of reconciliation.[3]

Things looked promising in the Korean peninsula, where, in an echo of the discussions that took place in 2018, an outline agreement was reached between the US and North Korea to great fanfare about the peaceful reunification of Korea and about a pathway for denuclearisation that was welcomed as a significant step forward for non-proliferation and also for a safer region and for a safer world.[4]

In 1993, an important agreement was also reached between China and India that established the framework for dealing with disputed border issues that had been a source of rivalry and bitterness for three decades – while both sides also agreed to reduce troop levels along the frontier and work together towards a conclusion that was mutually acceptable.[5] This was important for both countries at a time when economic expansion and liberalisation was at the forefront for their respective political leaders. In China, Deng Xiaoping had recently undertaken a tour of the southern provinces to press for faster reforms, and to deal with hardliners who opposed the liberalisation of markets that had seen the stock exchange open in communist China in Shanghai in 1990.[6]

South Korea's transformation was already well underway. In the 1960s, the country had been one of the poorest in the world, with no natural resources and an unpromising location at the eastern extremity of Asia. Its transformation into an economic superpower that is home to companies like Samsung, Hyundai Motor and Hanwha Corporation – each of which has more than $100bn in assets – has led some commentators to talk of South Korea as 'the most successful country in the world'.[7]

In India, as elsewhere, there was a push for growth in the early 1990s – although few expected much from a small software company that struggled to list its stock in Mumbai in February 1993. Despite its size and potential, India was an economic minnow and the technology sector was tiny and untested. Those who were brave and bought shares in Infosys Technologies did well if they held on to their stock. The company reported an operating profit for the year ended 31 March 2018 of over $2.6bn – on turnover of more than $10bn.[8] Shares were worth 4,000 times more than they had been twenty-five years earlier.[9]

The foundation of a new airline in a small Gulf State seemed like a long shot, too. Founded in November 1993, Qatar Airways began operating two months later in what many assumed would be a modest operation that handled a few local routes, for which demand would be minimal. Today, the airline has a fleet of over 200 aircraft, more than 40,000 staff and flies to over 150 destinations – winning armfuls of accolades that few would have thought possible two and a half decades ago.[10] It is also the largest shareholder in International Airlines Group (the owner of British Airways, Iberia and Aer Lingus) – as well as holding a 10 per cent stake in Cathay Pacific.[11] In April 2018, it agreed to buy 25 per cent of the shares of Moscow's Vnukovo international airport – the third largest in Russia.[12]

Of course, good news did not abound everywhere in 1993, as a truck bomb at the World Trade Center in New York and a coordinated series of bombings in Mumbai that killed more than 250 people showed. Sarajevo, a city already famous for the assassination of Franz Ferdinand and the road to war in 1914, was submitted to a siege by Bosnian Serb forces that lasted longer than the Battle of Stalingrad during the Second World War. Scenes of snipers shooting at civilians as they crossed the streets became commonplace, as did terrible images of the devastation caused by mortars being fired into the city from the neighbouring hills. The reappearance of concentration camps in Europe, and of genocide at Srebrenica and Gorazde in the mid-1990s provided a brutal reminder that even the most horrifying lessons from the past can be easily forgotten.

Some of the troubles of the early 1990s were more familiar. In Britain, for example, political discourse was shaped by poisonous debates about membership of the European Union and calls for a referendum. These almost brought down the government, and led to the prime minister, John Major, referring to members of his own cabinet as 'bastards'.[13]

*

These events are all in the recent past. And yet they now feel distant and seem to evoke a different age. I listened to an album called *Pablo Honey* by a promising new band called Radiohead as I prepared for my final exams in the summer of 1993. Little did I know that the most prophetic song of the year was not 'Creep' – which has gone on to have been streamed more than a quarter of a billion times on Spotify – but one that won at the Oscars that year. 'A whole new world,' Aladdin promised Jasmine, 'a new fantastic point of view.' Indeed, she agreed. 'A whole new world, a dazzling place I never knew.' A song based on a story from and set along the past of the Silk Roads foretold its future.

That whole new world can be seen nowhere more clearly than by comparing the game of football in England in 1993 and today. A week before Finals started in Cambridge, I watched a replay of the FA Cup final between Arsenal and Sheffield Wednesday, which was almost as dull and dour as the drawn first match. Of the players who featured in the match (including substitutes), all but three came from the British Isles. Twenty-five years later, the final between Chelsea and Manchester United was an equally underwhelming occasion – but the composition of the teams was radically different: just six of the twenty-seven who played at Wembley were born in the United Kingdom or Ireland. The others came from all over the world, including Spain, France, Nigeria and Ecuador.

If that tells a story about the pace of globalisation in the course of a generation, then perhaps even more striking is the dramatic change in the ownership of English football clubs over the same period. Not long ago, the idea that leading teams would have foreign owners would have been dismissed as the stuff of fantasy – at a time when even a foreign accent in the boardroom would have had club directors spluttering into their tea and choking on their pork pies at half-time. But today, many of the most famous names in English and European football have owners from abroad. And many come from the lands of the Silk Roads.

In some ways, that is not surprising. After all, although the game was codified in London in 1863, football was not invented in England. According to FIFA, the international body that governs the sport, football is first attested in Han-dynasty China (206 BC–AD 220), where a game that involved players kicking a leather ball filled with feathers into a net held up by two bamboo rods was known as *cuju*.[14]

Even so, it is a long way to go from the origins of the game to noting that all the great teams from in and around Birmingham – including Aston Villa, West Bromwich Albion, Birmingham City and Wolverhampton Wanderers – have been bought by

Chinese owners since *The Silk Roads* was published in 2015. In 2017, meanwhile, two of the giants of Italian football that share the magnificent San Siro stadium – AC and Inter Milan – were also sold to Chinese buyers.

Then there are the owners of England's – and Europe's – finest teams who come from the Gulf. Manchester City, who dominated all domestic competition to win the English Premier League in 2018 by a record margin, are owned by Mansour bin Zayed al Nayhan, who is also deputy prime minister of the United Arab Emirates. The team has a parallel in Paris Saint-Germain, who strolled to the French Ligue 1 title in the same year with equal ease, and whose Qatari owners were able to provide the team with two new players – Neymar and Kylian Mbappé – by signing them the previous summer for transfer fees that exceeded more than €350m (before salaries and bonuses).

Everton FC's majority owner is Farhad Moshiri, who was born in Iran but now lives in Monaco, who made his fortune working alongside Alisher Usmanov, a businessman from Uzbekistan, whose investments in Russia, Central Asia and elsewhere have made him worth more than $15bn – and enabled him to buy a significant stake in Arsenal Football Club. For a time, Usmanov wanted to buy control, but was thwarted by the complex shareholder structure. Arsenal fans had pleaded with him not to sell his shares before he finally disposed of them in the summer of 2018. But for years, the fate of a proud and famous football club hung on the decision of an Uzbek magnate.[15]

That of the Gunners' London rivals, Chelsea FC, rests with Roman Abramovich, who bought the Blues in 2003 and then spent more than $1bn turning the club into one of the best in the world – winning seventeen major domestic and international trophies in fifteen years. To these can be added any number of the most famous names in English football whose owners are from the rising east. Sheffield Wednesday – whose last brush with glory came with that losing final in 1993 – have owners from Thailand, while their perennial city rivals, Sheffield United, are half owned by a member of the Saudi royal family. Queens Park Rangers are owned by Tony Fernandes, the Malaysian entrepreneur, alongside Indian steel magnate Lakshmi Mittal. The list goes on and on.

Once upon a time, rich Englishmen would head to Europe as part of the Grand Tour, frolicking in cities like Venice, Naples, Florence and Rome, admiring and being inspired by their art and architecture, and with some buying up paintings, drawings, sculptures, manuscripts and even entire contents of houses to take home with them.[16] These were the spoils of the rising wealth and commercial and military success that turned a small island in the North Atlantic into a global super power. Now the trophies to show off are the World Cup football tournament, successfully bid for by Russia and Qatar, the Winter Olympics (held at Sochi in 2014) and magnificent art galleries – such as the new Louvre, located not in Paris but Abu Dhabi, or the new V&A museum that is not in London's Albertopolis but in Shenzhen. Then there is the stunning Rem Koolhaas-designed Garage Museum of Modern Art in Moscow, or the Winter Sports Complex in Ashgabat, Turkmenistan, a venue that is considerably bigger than Madison Square Garden.

In the eighteenth century, one British traveller set off on his journey to Italy 'being impatiently desirous of viewing a country so famous in history, which once gave laws to the world'.[17] Today that has changed, and now it is Britain's history that has come to be admired, its laws and its courts used to settle disputes and agree divorce settlements, and its trophies hunted and bought by the new great and good – such as football clubs or statement assets like world-famous flagship stores Harrods and Hamleys, Canary Wharf, 'the Walkie-Talkie' building at 20 Fenchurch Street in the City, or media outlets like the *Independent* and the *Evening Standard*, all of which have owners with Chinese, Russian or Emirati backgrounds.

It is the same story in the United States, where the Brooklyn Nets basketball franchise, the *New York Post*, the Waldorf Astoria and the Plaza Hotel in New York, and Warner Music are just some of the flagship businesses and brands that have been bought outright or as partnerships by investors both from and with close links to Russia, the Middle East and China.

These also include, as it happens, Legendary Entertainment, the Hollywood studio behind *Jurassic Park*, which was the box-office smash of the summer of 1993 – and one of the rewards I enjoyed after finishing my exams. That is now part of Wang Jianlin's Dalian Wanda Group Company – which also owns the Odeon, UCI, Carmike and Hoyts cinema chains in Europe, the US and Australia (with a total of more than 14,000 screens), as well as Sunseeker yachts and Infront Sports and Media – which holds the exclusive broadcast rights to sporting events that include the 2018 and 2022 football World Cup.

Naturally, while some of these businesses might qualify as hobbies and passions to be indulged, many represent serious as well as big-ticket investments. They are based on a great movement of global GDP over the last twenty-five years, with more than 800 million being lifted above the poverty line since the 1980s in China alone.[18] While the setting of what constitutes 'poverty' is a matter of debate for development economists and others, there can be little doubt that the pace as well as the extent of China's growth is astonishing. In 2001, China's GDP was 39 per cent of that of the US (on a purchasing power parity); that rose to 62 per cent by 2008. By 2016, China's GDP was 114 per cent that of the United States, measured on the same basis – and is likely to rise both further and sharply in the next five years.[19]

This change is not just transformational for China; it is transformational for the rest of the world. For example, in anticipation of the further rise of the Chinese middle class, one entrepreneur based in Beijing has bought 3,000 hectares of land in central France, with the aim of providing flour for a chain of more than a thousand *boulangeries* that he is planning to open across China. The expectation is that Chinese tastes will evolve from rice-based food – and that, when they do, 'the potential is immense', according to Hu Keqin, the owner in question.[20]

If that brings concerns in France about rising prices for bread, as flour is exported rather than being used in local *boulangeries*, then the same can be said for the wine industry – where exports to China rose by 14 per cent in 2017 alone to nearly 220 million litres. French wine exports to China are expected to be worth more than $20bn in five years' time, something that is better news for wine growers in France than for wine drinkers.[21]

What also irks is not just that many of the most famous vineyards in Bordeaux have changed hands in the last few years and been bought by famous personalities like the actress Zhao Wei or the tycoon Jack Ma (who owns four, including the celebrated Château de Sours), but some have also changed names in order to be more appealing to drinkers in China. Château Senilhac in Médoc has been renamed Chateau Antilope Tibetaine (Tibetan Antelope), Château La Tour Saint-Pierre has become Château Lapin d'Or (Golden Rabbit), while Château Clos Bel-Air is now Château Grande Antilope (Big Antelope).[22]

That might annoy purists who see proud names that have earned respect and fame over centuries being dropped, but the rise of the east has other effects that change what seem to be mundane elements of the world around us. Qatar Airways is just one of a large clutch of airlines whose operations have fuelled demand for commercial jets – demand that will only continue to rise. The International Air Transport Association (IATA) expects that the numbers of passengers travelling by plane will nearly double to 7.8 billion a year by 2036, with the growing and increasingly affluent populations of Asia, with China, India, Turkey and Thailand driving this increase.[23]

According to Boeing's separate analysis, that means 500,000 new pilots will be needed over the next twenty years.[24] But the consequences are being felt already: there are not enough pilots to go round as it is. This has pushed wages sky-high, with salaries of $400,000 being offered by Xiamen Air for Boeing 737 pilots – and offers as high as $750,000 a year being reported in some quarters.[25]

Salary inflation on this scale has obvious implications for the cost of travel. But the pressure caused by the shortage of pilots worldwide has already seen established and well-resourced operators cancelling flights as a result of staff shortages.[26] It might seem hard to believe, but when a plane gets cancelled on a business trip to the American Midwest, on the way back from a skiing holiday in the Alps, or before a dream holiday on the other side of the world, the rise of the Silk Roads will have something to do with it.

How that hotel room looks, what music is playing in the lobby and what drinks are available in the bar will also be influenced by the same factors. In 1990, the numbers of Chinese visitors to foreign countries were minimal, principally limited to state-related activities, spending around $500 million abroad in total.[27] By 2017, that figure had risen by 500 times to more than $250bn per year – roughly double what American travellers spend abroad annually.[28] These figures will rocket in the future, given that only around 5 per cent of Chinese citizens currently have passports. According to some estimates, 200 million Chinese will travel abroad in 2020, with research suggesting this will open up particularly rich opportunities in the gaming and cosmetics sectors, as well as boosting airlines flying to the right places, hotels that cater for Chinese tastes and online booking agents that arrange travel abroad – like Skyscanner, which was acquired by Chinese company Ctrip at the end of 2016 in a deal worth $1.7bn.[29]

The changing world also offers challenges – often in unexpected places and in unexpected ways. China's rise has presented extraordinary problems for donkeys and donkey breeders from Central Asia to West Africa. Donkey hides are an ingredient in *ejiao*, an alternative medicine popular in China that is purported to dull pain but also treat acne, prevent cancer and improve the libido. Demand for *ejiao* has led to a halving of the donkey population in China in the last twenty-five years and new sources of donkeys being identified elsewhere.[30] Rising demand has led to new sources of donkeys being identified elsewhere. Prices for donkeys has quadrupled in Tajikistan, and there have been sharp rises in Africa as well. This is not necessarily good news. Because donkeys are used as pack animals and play an important role in agricultural production and in bringing food to market, the sudden and sharp decrease in their numbers (and the rise in their price) has threatened to destabilise the agrarian economy in countries where the balance can often be precarious. For this reason, export bans of donkeys to China have been introduced in Niger, Burkina Faso and elsewhere in Africa.[31] One effect of the rise of the Silk Roads has been the emergence of a black market in donkey hides.[32]

Linking the trade in donkeys and the difficulties of first-time buyers in acquiring property in London may not seem an obvious step to make. Yet the amount of money that has been poured into Central London real estate has been a factor in driving prices up to the point of unaffordability. The surge of foreign capital between 1999 and 2014 played a role in increasing the prices of expensive homes, as well as producing a 'trickle-down' effect on less expensive properties. According to the workings of one scholar, prices would have been 19 per cent lower in the absence of the foreign investment that poured into the city in that period.[33]

A substantial amount of that came from Russia. Between 2007 and 2014, almost 10 per cent of all money spent on property in London was Russian – with that figure rising to more than 20 per cent on homes worth more than £10m.[34] Inflows of capital into overseas residential property markets from China have also been soaring, with Chinese citizens buying more than $50bn of homes abroad in 2016 and $40bn the following year.[35] This does not include capital that accounted for a third of all investment in London commercial real estate in 2017.[36]

It is a similar story elsewhere. Chinese buyers bought properties in Vancouver in such volume in 2016 that prices escalated at a rate of 30 per cent per month compared with the previous year, leading city authorities to introduce a 15 per cent tax on real estate bought by foreign buyers in an attempt to cool the market. Similar pressures can be found elsewhere in Canada – as well as in San Francisco, Australia, New Zealand, and now in South East Asia too.[37] Not being able to afford a home may not have its roots along the Silk Roads, but it is part of the narrative of a world that is moving its economic centre of gravity away from the west.

*

The rising wealth in the east is eye-opening in its scale. In February 2017, Mehrdad Safari, an Iranian businessman who had rented an apartment in a tower in Istanbul, enjoyed living there so much that he bought the entire block for $90m (excluding VAT). Once it was only Americans who liked something so much they bought the entire company – as Victor Kiam famously claimed about Remington, the electric razor business; now others have the inclination and the means to do so.[38]

The changing world means changing spending patterns and living habits at home as well as abroad. Pakistan is now the world's fastest-growing retail market, partly thanks to the fact that disposable income has doubled since 2010. The number of retail stores, which is forecast to rise by 50 per cent between 2017 and 2021, is also being driven by the two-thirds of the populace under the age of thirty – and by the changing attitude to money among the young, who want to enjoy a good lifestyle now rather than save to enjoy one later.[39]

In India the dramatic expansion of the middle class that has happened in the last three decades is continuing at an extraordinary pace. Although some economists note the highly uneven distribution of wealth in India, which has seen disproportionate gains going to the rich, the fact that the number of households in India with disposable incomes of more than $10,000 a year rose from 2 million in 1990 to 50 million by 2014 tells its own story.[40] This is just the start of a transformation that is seismic in scale and significance. Recent research estimates that consumer spending will treble in the next eight years before reaching $4tr by 2025. Such changes are affecting the way that people in India live: the traditional model of extended families cohabiting is being replaced by households of single people or couples, both with and without children. This naturally has an important impact on family life and presents challenges for the housing market and for infrastructure such as transport, electricity, water, health and education. But it also presents immense opportunities, not least since market research estimates that small households spend 20 to 30 per cent more per capita than joint families.[41]

These shifts are not lost on the luxury goods industry, where patterns of demand have changed beyond all recognition since the early 1990s. At that time, Chinese customers accounted for a negligible percentage of buyers of luxury goods. Now they account for a full third of the global total – and by 2025 will buy 44 per cent of all luxury goods.[42] This is one reason why Prada Group is opening seven stores in 2018 in just one city – Xi'an.[43] It also explains business decisions made by Chanel, for example, to buy a series of silk manufacturers in order to guarantee supply for their products, something that is not surprising given the brand's popularity in China and elsewhere around the world.[44]

These trends are clear too to Starbucks, the chain of coffee houses, which has set its sights on expansion in China. The scale of its ambitions shows just how big it believes the opportunities are in the world's most populous country at a time of change. In 2017, the company announced that it would open 2,000 stores in China by 2021 – or the equivalent of one new Starbucks coffee shop every fifteen hours.[45] China is a market that not only offers the prospect of lucrative returns; it is one that cannot be ignored.

It is a similar story in India, Pakistan, Russia or the Gulf – where customers in the United Arab Emirates alone spend almost $3bn a year on high-end cars. Getting things right in the east makes – and breaks – leading brands.[46] The same applies to almost every sector in the economy, including music and culture. For example, when the Chinese government dropped its One Child policy at the end of 2015, shares in companies that make prams, nappies and baby formula soared – while those of popular brands of condoms fell sharply.[47] A report by Credit Suisse suggested the surge in births would result in hundreds of billions of yuan being spent on retail goods related to babies, infants and children.[48] There are fortunes to be made by being in the right place at the right time as spending habits change – and consequences for failing to adapt or respond in the right way.

Winners and losers in the tourism sector in the future will be determined by which locations, hotels, facilities, menus and tourist attractions most appeal to the population of Asia, which currently stands at nearly 4.5 billion and is becoming more numerous – as well as richer.[49] To put this it into perspective, judging from World Bank and Organisation for Economic Cooperation and Development (OECD) data, not one of the ten fastest-growing economies of 2017 is located in the western hemisphere, nor has one been for the last decade.[50] Tastes, trends and appetites will be made in the east – and not in the west.

Changing aspirations, appetites and tastes will drive demand – as they always have done. But the speed of transformation is striking. A recent report by McKinsey & Company noted a shift in the way that Chinese consumers choose between products. In almost half the categories surveyed by the company, including food, electronics, personal care and beer, respondents expressed a clear preference for local brands over foreign peers.[51] Corporate fortunes and failures will be made in the east – and not in the west.

*

Economic and demographic growth provide one part of the picture of change. It is important, however, to recognise that both bring growing pains as well. Building infrastructure to support booming populations is logistically difficult, expensive to do and requires not just advance planning but a considerable degree of luck in being able to anticipate what the future will look like in terms of what energy, technology and transport needs might be.

Ironically, therefore, building smart cities from scratch can be easier than upgrading existing urban centres. In Bangalore, for example, difficulties caused by rapid urbanisation and the success of the city's IT sector has put an extraordinary strain on water resources. While the city's water board has prepared detailed proposals that they claim can not only improve supply for the current population of around 8 million but also a population that is forecast to more than double by

2050, some senior officials have spoken about the need to have a plan to evacuate the city before 'Day Zero' – the day that all taps run dry – which might come as early as 2025.[52]

Bangalore is an extreme case, but it is illustrative of the wider challenges facing urban growth as well as economic, demographic and even political stability in the future. The link between rapid urbanisation and radicalisation is one that is as familiar to historians of Russia in the early twentieth century as it is to those working on Turkey in the 1970s.[53] Not surprisingly, it is also a subject of considerable interest to scholars working on the world of today and tomorrow.[54] A recent UN report on cities did not pull its punches. 'Many cities all over the world,' it states, 'are grossly unprepared for the multi-dimensional challenges associated with urbanisation.'[55]

Peace and stability are not to be taken for granted – as even the most cursory look at Syria, Iraq, Yemen and Afghanistan show. The limited development of democratic traditions, the diffusion of power and wealth from small elites and the emergence of professional middle classes means that across Asia there is a series of powerful leaders – and obvious fragilities too that can mean states fail quickly and dramatically.

Those who do try to adapt find that it is not always easy to manage change. A series of reforms announced in Saudi Arabia at the end of 2017, which included opening the first cinemas in forty-four years, allowing women into a sports stadium and issuing driving

36

permits for women, was greeted as a sign of progress in a country long derided for the lack of any form of gender equality.

The hopes and expectations, however, were quickly tempered by the arrest of ten of the country's most prominent activists, mostly women. The fact that they were denounced in the Saudi press first as 'traitors' who have 'no place among us', and by the Ministry of the Interior as being members of a 'spy cell', who had had 'suspicious communication with foreign entities with the aim of undermining the country's stability and social fabric', was a classic case of one step forward and at least two steps back.[56]

The difficulty of championing progress while practising repression is nowhere better shown than by the fact that on the same day that the foreign minister of the United Arab Emirates, Abdullah bin Zayed Al Nahyan, wrote a passionate column for the leading Canadian daily the *Globe and Mail*, arguing that it was vital that women be empowered across the Middle East and warning that momentum 'needs to be protected from powerful forces in the region that still resist change' and 'push back against women's rights', it was announced that one of the most prominent human rights activists in the UAE had been sentenced to ten years in prison – and heavily fined for insulting the 'status and prestige of the UAE and its symbols'.[57]

Unregulated, accelerated change has proved unnerving to others in different ways. In China, for example, concern over city development led the highest body in the country, the State Council, to issue guidelines to tighten up planning rules and ordering a greater emphasis on promoting 'construction techniques that generate less waste and use fewer resources, such as the use of prefabricated buildings'. That seems laudable enough. More eccentric, however, was the fact that the clampdown was also used to issue a stern line about strange-looking buildings, with a ban issued on 'bizarre architecture that is not economical, functional, aesthetically pleasing or environmentally friendly'. To ensure compliance, remote satellite sensing will be used 'to locate buildings that violate existing urban-planning policies'. Drones flying overhead will not just be watching who you talk to, or where you are in other words, but also what you might choose to do with your chimney pots or patio extension.[58]

A new world is coming, one that seems unfamiliar to most but also in turns exotic and worrying. It is perhaps hard to believe that one of the most vibrant centres for tech start-ups in the world today is Iran, where one unexpected side effect of being distanced from western competition has been a surge in new businesses and incubators for start-up companies, like Sarava, that help fledgling concepts off the ground.[59] Among those selected to appear at the appropriately named Silk Road Startup in Kish in the spring of 2018 were a marketplace for water-friendly food and agriculture products, an eco-friendly and online fashion marketplace for women to buy and sell pre-owned wearables, and a handheld device that measures the level of blood glucose with infrared spectroscopy and artificial intelligence.[60]

Such successes do not scratch the surface of what is going on India and China, whose adoption rates of new financial technologies (FinTech) for money transfers and payments, savings and investments and borrowing are far higher than any other country in the world – including the US.[61] In both countries, the scope for growth seems to be almost limitless. Ant Financial, hived off from the e-commerce giant Alibaba before the latter floated in the world's largest initial public offering (or IPO) in history in 2014, is itself preparing to undertake a fundraising round that will value the cashless payment business at a jaw-dropping $150bn.[62] This makes the valuation of India's Paytm (in which Alibaba is a shareholder) of just $10bn look conservative – not bad for a company only founded a few months before Prince William and Kate Middleton got engaged in autumn 2010.[63]

This all sounds impressive – because it is. But the success of new businesses should not mask the fact that in most sectors and most industries, the west still leads the way. That is not lost on Vladimir Putin, who has directed Russian state institutions to switch to domestic technology as a means to cut imports – though few expect this order to bear meaningful fruit, given how underfunded research and development have been in the past, and how limited a role entrepreneurs and businesses play in investing in innovation.[64]

Nevertheless, Russia's awareness of the need to develop its own capabilities is a key theme in Moscow's thinking. Significant resources have been spent on developing cyber-technologies. At confirmation hearings to the position of Commander, US Cyber Command and Director of the National Security Agency, Lt General Paul Nakasone noted that Kremlin is the 'most technically advanced potential adversary' that the US faces, capable of using sophisticated tactics, techniques and procedures against 'US and foreign military, diplomatic and commercial targets'.[65]

As well as developing tools to use against foreign and domestic targets, Russia has also been working on improving its own defences to protect from attacks from outside.[66] That might seem ironic given Russia's own use of cyber technology in everything from presidential elections, to the Brexit campaign in the UK, to ransoming businesses and the theft of intellectual property. Indeed, in April 2018, the US Department of Homeland Security, the FBI and the United Kingdom's National Cyber Security Centre issued a formal alert about Russian state-sponsored attempts to target hardware that controls internet traffic.[67] Nevertheless, like other countries, Russia has experience of having to deal with ransomware and with hacks on its banking system, mobile telephony and government agencies, which it is keen to avoid or prevent in the future.[68]

In the west, one of the most important contemporary questions concerns the monetisation of data – and about the legality and ethics of corporations like Facebook gathering and deploying information about users and even about users' friends and contacts who are not on social networks. In the east, the issue is about the weaponisation of data and the relationship between the digital world and state interests, perceived or otherwise.

In Russia, for example, Facebook was told that if the personal data of those who used the business were not stored on Russian servers, access to the site would be blocked.[69] Not only that, but it recently emerged that Facebook had also been allowing Russia's largest technology corporation, Mail.Ru Group, to have access to personal user data. 'We have a responsibility to protect your data,' wrote Mark Zuckerberg in a Facebook post – while not admitting that his company had been sharing it with a company with deep and close links with the Kremlin, a fact that emerged only later.[70]

Russia's way of monitoring the digital activities of its own citizens and, presumably, those of others too, lay behind the blocking of the encrypted Telegram messaging service, as well as virtual private networks (VPNs) that enable the bypassing or concealment of localisation services.[71] In Turkey, meanwhile, regular state interference with social media sites is coupled with government actions that purport to prevent 'abnormal' messages on the day of presidential elections.[72]

Then there is China, where the three largest telecoms companies – China Mobile, China Unicom and China

Telecom – are state-owned, where the government has taken steps to block VPNs as part of an internet 'clean-up', and where access to sites like Google, Facebook and Twitter is blocked.[73] In one part of the world, monitoring what citizens routinely do online is used to drive corporate revenues; in another it is considered a matter of national security.

Not in US too! Stupid!

This is about more than just noting different approaches to the same question. In fact, it is closely linked to the wider changes that have been taking place over the last twenty-five years. We are living through a transformation and a shift that is epochal in its scale and character, similar to what happened in the decades that followed the crossing of the Atlantic by Columbus and those who soon followed him, and the near-simultaneous rounding of the southern tip of Africa by Vasco da Gama that opened up new maritime trade routes between Europe, the Indian Ocean, South Asia and beyond. Those twin expeditions, just over 500 years ago, laid the ground for a dramatic shift in the world's centre of economic and political gravity, placing western Europe at the heart of global trade routes for the first time in history.[74]

Something similar is happening today, albeit in reverse. Asia and the Silk Roads are rising – and they are rising fast. They are not doing so in isolation from the west, nor even in competition with it. In fact, quite the opposite: Asia's rise is closely linked with the developed economies of the United States, Europe and beyond. The demand and needs for resources, goods, services and skills in the latter have stimulated growth in the former, creating jobs and opportunities and serving as a catalyst for change. The success of one part of the world is connected to that of the other – rather than coming at its expense. The sun rising in the east does not mean that it is setting on the west. Not yet, at least.

What is striking, however, are the reactions to change in east and west. In one, there is hope and optimism about what tomorrow will bring, while in the other anxiety that is so acute that countries are more and more divided, to the point that some senior politicians like Madeleine Albright, formerly US Secretary of State, have openly questioned whether 'the democratic banner can remain aloft' in the west amid the 'storm clouds that have gathered' – and warned that we should be vigilant of the lessons of history in order to prevent the return of fascism.[75]

Some might consider such alarm as overstated. But the fact that comments like these are being aired in the mainstream media is itself revealing of the crisis of confidence and the concern about the direction of travel in the west in a time of change. Whatever one's own political persuasion and views, it is not hard to see that something important is happening in the world.

'It's crystal clear,' Aladdin sang to Princess Jasmine twenty-five years ago, 'that now I'm in a whole new world with you.' It is worthwhile trying to understand what that is – and to consider the implications and consequences.

The Roads to the Heart of the World

Events of recent years make it hard to argue with the assesssment that the age of the west is at a crossroads. In the United States, Donald Trump was elected president after campaigning to 'Make America Great Again'. It was essential that the US change direction, he had said repeatedly during the election campaign. The very future of the country hung by a thread. 'Either we win this election,' he told voters in Colorado Springs three weeks before polling day, 'or we lose the country.'[1]

The US was in freefall, he said time and again during the campaign. Desperate measures were needed to save the country, Trump declared when announcing his candidacy in the summer of 2015. 'Our country is in serious trouble,' he said. 'We don't have victories any more. We used to have victories, but we don't have them.' Other countries had grown rich at America's expense. 'When did we beat Japan at anything?' he asked. 'They send their cars over by the millions, and what do we do? When was the last time you saw a Chevrolet in Tokyo? It doesn't exist, folks. They beat us all the time.'

Mexico was a problem, too. 'When Mexico sends its people, they're not sending their best,' he declared. 'They're sending people that have lots of problems, and they're bringing those problems with us. They're bringing drugs. They're bringing crime. They're rapists. And some, I assume, are good people.' China was a problem, too. 'When was the last time anybody saw us beating ... China in a trade deal? They kill us. I beat China all the time. All the time.' Engagements overseas, meanwhile, had been costly and achieved nothing. 'We spent $2 trillion in Iraq, $2 trillion. We lost thousands of lives, thousands in Iraq. We have wounded soldiers, who I love, I love – they're great – all over the place, thousands and thousands of wounded soldiers.'[2]

It was time for dramatic action – or the US was doomed. 'I would bring back waterboarding,' Trump said in one televised debate with Republican rivals, 'and I'd bring back a hell of a lot worse than waterboarding.'[3] Then there were the infamous plans to build a wall with Mexico that Trump promised would be 'an impenetrable, physical, tall, powerful, beautiful, southern border wall'. The Mexicans 'are great people and great leaders', he said. 'They don't know it yet, but they're going to pay for it.'[4] Former Mexican president Vincente Fox was incandescent: 'We are not, I am not going to pay for that fucking wall,' he told television reporters. 'And I am not going to apologise' for swearing, he added defiantly.[5]

Action was needed against China too, Trump repeatedly said. 'We can't continue to allow China to rape our country and that's what they're doing.'[6] The Chinese 'have taken advantage of us like nobody in history', Trump told ABC's *Good Morning America*. 'They have; it's the greatest theft in the history of the world what they've done to the United States. They've taken our jobs.'[7] It was black and white. 'There are people who wish I wouldn't refer to China as our enemy', Trump wrote in a book that was designed to serve as his presidential manifesto. 'But that's exactly what they are.'[8]

The US was on its knees. 'This American carnage stops right here and stops right now ... From this day forward, a new vision will govern,' Trump stated at his inauguration in January 2017. 'It's going to be only America first, America first.'[9] The mantra of 'America First' – a slogan with deep roots to the inter-war period and long-standing isolationist views that the US should stay out of international affairs, as well as to the Ku Klux Klan and to anti-Semitic views – infused the White House. Indeed, the first budget Trump presented to Congress in the spring of 2017 was simply entitled 'America First. A Budget Blueprint to Make America Great Again'.[10]

As he had promised during the election, Trump promptly set about pulling out of multiple agreements that the previous administration had signed up to, detaching the United States from the international mainstream in the process. This included signing an order to 'permanently withdraw' from the Trans-Pacific Partnership on his first day in office, promising that this was a necessary step if he was to 'promote American industry, protect American workers, and raise American wages'.[11]

Then there was the Paris Climate Accord, which Trump described as 'simply the latest example of Washington entering into an agreement that disadvantages the United States to the exclusive benefit of other countries, leaving American workers – who I love – and taxpayers to absorb the cost in terms of lost jobs, lower wages, shuttered factories, and vastly diminished economic production'. As a result, he announced in June 2017, the United States 'will cease all implementation' of the Accord with immediate effect and thereby avoid the 'draconian financial and economic burdens the agreement imposes on our country'.[12]

In addition to these withdrawals were steps such as issuing an executive order banning all nationals from Iraq, Syria, Iran, Libya, Somalia, Sudan and Yemen from travelling to the US;[13] instructions to cancel 'the last administration's completely one-sided deal' with Cuba ('effective immediately');[14] and steps – the 'first of many' – to impose tariffs on more than a thousand products that would eventually affect some $50–60bn of imports from China.[15]

These dramatic switches of direction point to a world that is changing fast and where political leaders – and voters – are both demanding and choosing sharp changes of course. Europe has seen the rise of the far right, with Marine Le Pen of the National Front (FN) contesting the French presidential election as one of the two highest-ranked candidates in the preliminary round in mid-2017; in Germany, the Alternative für Deutschland (AfD) not only won its first ever seats in the Bundestag elections in September of the same year but became the third largest party in the process – with ninety-four MPs elected to parliament.

Frictions in Europe centre on questions about immigration and national identities. But they are fuelled by the fear – real or imagined – that radical action is needed either to slow down change or to reverse it. In Hungary, barbed-wire fencing has been constructed along the border with Croatia and Serbia, while the failure to ensure the independence of the judiciary and freedom of expression, and the growing lack of protection for minorities, has led to calls in the European Parliament for sanctions to be imposed by the EU on one of its own members – so dramatic is the 'clear breach ... of the values on which the Union is founded'.[16]

This followed calls to punish Poland over similar concerns about the rejection of liberal values that were so intense that, in December 2017, the EU deployed Article 7 of the Lisbon Treaty, obliging Warsaw to reverse judicial reforms. 'We have a dispute with the Polish government,' said Jean-Claude Juncker, the President of the European Commission; at least, he added reassuringly, 'we are not at war'.[17]

The stresses and tensions within Europe, the difficulties of member states to see eye to eye about major internal issues and the failure to deal effectively with arrivals of refugees and economic migrants from outside Europe have put an enormous strain on the ideals and integrity of the European Union itself. The EU seems to have 'serious problems with its founding principles', declared Italy's Deputy Prime Minister, Luigi di Maio, in the summer of 2018. Perhaps the time has come, he said, to no longer make contributions to the European Union's annual budget.[18]

The breakdown in confidence was epitomised, however, by the referendum campaign held in Britain in the summer of 2016, when 52 per cent of those who voted chose to recommend leaving the EU – even though the process and consequences of doing so remained not so much obtuse as unknown. Most people in Britain were 'suffering because of our membership of the EU', Michael Gove, then secretary of state for justice, stated baldly in a televised interview shortly before the referendum, offering no evidence to support his claim.[19] The European Union, he had said previously, had 'proved a failure on so many fronts' – and was not only holding Britain back, but doing so to all its members. By leaving, he claimed, 'we can show the rest of Europe the way to flourish'.[20]

50

In the build-up to the referendum, the European Union was presented as being part of the problem, not part of the solution for Britain's future. The EU, said Boris Johnson, was 'a job-destroyer engine', that did deep damage to the British economy.[21] The customs union between all the members of the EU was a 'complete sell-out of Britain's national interests', said another prominent proponent of Brexit; 'luckily', however, noted yet another senior politician, Britain has 'old friendships' with other countries that could be rekindled and with whom better trade agreements could be reached – countries, as it so happened, that had almost all once been British colonies.[22] To advance into the future meant looking to the past.

*

Whatever the long-term significance of Brexit turns out to be, the fact is that across many parts of the developed world in the west, politicians, voters and governments are taking steps to diminish cooperation with each other, to disengage from agreements that were made in the past and which now appear to be unwanted, imperfect and, indeed, counterproductive. The hopeful optimism of working towards common interests and mutual benefits has given way to suspicion and distrust and, more importantly, towards action designed to allow each to go their own way. Theresa May used her first visit to a G20 summit as prime minister in the autumn of 2016 to inform the startled heads of the world's most powerful countries that Britain would become 'the global leader in free trade' – an aspiration not lacking ambition or nerve in the circumstances: it is hard to offer to lead others when one's own house is in an obvious state of chaos.[23]

The relentless focus on the White House, on Brexit and on the day's latest breaking news in the familiar corridors of power in the west means there is limited focus on what is going on elsewhere in the world. This blindness is particularly strong when it comes to large-scale developments that have regional, and indeed trans-continental consequences. Following the same stories and same personalities comes at the cost of being able to see the big picture.

*

The themes of isolation and fragmentation in the west stand in sharp contrast to what has been happening along the Silk Roads since 2015. The story across large parts of the region linking the Pacific through to the Mediterranean has been about consolidation and trying to find ways to collaborate more effectively; the trend has been about defusing tensions and of building alliances; the discussions have been about solutions that are mutually beneficial and provide the platform for long-term cooperation and collaboration.

These have been facilitated by multiple institutions that both enable dialogue and take practical steps to deepen ties between states – multilateral financial institutions such as the Asian Development Bank and the new Asian Infrastructure Investment Bank, but also groups like the Shanghai Cooperation Organisation, the Eurasian Economic Union, the BRICS summits, the Trans-Pacific Partnership (albeit without US participation) and the Regional Comprehensive Economic Partnership – the last of which includes countries from South East Asia along with China, India, South Korea, Japan, Australia and New Zealand. Together, these have a combined GDP of almost $30tr – or 30 per cent of global GDP – and represent 3.5 billion people. Negotiations to create a 'modern, comprehensive, high-quality and mutually beneficial economic partnership agreement' have intensified, raising the prospect of what one economist has called the largest free trade deal in history.[24]

Not surprisingly, progress towards collaboration has not been uniform across Asia and beyond. Nor would it be fair to make light of a series of very significant hurdles, antagonisms and rivalries between peoples and individuals that have the potential to be so destabilising as to have a regional and in some cases a global impact. Nevertheless, it is striking that the world is spinning in two different directions: de-coupling and going it alone in one, and deepening ties and trying to work together in another.

Many of the resource-rich states in Central Asia, for example, have been exploring ways of working together practically and with some effect. In March 2017 the presidents of Turkmenistan and Uzbekistan inaugurated a new railway bridge across the Amu Darya River at Turkmenabat–Farab – an important intersection that will help improve connections not only between the two countries but open possibilities for long-distance trade too.[25] Then there is the cooperation by Central Asian republics with initiatives such as those intended to help Tajikistan reinforce its southern border with Afghanistan, including an operation aimed at blocking drug smuggling, or the opening up of new checkpoints in the second half of 2017 in Osh, Batken and Jalal-Abad districts in Kyrgyzstan to make crossing the border to Uzbekistan easier and quicker.[26]

Improving relations boosts exchanges. For example, bilateral trade between Kazakhstan and Uzbekistan increased by 31.2 per cent in 2017 alone, while new initiatives aim to increase this further still in the coming years.[27] Whether the declaration in Kazakhstan that 2018 will be the Year of Uzbekistan and the reciprocal nomination of 2019 in Uzbekistan as the Year of Kazakhstan will make a material difference remains to be seen.[28] Statements about 'two fraternal people … marching side by side on the path of economic development' and seeking mutual advancement based on 'eternal friendship and strategic partnership' help create a common narrative that talks of mutual interests, common pasts and a joint future.[29]

It is a similar story elsewhere. The turnover of trade between Uzbekistan and Tajikistan doubled in the first six months of 2018 compared to the same period the year before.[30] In Iran and Azerbaijan, meanwhile, 'all necessary preparations have been made for cooperation in strategic projects such as in the energy sector', according to Mahmoud Vaezi, chief of staff to the President of Iran, following a meeting in Baku in the early summer of 2018.[31]

Agreements concerning academic cooperation as well as those relating to pipeline construction have heralded a period of closer ties between Afghanistan and Tajikistan in the years ahead.[32] More important is the Trans-Anatolian Pipeline (TANAP), which became operational in June 2018, that links the Shah Deniz II gas field in Azerbaijan with south-eastern Europe – even if some argue that its long-term role in the energy supply for Europe as a whole may be limited in the medium term.[33]

TANAP is just one of many similar projects at various stages of development that connect to resource-rich countries lying in the centre of Asia. Another is the Central Asia–South Asia power project (CASA-1000), which will transmit surplus energy generated from hydroelectric power plants in Tajikistan and Kyrgyzstan to Pakistan and Afghanistan by 2020.[34] Such is the strengthening of ties that the Kyrgyz ambassador to Pakistan, Erik Beishembiev, recently talked about improving bilateral links between the governments in Bishkek and Islamabad, because the two countries 'have historical roots, common religion, similar traditions and worldview on many issues'.[35]

Shared mutual interests have also underpinned talks between Russia and the other members of the Eurasian Economic Union (Kazakhstan, Kyrgyzstan, Armenia and Belarus) with Iran about the creation of a free-trade zone, joint investments and interbank agreements – a key stumbling block – that would be mutually beneficial, but also important, according to Vyacheslav Volodin, Speaker of the Russian Duma.[36]

This is part of a wider consolidation in Central Asia in which Russia and Iran also play a key role. Increasing trade, improving relations and working to cut down cross-border smuggling are not just theoretical priorities but are being actively worked on and developed through institutional reforms and through the establishment of bodies to oversee and coordinate areas of obvious mutual interest. These serve as sign parts of a desire to strengthen ties and improve political ties, too.[37]

A typical example of the way in which the heart of the world is being knitted together comes from a conference held in Samarkand in November 2017 where senior officials from the Central Asian Republics, as well as from Afghanistan, Russia, China, Turkey, Iran, India and Pakistan, met to discuss ways of working together to deal with terrorism, religious extremism, transnational organised crime and drug trafficking – under the theme 'Central Asia: one past and a common future, cooperation for sustainable development and mutual prosperity'.[38]

Of course, such conferences – and frothy statements about the solidarity of peoples living along the Silk Roads – can flatter to deceive and are expressions of goodwill as much as an attempt to resolve substantive issues. In the case of Central Asia, however, there has been progress with the thorny issue of border disputes, where historical and ethnic tensions have often soured relations to the point where some observers have warned of the potential for military conflict.[39] These too have started to be settled. Perhaps the most significant step in the consolidation in the heart of the world is an agreement over the legal status of the Caspian Sea, an issue that has been a stumbling block for large-scale co-operation between Russia, Iran, Turkmenistan, Kazakhstan and Azerbaijan – especially in the energy sector. Striking outline terms that are mutually acceptable to all sides has taken decades; but the landmark agreement may well serve to transform oil and gas supplies not just across the region but for markets all around the world, so great are the hydrocarbon resources of the Caspian littoral countries and of the Caspian itself.[40] However, as some observers point out, although the agreement signed in August 2018 is clearly an important step forward, much remains unresolved and it is by no means certain when, if or how all the issues that were not addressed will finally be dealt with.[41]

The agreements that were reached were nevertheless the latest in a series of steps forward that have started removing obstacles and improved long-term prospects for cooperation across the spine of Asia. One example comes with discussions about a possible land swap between Kyrgyzstan and Uzbekistan as part of the process of agreeing the border between the two countries.[42] Another example comes with a meeting held in Astana in April 2018 that enabled Kazakhstan, Uzbekistan and Turkmenistan to sign off on an agreed set of frontiers. 'There are no unresolved border issues,' announced President Nazarbayev of Kazakhstan, while noting, along with his counterpart, President Rahmon of Tajikistan, a renewed commitment to cooperate closely on the question of water resources in the region.[43]

The issue of water is one of the most significant across Central Asia – starkly illustrated by the near-disappearance of the Aral Sea since the 1960s, when the rivers that fed it were diverted to support misguided Soviet agricultural initiatives. The tensions and practical difficulties this caused are hard to underestimate, in terms of the devastation of the physical landscape, environmental pollution as well as public-health issues that range from respiratory diseases and cancer to infant mortality rates.[44]

At the end of May 2018, storms blew salt from the now dried-up sea floor and enveloped parts of Uzbekistan and Turkmenistan, covering wheat and cotton fields with as much as a centimetre of salt – at a time when water shortages had already resulted in crop failures in the season.[45] The fact that efforts to restore water levels appear to be having an effect, albeit slowly, is therefore welcome news indeed.[46]

This does not help Afghanistan, though, where a precipitation deficit of 70 per cent led to the United Nations issuing a warning in June 2018 that harvests had failed, rivers had dried up and 2 million people were expected to become food insecure by the end of the year – a catastrophic humanitarian crisis in the making in a country that has been ravaged by almost non-stop war for four decades.[47] 'I would do anything to save my son from hunger,' one farmer said. 'I would join Daesh or the Taliban.'[48]

Part of the problem is that the three major rivers in Central Asia – the Syr Darya, Amu Darya and Irtysh – are transboundary waterways, which means that decisions in one country have an impact on what happens downstream. The significance of this can be shown by noting that about 70 per cent of developmental problems in the region are caused by freshwater shortages.[49] As a result, finding a way to resolve water management in the optimum fashion has, not surprisingly, been a matter of particular interest and concern for some time.[50]

Water is also a problem in South Asia, where India's construction of the Kishanganga dam and hydroelectric plant has been a source of great concern for the government of Pakistan, who argue that these projects violate the treaty of 1960 that split the water resources of the Indus River between Pakistan and India. Anxieties about the dam, which was formally opened in May

2018, have been heightened by proposals to build as many as twelve hydroelectric plants on the River Kabul in Afghanistan – which would put further pressure on the resources of cities like Karachi, whose population is growing at more than 5 per cent per year and whose water board is only able to supply 50 per cent of its needs as it is.[51] Not surprisingly, the Kishanganga dam has been referred to the International Court for Arbitration, and, perhaps equally unsurprisingly, the dispute has resulted in recriminations, soul-searching and suspicions of sabotage and conspiracy in the press in both India and Pakistan.[52]

Then there is the impact of climate change, which according to recent research will cause the Urumqi Glacier No 1 to lose some 80% of its ice volume in the next three decades – which will have obvious implications for Central Asia as well as for western China, where this and other glaciers play an important role in providing water for rivers but also as standby resources in times of drought.[53]

The problems posed by water shortages can be illustrated by the protests that broke out in Iran in the spring of 2018. With the Islamic Republic of Iran Meteorological Organization estimating that 97 per cent of the country is experiencing drought to some degree, entire towns and villages have been abandoned by their population. Shortages led to riots, which were strongly repressed by security forces in some parts of the country.[54] The situation was so acute that Iran's

Supreme Leader, Ayatollah Khamenei, mentioned it in his Nowruz (New Year) address, acknowledging that the dry conditions had brought hardship, and praying that 'divine grace' would resolve the problem shortly.[55]

In addition to the prayers, Iran has also taken more constructive steps to resolve the water conditions, which are so dire that some of the country's energy supply has been affected by hydroelectric plants that have stopped working properly.[56] Discussions with neighbouring Afghanistan have intensified recently about restoring the flow of the Helmand River and the supply of water to the Hamoon wetlands. According to Iran's foreign minister, Mohammad Javad Zarif, an agreement has been reached that will result in 850 million cubic metres of water a year flowing into Iran in the future.[57]

*

Progress has been made elsewhere to move beyond framework agreements that have been signed in the past but were then held back by the lack of political goodwill between states – and their leaders – which often perceived and treated each other as rivals. The death of President Karimov of Uzbekistan in 2016 and his replacement by Shavkat Mirziyoyev has helped break the stalemate and brought about new opportunities for discussion and action. 'Problems of water, peace and security are inextricably linked,' Mirziyoyev told the General Assembly at the United Nations in New York in

September 2017. 'There is no alternative to addressing the water problem other than equally taking into account the interests of the countries and nations of the region.'[58]

The new administration of Mirziyoyev has blown other winds of change into Uzbekistan, including steps towards long-hoped-for improvements on human rights, press freedoms and other indices where the country – like many of its neighbours – has traditionally scored very poorly.[59] For the first time since the fall of the Soviet Union, for example, there were no journalists behind bars as of May 2018, when a judge released two men who had been accused of writing articles that were critical of the government and plotting its overthrow.[60]

According to a report by US-based Freedom House in the autumn of 2017, subjects that were previously taboo in public, such as 'failing currency-exchange policies' and 'the large number of Uzbek labour migrants in Russia' are now discussed openly, while 'a slight opening for civic activism' was also noteworthy, alongside a relaxing of the hard-line attitudes towards religious freedom.[61]

That improvements such as these have caught the attention of mainstream media outlets on the other side of the world shows just how significant the transformation may turn out to be. Indeed, within less than a fortnight the *New York Times* carried two major features on the positive changes in Uzbekistan and heralded the dawn of a new era of openness.[62] Others have been more circumspect. While welcoming the steps taken to improve human rights, a joint statement by a group of twelve non-governmental organisations (NGOs) pointed out that 'internet censorship, politically motivated imprisonment, torture, a lack of competitive electoral processes, and a lack of justice for serious past abuses remain to be addressed'.[63] Whether the reforms are real, or a case of window-dressing, is still not clear. Some experts are prepared to concede positive steps have been taken but remain unconvinced that a decisive corner has been turned.[64]

More is going on, however, beyond eye-catching headlines, speeches at the UN and apparent steps forward in human rights. Removing barriers, increasing cooperation and helping facilitate trade requires discussions and decisions at every level. Recent discussions between officials from Tajikistan and Turkmenistan about consular issues between the two countries were noteworthy in this regard – as was mention of 'the mining and oil and gas industry, energy sector and mineral resources processing' and 'infrastructure projects of regional importance'.[65]

This provides one example of closer ties being sought across the length of the Silk Roads. A joint venture by the state-owned oil companies of Turkmenistan, Azerbaijan and Uzbekistan to develop fields in the Caspian provides another.[66] So do the new train lines that have been built criss-crossing the Silk Roads. These include the Baku–Tbilisi–Kars track that was inaugurated in October 2017, new tracks connecting Yiwu with Tehran in Iran and also the upgrading of rail lines that transport freight to Europe.[67]

'There is much scope for increasing cooperation,' said President Rouhani of Iran at a meeting of the heads of the states bordering the Caspian in August 2018. If Kazakhstan and Iran built transit networks, 'Kazakhstan may be linked to the Southern waters through Iran, and Iran can be connected to China via Kazakhstan', he said – urging investment into new transport infrastructure to tie not just two countries, but a wider region together.[68]

The development of a new 'International North–South transport corridor' that connects South East Asia and northern Europe has also made progress and seen government bodies in Azerbaijan, Russia and Iran working closely with each other. 'This project will involve our transport ministries,' said Sergei Lavrov, Russian's foreign minister, 'which will consider technical and financial aspects, as well as interaction between our customs and consular services.'[69] Discussions are also continuing about expanding this corridor to enable the participation of Indian goods and services.[70]

The significance of the corridor is clear from the fact that some estimates suggest that if accompanied by investment into new rail lines, it might boost India's trade with countries in Eurasia from around $30bn a year by nearly six times.[71] Separate analysis suggests that Iran alone might generate $2bn of transit fees from the rise in trade across the region – with some officials stating that the country could expect fees of $50 per ton.[72]

Even if such figures are wildly optimistic, they point to expectations of what improved infrastructure, transport and communication ties might deliver.

Then there is the 'Ashgabat agreement' that was signed in 2011 by India, Iran, Kazakhstan, Turkmenistan, Uzbekistan and Oman, which seeks to deepen cooperation, facilitate the movement of goods and enable visa-free travel between the countries.[73] Another among the plethora of schemes intended to tie the heart of the world together is the 'Lapis Lazuli' corridor that connects Afghanistan, Turkmenistan, Azerbaijan, Georgia and Turkey. The $2bn proposal, which took four years to negotiate, aims to establish motorway and rail links between the city of Torgundi in the Afghan province of Herat with Ashgabat and the port of Turkmenbashi on the Caspian Sea. The corridor would then connect Baku with Tbilisi and Ankara with branches to Poti and Batumi, and then from the Turkish capital to Istanbul.[74]

This is to be supplemented, according to reports, by a new sixteen-lane expressway costing $2.4bn that will link Ashgabat with Turkmenabat on the border with Uzbekistan – and be studded with recreation centres, shops, restaurants, motels, open and covered parking lots, fuel stations and more besides – in a utopian vision of what motorway travel might be like in a country where summer temperatures regularly exceed 40°C.[75]

This extravagant building is part of a pattern that includes new port facilities at Turkmenbashi on the

Caspian Sea, constructed at a reported cost of $1.5bn. Such projects show that significant investment is going into large-scale infrastructure projects – even if, in the case of Turkmenistan at least, most commentators doubt whether the volume of cargo or passenger numbers will ever reach the levels that justify the outlay.[76]

Indeed, the opening ceremony of the new facilities in May 2018 focused less on the port playing a central role as a logistics hub than on the perennial favourite pursuit of Turkmen leaders: setting world records. The first guest introduced at the port's opening was a representative of the *Guinness Book of Records*, who was there to note the facility was the largest built below sea level in the world – an anomaly of Turkmenbashi's physical position.[77] This earned the port a place alongside earlier awards that include the world's highest concentration of buildings lined with white marble, the world's tallest flagpole (a title subsequently ceded to Tajikistan), the largest handmade woven carpet, the largest indoor Ferris wheel, the most number of people singing in the round, the largest star-shaped roof on a building and the largest symbol of a horse in the world.[78]

More substantive progress is apparent elsewhere, however. Discussions about mutual interests in the energy sector have led to proposals to connect the electrical grids of Russia, Azerbaijan and Iran to enable the latter to export electricity – as it already does to Iraq and Afghanistan.[79] Negotiations advanced quickly, with the first sale taking place between Iran and Azerbaijan just months after terms were agreed.[80]

The fruits of such large-scale infrastructure projects have been borne quickly. In the summer of 2017, Ebrahim Mohammadi, the deputy head of the Islamic Republic of Iran Railways, noted that freight transport was up 55 per cent compared to the same period a year before.[81] According to Iran's Trade Promotion Organisation, in the fiscal year ending 20 March 2018 transit revenues were up by 20 per cent compared to the previous twelve-month period.[82]

The prospects of future growth across Central Asia have been discerned by many. At a summit in Astana in the spring of 2018, the Turkish foreign minister, Mevlüt Çavuşoğlu, talked about boosting bilateral trade between Turkey and Kazakhstan to $5bn or even $10bn in the future, a significant improvement on current figures. 'Turkish companies have played a very important role in the development of Kazakhstan,' he noted, and had excellent potential to grow further in the future.[83] This is part of the wider emergence of a pan-Turkic sentiment and of the desire of Central Asian states – and Turkey – to collaborate and work more closely together economically, politically and culturally.

One way to help facilitate the intensification of exchange is the provision of a reliable legal system. In the case of Kazakhstan, one innovative solution has been the creation of the Astana International Financial Centre. The centre has a court presided over by some of the most distinguished British lawyers of recent decades, headed by Lord Woolf, the first Lord Supreme Court Judge in England and Wales. The court's mandate is to consider commercial and civil disputes based on the principles of English legal proceedings – and offer comfort to investors wary of being trapped by local laws that are hard to understand and a judiciary that may not appear to be as independent as it should be.[84] This is aimed at attracting foreign investors in general but also with one eye on the floats of state-owned businesses like Air Astana, the Kazakh national carrier, Kazakhtelecom, the biggest mobile operator in the country, and Kazatomprom, the world's biggest uranium miner.

The possibility of doing well from large-scale infrastructure investments has drawn attention from surprising sources. The launch of the construction of the section of a major new gas pipeline linking the Galkynysh field in Turkmenistan to Pakistan and India drew optimistic comments from the Afghan president, Ashraf Ghani, in words that come as a welcome change from reports of violence and instability in Afghanistan. 'South Asia is being connected with Central Asia through Afghanistan,' he said, 'after more than a century of division.' In a rare show of solidarity between India and Pakistan, the minister of state for external affairs in India praised the pipeline as 'a symbol of our goals' and 'a new page in cooperation', while the then prime minister of Pakistan, Shahid Khaqan Abbasi, voiced his belief that the Turkmenistan–Afghanistan–Pakistan– India (TAPI) pipeline 'will lead from a gas pipeline into an energy and communication corridor'.[85]

Such optimistic noises prompted sour faces in Iran, where the head of the National Iran Gas Company, Hamidreza Araqi, said that the pipeline would never be built. Far more sensible, he said, was for Turkmenistan to send gas to Iran and to swap it for gas that Iran would in turn send on to Pakistan directly. Apart from the fact that this proposal depends on a pipeline between Iran and Pakistan that does itself not exist, it has since been reported that progress has been made with the TAPI line after all, and that it will open in 2019 – albeit without the compressor stations that would allow it to operate at full capacity. But such is the demand for energy in Pakistan that it has been thought better to cut corners and open quickly than take the time needed to make operations run at optimal capacity.[86]

In any event, and rather surprisingly, the fears that instability in Afghanistan would preclude a major infrastructure project ever leaving the drawing board were assuaged by warm words offered by none other than the Taliban. 'The TAPI pipeline is an important regional project whose groundwork was initiated during the Islamic Emirate's rule,' said the Taliban in a statement released in early 2018. Construction work had been delayed because of US military presence. 'In areas under its control, the Islamic Emirate announces full cooperation on implementation of the project,' the statement added. As a result, said the Taliban, 'there will be no delay in this important national project'.[87]

This is one element of an apparent change in Afghanistan that has seen signs of what some regard as encouraging dialogue between the Taliban and the government. 'We have held discussions with the leaders of the tribes, politicians, teachers and members of civil-society institutions,' said Gul Agha Sherzai, minister for borders and tribal affairs, in the spring of 2018.[88] The fact that neighbouring countries have not just encouraged such dialogue, but offered to host discussions can also be seen as a sign of determination of multiple countries to conciliate and consolidate and work together to resolve problems.[89]

The noises from inside Afghanistan have been encouraging enough for General John Nicholson, head of US and NATO forces in the war-torn country, to say that discussion of peace 'gives us hope that this is an unprecedented moment'. NATO's senior civilian representative, Cornelius Zimmermann, agreed, adding that 'in my time in Afghanistan, I have never heard or experienced such a bold move as the one by President Ghani'.[90]

That assessment is based in part on more bullish views about what is happening in Afghanistan. Recent months have seen momentum 'shifted in favour of Afghan security forces', says a recent military update prepared for the US Congress. The Taliban's 'lowering expectations' can be seen from the move away from all-out confrontation to 'guerrilla tactics and suicide attacks'. Even after a major attack on Ghazni in the summer of 2018, western military commanders stayed upbeat. 'We have an unprecedented opportunity, a window of opportunity for peace right now.'[91]

That may be the case. But the fact that US officials increasingly travel around Kabul 'by air to avoid suicide attacks on the streets' reveals much about the frequency and scale of disruption just within the Afghan capital itself – and how important it is to treat the enthusiastic noises about a supposedly improving situation with caution.[92] One who does so is President Trump, who reportedly let his feelings about General Nicholson be known in a meeting at the Pentagon in July 2018. 'I don't think he knows how to win,' said Trump. 'I don't know if he's a winner. There's no victories.'[93]

In any event, only the most determined optimist would be brave enough to bet on a swift or binding solution in Afghanistan, given the history of the last four decades. And while the words of conciliation and support might seem encouraging, the reality of relying on the Taliban – a label that belies the disparate group of individuals who choose to cooperate as and when interests elide – requires a stern constitution, especially at a time when, regardless of the upbeat US military assessment, pressure on districts across Afghanistan remains intense.[94]

The Taliban's interest in supporting the pipeline should also be understood for what it is. Rather than being a gesture of solidarity with the Afghan people or an expression of a willingness to cooperate with the government, the purported backing for the TAPI pipeline also points to a sophisticated awareness of how to take advantage of the vast mineral wealth of the country, which has been estimated as being worth not billions, but trillions of dollars. According to the US Geological Survey, Afghanistan may hold nearly 60 million metric tons of copper, 2,200 million tons of iron deposits, 32,000 tons of mercury, millions of tons of potash as well as huge reserves of rare earths such as lithium, beryllium, niobium and caesium.[95]

The Taliban has realised that Afghanistan's mineral wealth offers opportunities to get rich – as well as to buy more weapons, recruit more supporters and build stronger power bases. As a result, they have paid particular attention to securing regions that have existing mining activities, with an eye on continuing to exploit the resources and even to expand operations. According to one report, in 2014, 'the two mining areas of Deodarra and Kuran wa Munjan alone provided around $20m to armed groups, according to rough but conservative estimates – equivalent to the government's declared revenue from the entire extractive sector' for the whole of the previous year. In 2016, meanwhile, fully half of all the revenue from lapis mines went to the Taliban – a sum again to be measured in millions, if not tens of millions, of dollars.[96]

The same is true of the funds that flow from hydrated magnesium silicate, the 'softest mineral known to

72

man', more familiar to consumers as talcum powder. Afghanistan is blessed with significant deposits that can be translated into hard cash. As with other natural resources, militant forces in the country have been quick to understand that controlling minerals generates revenue streams that can help fuel armed insurgency as well as establishing, propping up and expanding individual fiefdoms. It is not just the Taliban leaders who have moved in on hydrated magnesium silicate mines; so too have members of the Islamic State of Iraq and the Levant–Khorasan province (ISIS-K), many of whom were part of the failed attempt to create a caliphate centred on Raqqa and Mosul following the disintegration of Syria and northern Iraq in 2013. ISIS-K has focused on gaining hold of resource-rich territories and in some cases doubling the workforce to make mines not only stay open but to expand production.[97] Strange as it may seem, parents powdering a baby's bottom in Bogotà, San Francisco, Lagos, Kolkata or Wuhan to combat nappy rash are involved, albeit unwittingly, in a chain that connects them to the struggle for power in the heart of the world.

*

The success of both the Taliban and ISIS has raised fears of contagion – not only by fundamentalist ideas but also by disruptive and militant techniques and tactics inside Afghanistan as well as outside it. It is striking, for example, that some studies note that significant numbers of ISIS supporters who fought in Syria and Iraq had Central Asian backgrounds and many of them were used for suicide missions.[98] Terror attacks committed in New York, Stockholm, St Petersburg and Istanbul in 2017 were perpetrated by men from or with strong links to Central Asia.[99]

This is one reason why there has been a sharp rise in the willingness of countries of the Silk Roads to work together on intelligence matters, including cooperation between armed forces. In addition to Uzbek and Tajik forces announcing plans to conduct joint operations for the first time, for example, initiatives have been announced for manoeuvres of Russian and Uzbek troops in the Forish mountain range, and for combined exercises of the armed forces of Tajikistan, Pakistan, Afghanistan and China.[100] These follow the Prabal Dostyk (literally 'robust friendship') exercises which have been carried out by soldiers from Kazakhstan and India since 2016, whose aims are 'to enhance [the] existing military relationship ... and achieve synergy for joint conduct of operations as and when the requirement arises'.[101]

In the summer of 2018, combined military exercises by forces from the countries of the Silk Roads that are members of the Shanghai Cooperation Organisation took place near Chelyabinsk in the Urals. These included soldiers from Russia and China,[102] and they also saw the presence of troops from India and Pakistan – the first time that the two countries have ever taken part in a joint military exercise.[103]

A spate of incidents in the last few years on Iran's border with Pakistan have resulted in commitments from both countries to work more closely to deal with militants who have regularly targeted border guards. In April 2017, for example, the killing of ten border guards of Mirjaveh county in Iran's Sistan-Baluchestan province in an ambush by militants operating from inside Pakistan prompted politicians, diplomats and army chiefs in Tehran and Islamabad to resolve to work more closely together in the future – although not before the Iranian ambassador was summoned to explain comments by a senior Iranian general that military action would be taken against Pakistan if there were any further attacks.[104]

To suggest that the countries across the heart of the Silk Roads work together, see eye to eye and focus on mutual benefits is not just an oversimplification, but also understates the structural problems, petty rivalries, personal animosities and difficulties that could equally be used to characterise the region. Highlighting recent proposals to enable gas-swap deals between Iran and Turkmenistan, for example, masks the fact that the two countries have been locked in dispute since the start of 2017; then the latter claimed it was owed $1.5bn dating back to sales a decade earlier, when a cold winter forced Tehran to import gas – whose price Ashgabat promptly increased by nine times to take advantage of its neighbour's predicament.[105] The lack of progress in discussions to settle matters has now led to a lawsuit being filed at the International Court of Arbitration.[106]

Relations between Turkey and Turkmenistan likewise have become strained after Polimeks, a leading Turkish contractor that has carried out billions of dollars' worth of construction projects, including hotels, monuments and highways, was accused of defects relating to the roof, pipes and water supply of the new falcon-shaped airport in Ashgabat.[107] Failure to pay Polimeks and other companies hundreds of millions of dollars has led to the downing of tools in an embarrassing revelation of the consequences of persistent financial mismanagement that has put extraordinary strain on the economy of Turkmenistan, where having the fourth-largest gas reserves in the world has not prevented rampant inflation, a high unemployment rate and reports of food shortages and of medicine supplies running so low that medication for diabetes and cardiovascular disease is impossible to come by, while the cost of aspirin has trebled.[108]

Part of the problem lies with low hydrocarbon prices, as revenues from oil and gas collapsed in 2014, halving in the space of six months – and remaining low thereafter. Across Central Asia, the slump in commodity prices had a significant impact on public debt, putting strains on the economy and not so much forcing a check on ambitions as pushing them into reverse.[109]

In the case of Turkmenistan, the relentless pursuit of expensive vanity projects has not helped. These include an Olympic stadium (that has never hosted or even bid to host the Olympic Games), a winter sports arena (in a country where, as we have seen, temperatures in the summer touch 40°C and rarely dip below a mild 10°C in winter), and the new $2.3bn airport at Ashgabat that is capable of handling 17 million passengers a year – which should definitely be able to cope if there is a sharp spike in the 105,000 visitors who arrived in the city in 2015.[110] With any luck, by the time numbers rise, a solution will be found to resolve the fact that the new airport appears to be sinking into the sand.[111]

Disillusion is such that opposition groups outside the country have reported that citizens have been using newspapers to wipe their backsides as a form of protest, which has in turn led to police being dispatched house to house to inspect toilet facilities in the search for culprits. They have done so because it appears that the tumbling value of the currency, the manat, had led to a rise in the price of basic commodities, including toilet paper. But another reason, according to opposition groups outside the country, is that newspaper is being used because it features an image of president Berdymukhamedov on the front page every day. Given the president received a mere 97 per cent of the vote in the most recent election in 2017, there cannot presumably be many suspects to track down – even if the volume of the soiled newspapers apparently suggests otherwise.[112] Difficulties in gathering reliable information from inside Turkmenistan make it hard to confirm whether this is a tall story – and a case of dirty smears appearing in the press.

In some cases, the dramatic fall in gas, oil and commodity prices during 2015 was the catalyst for a process of professionalisation, of clearing out poor practices and stamping down on corruption. Expectations had to be quickly reduced in Kazakhstan, for example, which is heavily dependent on sales of fossil fuels, as the price of oil fell from $115 to $33 per barrel in the space of eighteen months. This led to a squeeze on the sovereign wealth fund that was raided in order to help meet government obligations – with the result that assets fell by nearly 20 per cent in just over a year.[113] Inevitably, this led not only to a recalibration of projected spending, but also to a clampdown on those who had done too well in times of plenty – men like Mukhtar Ablyazov, former chairman of BTA Bank, who is being pursued for the embezzlement of $4bn through courtrooms from Kazakhstan to Knightsbridge.[114]

A similar sobering process had begun in Russia following the slump in prices. The appointment of Elvira Nabiullina as governor of the Central Bank inaugurated a ferocious clean-up of the country's financial sector, with 276 banks closed in the course of three years and another twenty-eight forced into compulsory rehabilitation programmes – earning Nabiullina the praise of Vladimir Putin for her 'energetic efforts [against] banditry'.[115]

And then, for all the warm words about the joys of cooperation, major projects – including the TAPI pipeline – are neither easy to undertake, nor easy to pay for and in some cases never leave the drawing board. The cost of the TAPI pipeline alone is estimated to run to some $10bn, leading many observers to doubt whether it will ever be completed – and even wondering whether sections that have purportedly been built in Turkmenistan even exist at all.[116] Financing problems at least make that understandable. The same cannot be said for Line D of the Turkmenistan–China pipeline, which does not pass through war-torn Afghanistan, has an agreed route and has funding in place – and yet shows no sign of being implemented, presumably because of local rivalries in the region.[117]

Seasoned watchers of the Silk Roads also know that unpredictability and eccentricity are par for the course. In the summer of 2018, for example, Saidmukarram Abdulkodirzoda, the highest-ranking Islamic official in Tajikistan, declared that fighting sports – such as boxing – as well as 'games and duels' done for money were a waste of time and thus forbidden under Islamic law. This came as a surprise to Tajik boxers, who won medals at the 2008 and 2012 Olympics. (Wrestling is a different matter, according to Abdulkodirzoda, because it encourages physical and spiritual development, and inspires the young 'to proudly raise the flag of the country and enhance the image of the nation and state'.[118])

For all the positive stories about cooperation and progress, there are still uncomfortable realities to confront in the heart of the world. In the summer of 2018 it was reported that Tajiks crossing the border to Uzbekistan were being prevented from taking more than 40 kg of goods with them – including a maximum of two kilograms of meat and seven of flour.[119] This followed the announcement that university professors and students would not be allowed to leave Tajikistan without government permission – hardly a positive sign at a time when collaboration with scholars in neighbouring countries and beyond can surely only be of wider benefit.[120]

This has an echo in Turkmenistan, where it was reported that those under the age of thirty were being stopped from leaving the country in an attempt to arrest the brain drain and to prevent the workforce becoming depleted.[121] Or there is Pakistan and India, where intimidation of journalists is increasingly common and often violent.[122] Kazakhstan offers yet another case where protestors have been detained to prevent anti-government messages reaching a wider audience – which at least would seem to scotch suspicions that the opposition in the country had been set up by the government to provide the semblance of democratic reforms.[123]

There are basic and signficant problems too that may not just curtail progress so much as compromise it altogether. The uneven distribution of the natural resources in Central Asian republics has led to a lack of jobs – and prospects – for the young, raising questions about long-term political stability.[124] The inability to tolerate dissent in any form has led to children of activists being deprived of medical treatment or taken off planes out of the country, to jail sentences for those who dare to criticise the government and to the blocking of the internet.[125] Despite the welcome progress in Uzbekistan, meanwhile, indices such as those measuring press freedom across Asia – from Turkey to Thailand, Iran to India, Pakistan to the Phillipines, China to almost all the states of Central Asia – are not just failing to improve; they are in decline, in some cases dramatically.[126] A new world is emerging in Asia, but it is not a free one.

The question of whether to show the Silk Roads in the best or the worst possible light is a perennial concern for specialists who work on the bridge between east and west. It is perfectly possible to point to progress and to the opportunities that are not just emerging but already being taken advantage of; but it is equally true that the hot air of soundbites, the trail of broken promises and the very real frictions, dislocations and fragilities are also part of the reality of a region that has proved to be the bellwether for global affairs for millennia.[127]

Part of the difficulty of interpretation comes from the fact that Central Asia is a piece of a much bigger puzzle – and is affected by moving pieces at each end. To the west, of course, is the civil war in Syria, and the continued struggle in Iraq to rebuild a state more or less from scratch. For the last few years, things have looked more promising in Iran – at least superficially. After signing the Joint Comprehensive Plan of Action (JCPOA) in 2015 and the lifting of sanctions, the country was able to double exports of oil – helping the economy to grow by 12.5 per cent in the following twelve months.[128] Although the pace of growth had already slowed, the threat of the JCPOA deal being cancelled helped fuel already rising inflation to the point where the government has resorted to desperate measures to try to shore up the value of the rial, the Iranian currency.[129]

The uncertainties concerning the future of Iran's international relations, coupled with the failure of living standards to rise, unemployment figures that are far higher than official figures suggest, especially among the young, and increased mobile-device ownership have played a role in street protests at the end of 2017 and early 2018 that raised the familiar question of whether to concede grounds to protesters or to stamp out any dissent.[130] Much, though, depends on evaluating the motivations and aims of those who took to the streets – where at least some of the anger against the government seems to have come from those demanding the adoption of more, rather than less, conservative policies.[131]

Such nuances were lost on President Trump, who took to Twitter on 1 January 2018 to declare that 'the great Iranian people have been repressed for many years. They are hungry for food and for freedom. Along with human rights, the wealth of Iran is being looted. TIME FOR CHANGE!'[132] Trump's close adviser Rudy Giuliani put things more forcefully a few months later, when he told reporters that the president was committed to regime change in Tehran, and that not only was the fall of the Iranian government 'the only way to peace in the Middle East', but that it was more important than an agreement between Israelis and Palestinians – whose troubles have plagued the region for decades.[133] What is more, boasted Guiliani on another occasion, the street protests were neither spontaneous nor local. They were 'being co-ordinated', he said, 'by many of our people in Albania', a suggestion so odd as to beg simple questions not just about his basic grasp of geography but of reality.[134]

Of course, statements like these do more to unite Iranians than almost any policy that an Iranian government might adopt and implement. The same is true of the announcement made by President Trump that the US would withdraw from the JCPOA in May 2018, which he dismissed as a 'disastrous deal [that] gave this regime – and it's a regime of great terror – many billions of dollars, some of it in actual cash – a great embarrassment to me as a citizen and to all citizens of the United States'.[135]

As we shall see, the US withdrawal from the JCPOA, which came despite inspectors from the International Atomic Energy Agency verifying that Iran was compliant with the original agreement, has consequences that go beyond what the unilateral decision by the United States means for Iran.[136] The decision in Washington likewise plays into the hands of hardliners in Tehran by undermining the credibility and confidence in the current leadership of Iran under President Rouhani, who is a moderate and a reformer – at least by Iranian standards. Pulling out of the JCPOA strengthens the hand of hardliners and factions more likely to be much more hostile to the US. For all the gung-ho talk by American politicians, then, it would be ironic if the regime change is one that makes life for Iranians more oppressive and makes international agreements less, rather than more, likely to be reached in the future.

In fact, responses to the JCPOA withdrawal included calls in Tehran for more expenditure on the armed forces, defence and 'cultural and propaganda plans' and statements from the powerful Revolutionary Guards that trying to deal with 'the criminal, war-mongering, deceitful and reneging' US government is pointless.[137] The reimposition of sanctions during the course of 2018 on 6 August and 4 November (90 and 180 days after the US withdrawal from the agreement respectively) means that Iran faces difficult decisions as to how to prepare for and deal with a series of pressures in the coming months and years.

It may well be that the US is able to force Tehran to the negotiating table and perhaps even manage to demand stricter and better terms than had been the case when the JCPOA deal was agreed. But that comes at an expense of laying the seeds for bitterness in the future, and potentially for Iran to buckle under the strain of food shortages, civic unrest and the mass repression that is likely to follow. Those who look forward to the implosion of yet another state in this region might pause to reflect on the lessons of the recent histories of Syria, Iraq and Afghanistan.

*

Iran's problems are not confined to the fallout of the JCPOA or to domestic affairs. Support for President Assad of Syria and for disruptive parties across the Middle East also come at significant cost. According to H. R. McMaster, national security advisor, 'Iran has provided over $16 billion to the Assad regime and to other proxies in Syria, Iraq and Yemen' between 2012 and 2018, placing a heavy burden on an already strained economy.[138] Relations between Iran and Saudi Arabia have long been strained, but in recent years they have threatened not only to deteriorate but to lead to problems that would have major consequences across the region and beyond.

Name-calling is bad enough. 'I believe the Iranian supreme leader [Ayatollah Ali Khamenei] makes Hitler look good,' said the ambitious young Saudi crown prince, Mohammad bin Salman, in April 2018. Hitler only wanted to conquer Europe, said the prince, warming to his theme; but Iran's leader 'is trying to conquer the world'.[139] Previous remarks comparing Khamenei with Hitler had been dismissed by an Iranian foreign ministry spokesman as being the words of an 'adventurist' crown prince whose comments were 'immature, inconsiderate, and baseless'.[140]

At least this was better than the threats of direct action that were being openly bandied about in the middle of 2017. There was no prospect of dialogue with Iran, said the Saudi crown prince in a TV interview. 'We know we are a major target for the Iranian regime,' he said. As a result, he hinted strongly, plans were being made accordingly to pre-empt military action with a first strike: the Saudis would have no hesitation moving first, rather than being forced to respond. Far better, he said 'to have the battle in Iran rather than in Saudi Arabia'.[141] The from Tehran response was equally emphatic: 'If the Saudis do anything ignorant,' said an Iranian defence spokesman, 'we will leave no area untouched except Mecca and Medina.'[142]

The dramatic changes in the world's centre of economic, political and military gravity are prompting old alliances to be reviewed and new ones to be made. A case in point comes from the warming relations between the Saudis and Israel. For seven decades, Riyadh has refused to recognise the State of Israel or even to concede that country's right to exist, with the result that there have been no official diplomatic relations between the two. That has started to change as a result of the shadow cast by the fear of Iran.[143]

Years of the Saudis funding and supporting the Palestinian cause are giving way to trying to outmanoeuvre the regime in Tehran. The Saudis are looking to force a settlement between Israel and the Palestinians at almost any price: the Saudis 'don't care, they don't give a damn about what will be in the agreement,' said Yaakov Nagel, the former Israeli national security adviser – as long as one is reached quickly.[144] That might explain why the Grand Mufti of Saudi Arabia not only issued a fatwa declaring that it was inappropriate for Muslims to fight Israel and to kill Jews, but stated that Hamas was 'a terror organisation' – an important symbolic and legal statement, as well as a clear indicator of the shifting sands in the Middle East.[145]

Israel has played its own part in this fundamental reconfiguration of alliances and, indeed, the geopolitics of the Middle East. 'We have many contacts, partly secret, with many Muslim and Arab countries,' Yuval Steinitz, Israel's energy minister and member of the security cabinet, told Israeli Army Radio. The 'connection with the moderate Arab world, including Saudi Arabia, helps us block Iran'.[146]

While there are still regular diatribes again Israel in the Saudi press, such as a sustained attack on laws that the latter claim 'perpetuate racial discrimination', these can be set alongside more progressive signs of growing cooperation, which include allowing airlines to use Saudi airspace to fly between Tel Aviv and India – rather than forcing them to undertake a lengthy diversion, as has been the case in the past.[147]

Change in the twenty-first century is stimulated by many factors – from demographics to the shift of economic power, from the role played by digital technologies to climate change. The Silk Roads are rising fast because they are being galvanised. What happens in the heart of the world in the coming years will shape the next hundred.

The Roads to Beijing

Late on 6 September 2013, President Xi Jinping of China arrived in Astana, the gleaming new capital of Kazakhstan, which is adorned with modernist buildings such as the Shatyr shopping mall, the Palace of Peace and Reconciliation and the turquoise Kazakhstan Central Concert Hall – just three of the bold new structures constructed in the city since the late 1990s.

The following morning, Xi arrived at Nazarbayev University to give a speech with the title 'Promote People-to-People Friendship and Create a Better Future'. Few can have guessed its significance. It is a 'foreign policy priority,' said the president, for China to have good relations with its neighbours. Inspiration should be taken from the network of connections that bound people together in the past. 'Throughout the millennia,' said Xi, 'the people of various countries along the ancient Silk Road have jointly written a chapter of friendship that has been passed on to this very day.' Study of the Silk Roads showed that peoples of 'different races, beliefs and cultural backgrounds are fully capable of sharing peace and development'.

This was a model not just to study and admire – but one that should be replicated. It was time, he said, 'to forge closer economic ties, deepen cooperation and expand development space in the Eurasian region'. It was time to build an 'economic belt along the Silk Road'. To do so required taking several joint steps, such as improving policy communication and coordination, upgrading transport links, promoting unimpeded trade and enhancing monetary circulation. The time had come to reinvigorate the Silk Roads.[1]

Such initiatives had been suggested before. In the aftermath of the invasion of Iraq, US diplomats and policymakers began to talk with increasing frequency about reviving links across the heart of Asia as part of a formal policy: 'Our goal,' said Richard A. Boucher, assistant secretary of state for South and Central Asian affairs, in comments to the International Relations Committee in Congress in 2006, 'is to revive ancient ties between South and Central Asia and to help create new links in the areas of trade, transport, democracy, energy and communications.'[2]

Statements such as this – and in particular a position paper written the previous year by S. Frederick Starr an eminent scholar on Eurasian affairs – drew stinging reactions in China. 'US scheming for "Great Central Asia Strategy"', complained one headline in *People's*

Daily. 'It has always been a consistent goal of the United States to penetrate Central Asia and then control this region', said the editorial. 'The 9/11 incident', it went on, gave the United States the opportunity and excuse to gain a foothold in Central Asia and refashion the region to suit its own ends.[3]

Then there were speeches like those given by Hillary Clinton, when secretary of state, that talked about reviving the past. 'Historically, the nations of South and Central Asia were connected to each other and the rest of the continent by a sprawling trading network called the Silk Road,' Clinton said in Chennai in 2011. 'Let's work together to create a new Silk Road. Not a single thoroughfare like its namesake, but an international web and network of economic and transit connections. That means building more rail lines, highways, energy infrastructure … upgrading the facilities at border crossings … removing the bureaucratic barriers and other impediments to the free flow of goods and people … and casting aside the outdated trade policies.' This was nothing less than a 'vision for the twenty-first century'.[4]

Like many visions, however, this was more about hope than substance. Talking about improving connections is one thing; funding them quite another. So when President Xi followed up his talk at Astana with concrete proposals and the commitment of hard cash, it quickly became clear that something serious was afoot. Work had gone into preparing the framework for what quickly became known as the One Belt, One Road policy – the belt representing overland connections to China's neighbours and beyond, and the road a 'maritime sea road' ultimately linking waterways as far as the Indian Ocean, the Gulf and the Red Sea. As minutes of the Central Committee of the Communist Party of China from November 2013 testify, plans to implement these ideas were quickly being put into practice – which means they had been thought about for some time beforehand. 'We will set up development-oriented financial institutions, accelerate the construction of infrastructure connecting China with neighbouring countries and regions, and work hard to build a Silk Road Economic Belt and a Maritime Silk Road to form a new pattern of all-round opportunities.'[5]

The idea of encouraging Chinese businesses to look outside the country for new opportunities had been encouraged with the formal adoption of the 'going out' strategy (*zouchuqu zhanlue*) in 2000 as part of the Ninth National People's Congress and the adoption of the National Economy and Social Development Five-Year Plan. Xi's ambitions are much more expansive – and what is more, they have been made reality with astonishing speed and enthusiasm.

By the middle of 2015 the China Development Bank, one of the country's key financial institutions, declared that it had reserved $890bn to spend on some 900 projects mainly focusing on transportation, infrastructure and energy.[6] Six months later, the Export-Import Bank of China announced that it had begun the financing of what it expected to number more than 1,000 projects in forty-nine countries as part of the Belt and Road Initiative (as OBOR had been renamed).[7] As with the Silk Roads of the past, there is no specific geographical criterion to be part of the initiative; indeed, the maritime element of it is intended precisely to allow parameters of inclusion to be extended as far as the eastern coast of Africa and beyond.

Over eighty countries are now part of the initiative. These include the Central Asian republics, the countries of South and South East Asia, those of the Middle East, Turkey and Eastern Europe – as well as states in Africa and the Caribbean.[8] With a combined population of 4.4 billion, those living along the new Silk Roads between China and the Eastern Mediterranean account for more than 63 per cent of the world's population, with a collective total of $21tr – or 29 per cent of total global output.[9]

The sweeping scale and ambition of the Belt and Road Initiative was made clear at a major forum held in Beijing in May 2017. There was more at stake than money and investments. In fact, said President Xi, the initiative could change the world. 'Exchange will replace estrangement,' he said. 'Mutual learning will replace clashes, and coexistence will replace a sense of superiority.' It would bring peace, for it would 'boost mutual understanding, mutual respect and mutual trust among different countries'.[10] The Belt and Road Initiative, he said, would 'add splendour to human civilisation' and help build 'a new era of harmony and trade'.[11]

China's plans should encourage a new way of thinking and different behaviour, said President Xi. 'We should foster a new type of international relations featuring win-win cooperation,' he stated, 'and we should forge partnerships of dialogue with no confrontation and of friendship rather than alliance.'[12] This sought to capitalise on three wider trends. First, to provide hope at a time of change in the world; second, to fill the vacuum left by isolationist and self-indulgent politics dominating the narrative in developed economies; and third, to demonstrate that China should not only be part of the global community of nations but could and should provide leadership that emphasises the benefits of mutual cooperation. A video released at the Beijing Forum encapsulated this neatly: 'What's wrong with the world? What can we do?' runs the refrain. 'China has a solution: A community of shared future for mankind.'[13]

The Belt and Road Initiative, said President Xi in May 2017, is the 'project of the century'.[14] Many agree with him. Jin Liqun, President of the Asian Infrastructure and Investment Bank – a Chinese-led institution with more than eighty member countries – told the *Financial Times* that 'the Chinese experience illustrates that infrastructure investment paves the way for broad-based economic social development, and poverty alleviation comes as a natural consequence of that'. In other words, China had learned from its own experiences that building roads, train lines, energy plants and creating the ecosystem to enable cities to grow does more than just accelerate commercial exchange; it helps lift people out of poverty.[15] This conclusion is based on reality. China's own economic miracle from the 1980s onwards taught important lessons about how policy, infrastructure investment and poverty alleviation can all go hand in hand.[16] 'We Chinese often say that if you want to get rich, build roads first,' said Le Yucheng, China's vice-minister for foreign affairs. The 'under-development of infrastructure', he told the *Financial Times*, has been one of the most important reasons for why some parts of the world have been held back – something that the Belt and Road Initiative is designed to fix.[17]

In the words of one commentator, assessing the progress of the Belt and Road Initiative is 'part art, part science' because 'it is a moving target, loosely defined and ever expanding', to the point that it is no longer 'constrained by geography or even by gravity', as the vision has expanded since 2013 to include Africa, Europe, the Arctic, cyberspace and even outer space.[18] The Belt and Road is all-encompassing and can include anything and everything; but then again, that was the case too with the Silk Roads of the past as well – where events that took place in one part of the world were sometimes directly linked to consequences in another.[19]

One attraction of the Silk Roads as a catch-all for closer cooperation is the malleability of the message of a return to the past. When the first direct train from China arrived in Bandar Anzali on Iran's Caspian coast in the summer of 2018, for example, Iran's vice president, Es'haq Jahangiri, was quick to use the re-emergence of the new Silk Roads as an affirmation of Iran's own past. Rather than associating the train with President Xi's vision or that of the Chinese state, Jahangiri reached a different conclusion: the rebuilding of ties across the spine of Asia was a 'sign of Iran's cultural, historical and civilisational ties with neighbouring countries'.[20]

It is a message that can be found elsewhere too – such as in Turkmenabat in Turkmenistan, where a new 28-metre-high Silk Road sculpture was unveiled in the spring of 2018 with a lavish ceremony that included public bicycle contests as well as marathon races.[21] Then there is Tashkent in Uzbekistan, which will have twelve new gates built at entry points to the city to mark its position as 'the symbolic and actual heart of the "Great Silk Road" and commemorate the link between Uzbek culture and those of other peoples'.[22] While Chinese capital and leadership clearly play a fundamentally important role, for those living in the centre of Asia the revival of the Silk Roads is something that can be appropriated and moulded into a message that has a national and domestic resonance. As one leading commentator has put it, the Belt and Road Initiative has become 'the Baskin-Robbins of partnerships, offering flavours for everyone'.[23]

There can be little doubt, however, that in many if not most cases it is China that has been the catalyst in the reconfiguration of a part of the world that has played such an important role in world history. Although it is not easy to assess the precise amount of money that has been invested so far or earmarked for investment, some very major projects have got underway. These include the China–Pakistan Economic Corridor, which includes multiple major investments into roads, energy plants and the development of a deep-water port at Gwadar, on the coast of Balochistan in southern Pakistan, with a total value of these projects usually quoted at around the $60bn mark.[24] Some expect investments to top $100bn by 2030.[25]

Current schemes being funded include the 1,320-MW Port Qasim coal-fired power plant project, major wind farms in Sindh, multiple industrial parks and the construction of a freshwater treatment facility that will help address chronic water shortages that will stop Gwadar playing its proposed role as a 'mega-port' by 2030.[26] Plans are also being finalised for the construction and operation of a high-speed train line between Karachi and Peshawar that will increase freight traffic by five times, while passenger traffic would be increased from 55 to 88 million passengers a year. The time taken to journey along the 1,000 miles would be reduced by half, which would in turn reduce congestion at roads and ports, and help make the cost of doing business with and in Pakistan fall.[27]

There has already been a discernible pickup in economic growth as a result of rising levels of investment across the country that is best evidenced by the rising sales of cement – the use of which most obviously correlates with construction projects. According to the All-Pakistan Cement Manufacturers Association, year-on-year sales rose by nearly 20 per cent to the end of 2017 – a very significant boost, in other words.[28]

Other flagship proposals and investments include construction of high-speed and freight-train lines across South East Asia, including the 688-km East Coast Rail Link that is intended to connect Malaysia's east and west coasts and the peninsula's main shipping ports in a scheme costing $13bn.[29] Then there is a new line that will span Laos, costing $5.8bn, which will supposedly turn the landlocked country into one that is 'land-linked'.[30] Multibillion-dollar loans for motorways, bridges, power plants and deep-water ports have been approved in Bangladesh, Cambodia, Myanmar and Sri Lanka, with major projects in Indonesia, Vietnam, the Philippines and Thailand also underway. Projects are not limited to Asia, as the $8.7bn railway from Mombasa to the Ugandan border, Kenya's biggest infrastructure project since independence from Britain in 1963, shows.[31] These sit alongside the creation of new international commercial courts in Xi'an and Shenzhen, which will rule on disputes for projects that run into difficulty or disagreement along the land-based 'belt' and maritime 'road' respectively.[32]

New agreements seem to be put in place every day. In June 2018 alone, ten deals were signed off by the Nepalese and Chinese governments for projects ranging from energy and transport to a proposal to build a tunnel under the Himalayas to link Kathmandu with Tibet and beyond.[33] These were in addition to previous support given to Nepal that has included the construction of new police-training centres, hospitals and a metro system in the Nepalese capital.[34]

This is part of a mosaic of projects that includes the construction of freight-train facilities and 'dry ports' like Khorgos on China's border with Kazakhstan, which form a web of connections of new railway tracks that enable goods to be shipped overland not only across the spine of Asia but deep into Europe, too. The value of these lines is symbolic rather than of immediate practical use, given that shipping by land is significantly more expensive than by sea: quoted costs for sending containers by rail from China to Europe can be up to five times pricier than by sea. While rail lines may take business away from air routes, even operating at capacity, they are unlikely to account for more than 1–2 per cent of maritime cargo volumes.[35] This is partly due to current oversupply in the shipping industry but also because of the sheer size of modern vessels: a train that arrived from China in Barking in east London amid a blaze of publicity in January 2017 was pulling a mere thirty-four containers from its departure point in Yiwu.[36] Even small container ships carry hundreds of times more – with ultra-large container vessels (ULCVs) being able to take more than 10,000 containers per voyage.[37]

Overland routes, including those that go via Gwadar, are quicker than shipping by sea, but it is hard to see many goods for which the benefit of speed will be decisive. Just think, says a recent Chinese advert: when 'Belt and Road Initiative reaches Europe, Europe's red wine is delivered to the doorstep half a month earlier!'[38] Even if the Chinese middle classes grow at the speed some economists project, building costly train lines to get red wine to the dinner table slightly more quickly seems an expensive way to enjoy the finer things in life.[39]

*

There are three principal motivations underpinning the Belt and Road Initiative, which has become President Xi's – and China's – signature foreign and economic policy. The first revolves around long-term planning for the future and China's domestic needs. Particular attention has been paid to natural resources, especially relating to energy, where the country's demands are expected to treble by 2030.[40] Pipelines that enable gas and oil to be pumped from Central Asia and Russia to China have therefore been one focus, but so too have commercial agreements that guarantee large-scale shipments – such as those with oil companies in Russia and the Middle East, including Iran, Saudi Arabia and the UAE.[41]

These have helped fuel China's growth – and made the country the world's largest importer of crude oil in 2017, when it imported more than 8 million barrels per day on average.[42] Securing energy supplies goes hand in hand with projects in non-hydrocarbon fields, such as the joint venture between Kazakh state nuclear company Kazatomprom and China's CGNPC, which will produce nuclear fuel for Chinese power plants from 2019.[43]

Pressures on agricultural production as a result of a rapid urbanisation have also encouraged Chinese companies to look outside the country to ensure supply at a time when the spending powers of the middle classes are rising and eating habits are changing quickly as a result. Retail prices for beef and pork rose by 80 per cent between 2009 and 2013, while imports of dairy products grew fourfold in almost the same period.[44]

The dangers posed by high levels of pollution have also played a role in leading the Chinese authorities to look at food and water security as key areas that need to be addressed. According to official Chinese figures, more than 70 per cent of the country's groundwater in the North China Plain is so polluted that it is 'unfit for human touch', while the Ministry of Environmental Protection reported that a sixth of the agricultural land has been affected by soil contamination.[45] Worsening air-quality readings in the first months of 2018 across China's industrial heartlands and the Yangtze River Delta show the scale of the problem.[46] This is one reason why green and clean technologies are being actively championed at governmental level.[47] It is also why President Xi has spoken repeatedly of the need to address environmental problems including pollution, and to talk about the importance of ecological sustainability.[48]

A second motivation is the transition of China's own economy from manufacturing to services as a result of its transformation over the last three decades, which led to what the International Monetary Fund (IMF) has termed a decisive shift from 'high-speed to high-quality growth'.[49] This has in turn resulted in excess capacity in steel, cement and metals. These can be usefully deployed abroad – as can a workforce that has been instrumental in realising large-scale construction projects in China, which are now less numerous than in the recent past.[50]

Other parts of Asia, meanwhile, are hungry for upgraded infrastructure. According to figures from the Ministry of Transport and Communication in Kazakhstan, for example, a full third of Kazakh roads are in unsatisfactory condition; Chinese finance – and know-how – has been therefore offered to fill useful gaps.[51] The scale of potential is made clear by a recent report by the Asian Development Bank, which estimates that 'infrastructure needs in developing Asia and the Pacific will exceed $22.6 trillion through 2030, or $1.5 trillion per year, if the region is to maintain growth momentum', with that figure rising to $1.7tr per year if climate-change mitigation is included.[52]

By supporting large-scale projects, the Belt and Road also raises the prospects for Chinese businesses to open up new opportunities for the future, too. Penetration of household appliances in South Asia, for example, is extremely limited: less than 10 per cent of homeowners have a personal computer or a microwave, while just a third of families own a refrigerator.[53] The logic is that if more and better roads, transport links and reliable energy sources exist in countries with large and growing populations, their economies will expand quickly too, increasing the disposable wealth and stimulating demand for goods that Chinese businesses will be well placed to service.

Supporting infrastructure projects in neighbouring countries also has a knock-on effect for China's own centre of gravity, which is heavily centred on the eastern coastal region. The rapidity and extent of urbanisation have led to the authorities seeking to limit the size of cities like Beijing and Shanghai and to look to stimulate growth in smaller, poorer cities – locations that are less populous, less industrialised and where life is cheaper to live. This has had the effect of leading to average incomes rising faster in so-called 'third- and fourth-tier cities', and to higher growth rates than in the biggest, most established urban conurbations.[54] The issuing of residency permits has led to the population of cities like Xi'an surging – and with it, inevitably, a spike in house prices, which have risen by 50 per cent year on year.[55]

Investment in transportation, water conservancy, power generation and communication has led to a rash of new businesses being established in China's western provinces, including a tourism boom and higher levels of growth than in other parts of the country – at least until spending was curtailed in the wake of fears about a debt bubble brought on by excessively optimistic projections by local officials.[56]

*

Security plays an important part in the motivations for the Belt and Road, too. The chaotic situation in Afghanistan has long been a cause for concern for Beijing, because of fears of contagion from Islamic fundamentalism in western China. Concern about large numbers of Uighurs who travelled to Syria to fight for Islamic State has also worried the authorities, even if estimates of those involved vary from several thousand to many times that number.[57]

The importance of Xinjiang's energy reserves is one reason why the region has become the focus of considerable government focus, defence spending and political repression. According to local government figures, spending on security in Xinjiang doubled during 2017 alone to more than $9bn, part of a drive to protect any threat to China's largest gas fields, half its coal deposits and as much as a fifth of its oil reserves.[58]

Worries about the spread of instability have led to strict measures being imposed on the Muslim Uighurs in Xinjiang. These include travel bans, controls over names given to children and the shaving off of 'abnormal' beards.[59] According to reports, many hundreds of thousands of Uighurs have been sent to special 're-education camps', whose existence is not acknowledged by the government, and where detention – and release – are not subject to decisions made in a court of law but by party officials and police.[60] In some areas, it was reported that 80% of the adult population have been detained.[61] A report on the situation also found that Beijing had secured deportation of multiple members of the Uyghur population from other countries back to China.[62]

China has denied the existence of these camps, with a foreign-ministry spokesman stating that that reports were being circulated by 'anti-China forces' and that 'the people of all ethnic groups in Xinjiang cherish the current situation of living and working in peace'.[63] 'There are no such things as detention centres,' said Hu Lianhe, a member of the Chinese delegation to the UN. 'There is no suppression of ethnic minorities or violations of their freedom of religious belief,' he said, adding that those 'deceived by religious extremism' were being assisted 'through resettlement and education'.[64]

What this assistance means can be deduced from an audio recording reportedly made by the Communist Party Youth League at the end of 2017. 'Members of the public who have been chosen for re-education have been infected by an ideological illness,' said the speaker. Although many 'who have been indoctrinated with extremist ideology have not committed any crimes, they are already infected by the disease … That is why they must be admitted to a re-education hospital in time to treat and cleanse the virus from their brain and restore their normal mind.' Those being sent 'for treatment' were not being 'forcibly arrested' or detained; they were being rescued.[65]

The crackdown on the Uighurs follows a rash of bombings and knife attacks in Xinjiang, most notably a series of violent attacks that took place in 2009, which rattled the Chinese government into taking action. It was essential, said President Xi in 2014, to 'make terrorists become like rats scurrying across a street, with everybody shouting "beat them"!'[66] It was not long before this was being put into practice, with one senior official in the province telling a mass anti-terror rally in Urumqi that terrorists would be destroyed, whether with loaded guns, unsheathed knives or with bare fists if necessary.[67]

That the security of Xinjiang is a policy priority is clear from the appointment of Chen Quanguo as party secretary of the Xinjiang Uyghur Autonomous Region (effectively the province's governor). Chen is a rising star whose uncompromising tactics in Tibet brought him to Xi's attention and helped gain his admiration and confidence. In the space of a year after his arrival in Xinjiang in August 2016, Chen advertised for more than 90,000 new police and security-related positions – an astonishing rise and an emphatic statement of intent.[68] While the Uighurs bore the brunt of the persecution, other minorities have also been targeted. Tajiks studying in Xinjiang have been formally obliged not to fast during Ramadan – although the same restrictions have apparently not been applied in other regions of the country.[69] But some Kazakhs living in western China claim far worse, with reports including spells in re-education camps and being kept in deep wells filled with ice. 'It was like hell,' said one.[70]

These measures are all part of what the Chinese leadership has called a 'great wall of iron' being placed around the western provinces; this was essential, said President Xi, so that 'people of all ethnic groups feel the Party's care and the warmth of the motherland'.[71] Others have called it 'the largest mass incarceration of a minority population in the world today'.[72]

Concern about Afghanistan's instability has also played a role in Chinese efforts to reinforce the frontier, both through initiatives such as the Quadrilateral Cooperation and Coordination Mechanism, a joint project between China, Afghanistan, Tajikistan and Pakistan, and with support and training for border troops in neighbouring countries. It appears that the Chinese military have also begun to play a role on both sides of the borders, as part of an effort to prevent unauthorised movement of people, goods – and ideas.[73] Perhaps not surprisingly, getting precise details about what is going on in this region is not entirely straightforward.[74]

It is noteworthy too that Beijng has begun to play a more active role in Afghanistan itself, opening lines of communication with the Taliban and inviting leading members to the Chinese capital for discussions. According to some reports, China has not only become closely involved in trying to plan for a post-conflict future of Afghanistan, but has made better progress than others (notably the US) in trying to provide conditions for settlements to be reached that might restore stability to the war-torn country.[75]

If this points to a region becoming more closely knitted together, then so too do more practical steps taken to ensure peaceful conditions necessary for enabling and deepening ties. Providing security for personnel and investments that are part of the Belt and Road Initiative has also evolved in countries like Pakistan, where high-profile cases such as the kidnapping and murder of two schoolteachers in Balochistan in 2017 have led to the creation of a new 15,000-strong force Pakistani soldiers that will protect the China–Pakistan Economic Corridor and safeguard Chinese nationals working as contractors on projects that range from roads to rail to power-plant construction.[76]

*

The expansion of China's perception of its national security interests has played an important part in the development of locations in the South China Sea and beyond. In 2013, dredgers began creating a series of new, man-made islands that can serve as military bases. These steps prompted considerable concern from other countries in this region. Following an appeal by the Philippines that China's actions violated the United Nations Convention on the Law of the Sea, the Permanent Court of Arbitration ruled in 2016 that there was no legal basis for China to claim historic rights, while also finding that there had been several breaches of the obligations set out in the Convention. It also found that the fact that China's refusal to accept or participate in the Philippines' action did not prevent the court reaching its decisions, on the basis that Annex VII of the Convention states that the '[a]bsence of a party or failure of a party to defend its case shall not constitute a bar to the proceedings'.[77]

China's refusal to accept the court's ruling has raised tensions across the region, not least because of the continued militarisation of the artificial islands and construction of landing strips, aircraft hangars, underground fuel reservoirs, barracks – and the installation of radar-jamming equipment and underwater sensors, which was followed by the deployment of anti-ship cruise missiles and long-range surface-to-air missiles in the spring of 2018. This has gone a long way to turning the South China Sea into a zone of anti-access/area denial (A2/AD), in which military competitors (particularly the US Navy) are either seriously impeded in their freedom of action inside the region – or kept out of it altogether.[78]

The militarisation has caused alarm in Vietnam, for example, which has its own territorial claims on the

Paracel Islands, a small archipelago now occupied by China. Landing drills by Chinese bombers have led to the formal demand that 'China put an end to these activities immediately, stop militarisation and seriously respect Vietnam's sovereignty' over the islands.[79] This was echoed in Manila, where the government of President Duterte took 'appropriate diplomatic action' about the presence of the bombers – but resisted calls of senior politicians to take more direct steps 'to inflict, at the very least, a bloody nose on any attacker who is out to harm us'.[80]

Seen from the perspective of Beijing, the fortification of the islands is part of a defensive network that is essential to protect rather than enhance China's position. The South China Sea is so important that in 2014 Chuck Hagel, then US secretary of defence, declared that it was nothing less than 'the beating heart of Asia–Pacific and a crossroads of the global economy'.[81] That is an understatement. While the assertion by many commentators that half of the world's merchant fleet (by tonnage) passes through the South China Sea each year may be hyperbolic, the volume is nevertheless immense.[82] As well as almost 40 per cent of all China's trade, the waterway carries nearly a third of India's trade goods by value, almost a quarter of that of Brazil as well as around 10 per cent that of the UK, Italy and Germany.[83] This is not 'a' crossroads of the global economy. It is 'the' crossroads of the global economy.

If that in turn explains why control of the sea is so important to Beijing, then so too does the fact that the overwhelming majority of China's crude-oil imports reach the country via a sea route through the Strait of Malacca, the shortest and most economical passageway between the Pacific and Indian Oceans (although there are also entry points via the Sunda Strait and the Lombok Strait).[84] China is acutely aware of the strategic vulnerability that stems from its heavy dependence on maritime shipping in general and the pinch points that control access to the South China Sea. 'It is no exaggeration to say that whoever controls the Strait of Malacca will also have a stranglehold on the energy route of China', noted one Chinese newspaper more than a decade ago at a time when anxieties were already being expressed by the leadership that 'certain major powers' were determined to control the strait – and thereby control China.[85]

From Beijing's perspective, protecting the South China Sea is not just a question of an expression of newfound military and political power or even an issue of national security. It is far more important than that: China's present and future depends on being able to ensure that it can get what it needs, safely, securely and without interruption – and ensuring that those who are keen to manage or curtail economic growth are prevented from being able to threaten routes to and from markets elsewhere in the world.

This is why China also finds itself in an increasingly tense standoff over the Senkaku Islands in the East China Sea. Japanese plans to upgrade facilities have resulted in China seeking to challenge Tokyo's control of the islands. Japan's plans to build on the previously uninhabited islands were described by an article written in an internal publication of the Chinese People's Liberation Army as part of a plan 'to control its neighbouring ocean and expand its living space'. The could not be compared, wrote the authors, with China's actions elsewhere, however, since the purpose of the latter was that of 'safeguarding our sovereignty and territorial integrity'.[86] The fact that the Japanese military is developing supersonic 'glide bombs' to be able to protect remote islands – such as the Senkakus – show how much is at stake in this region.[87]

*

China's actions in the South and East China Seas are also part of a wider picture that includes efforts to diversify and open up new transit routes. This explains the heavy investment into freight and high-speed rail lines and roads criss-crossing the new Silk Roads – as well as building new entry and exit points that can offer alternative routes for goods and supplies to move to and from the country. The most obvious example is Gwadar on the coast of Pakistan, which could potentially, in due course, become a major entrepôt, a gateway and a new window on the world. Seventy-five years ago, when it was still a young city, Shanghai was described as the Paris of the east, the New York of the west.[88] Gwadar could have the same fate and one day become the new Shanghai of the west.

The vision is more expansive and ambitious than just creating new connections with neighbours like Pakistan, for the network that China has been building is one that spreads into the Pacific, the Indian Ocean and deep into Africa. Loans, grants and long-term leases have led to a series of ports either under direct Chinese control or heavily indebted to government-controlled companies in the Maldives, Sri Lanka, Vanuatu, Solomon Islands and Djibouti.

The overburden of debts and the muscling-in to control ports like Hambantota in Sri Lanka have led to accusations that far from helping other countries to develop, the Belt and Road is a programme that facilitates a form of colonialism that results in assets ending up in Chinese hands – in just the same way as the British had ended up in control of Hong Kong in the nineteenth century.[89]

The expansion of Chinese interests has not just been through loans, but also through acquisitions that seem to be part of a broad, joined-up strategy. For example, Chinese companies have acquired shipping terminals in Spain, Italy and Belgium either in full or in part.[90] In 2016, the Chinese shipping company Cosco took control of the Greek port of Piraeus, later announcing plans to spend an additional $620m to expand and upgrade the shipyard.[91] In the interim, Cosco bought Orient Overseas Container Line, to become one of the world's largest container carriers – impressive for a company founded only just over a decade earlier.[92]

*

The expansion of China's interests into Europe is mirrored in Africa, where extensive activities date back to well before the announcement of the Belt and Road Initiative. Between 2000 and 2014, some $20bn of financing was invested in the construction of roads and railways across Africa, and almost the same again into power plants, energy grids and pipelines. In the words of one commentator, 'Chinese loans are building the continent.'[93]

There is a sense in some quarters that Chinese investment in Africa dwarfs that of others – a suggestion Beijing sometimes seems to encourage. In fact, as one recent report put it, 'the notion that China has provided an overwhelming amount of finance and is buying up the whole continent is inaccurate'. Nor is it true that Chinese companies operating in Africa only employ Chinese contractors – another common assumption and much-quoted criticism. Nevertheless, there can be little doubt that this is a new era of substantial and significant Sino-African relations.[94]

When it comes to relations with Africa, said President Xi at the 2018 Beijing Summit of the Forum on

China-Africa Cooperation, China follows a 'five-no' approach: 'No interference in African countries' internal affairs; no imposition of our will on African countries; no attachment of political strings to assistance to Africa; and no seeking of selfish political gains in investment and financing cooperation with Africa.' China, said Xi, will always be 'Africa's good friend, good partner and good brother'.[95]

China's attentions have been welcomed by figures like Olusegun Obasanjo, President of Nigeria from 1999 to 2007, who has noted that China is a source of inspiration for African nations. 'China has been hugely successful in poverty reduction,' he said in a speech at Zhejiang University in 2018. 'China has a lesson to teach any developing country who cares to learn.' As well as listening to these lessons, he added, African nations could benefit from 'a strategic relationship and partnership'. This would be of great benefit to all concerned. 'I have no doubt in my mind,' said Obasanjo, 'that Africa needs China, indeed Asia, as they need us.' His personal recommendation about the best next move was that China should provide $100bn of funds for African nations in the next ten years.[96]

It is a similar story in the Caribbean and Central and South America, where China has played a major role in an array of projects, again mainly involving infrastructure but also energy. According to some estimates, more than $220bn of loans was issued to governments in Latin

America and the Caribbean over the last fifteen years.[97] This does not include a recent $5bn loan to cash-strapped, oil-rich and dysfunctional Venezuela, where annual inflation reached over 24,000 per cent in June 2018.[98] When Venezuela needs emergency funding to stay afloat, it turns to China for support – partly because there is no one else to turn to.[99] Bailing out a failed state says a lot about how keen Beijing is to get what it needs – around 700,000 barrels of oil per day, in the case of Venezuela's shipments to China.[100]

*

China has been very active in South America since the publication of a policy paper in 2008 that noted the 'abundant resources' of the region, but also observed that Latin America and the Caribbean were at 'a similar stage of development', and shared similar challenges and difficulties. This underpinned a common desire for 'win-win results' and for higher levels of economic cooperation that resulted in the doubling of trade in a decade and led to China becoming South America's leading trade partner in 2015.[101]

The countries of this region are also to become part of China's connected vision. We are living in a period of great change, President Xi told a meeting of the leaders of the thirty-three states that are members of the Community of Latin American and Caribbean States (CELAC) in a message sent from Beijing. It was sensible to try to prepare for the future. In order best to take advantage of the opportunities and challenges, he said, he was delighted to extend an invitation to the member states of CELAC, offering them the chance formally to join the Belt and Road Initiative.[102]

In other words, the Silk Roads are everywhere – not just in Central Asia, but across all of Asia, Africa, Europe and the Americas. Adverts in airports celebrate the Belt and Road Initiative; investment banks produce reports and host conferences about the challenges and opportunities of the New Silk Roads; newspapers and media outlets commission essays on the motivations and consequences of new and old connections being formed and re-formed in the twenty-first century. All roads used to lead to Rome. Today, they lead to Beijing.

Indeed, it is possible to go further. In today's world, while we think what matters is what goes on in Washington, London and Brussels, a new world is taking shape – a world that is changing quickly, a world that is commercially vibrant, a world that is being galvanised not only by enormous investment but by the shared belief that tomorrow will be better than today. Talk of the Silk Roads of the past is helpful in providing a common narrative that binds peoples and cultures together; but so too are the practical steps to create the Silk Roads of the future.

These include initiatives that seek to use artificial intelligence, nanotechnology and quantum computing to help create smart cities, part of an effort to find solutions to the challenges presented by the high densities of urban populations in Asia; using big data and satellite imagery to measure air pollutants and gases multiple times daily; and work on disaster-risk reduction across the centre of Asia, which is prone to regular earthquakes and natural disasters. This has led to the establishment of a Chinese-led digital belt and road science program which will use earth observation science and technology and big earth data to assist with 'infrastructure improvement, environmental protection, disaster risk reduction, water resource management, urban development, food security, coastal zone management, and the conservation and management of natural and cultural heritage site management'. Its aim, in other words, is to use data to improve connections, improve sustainability and respond better to crises as and when they arise along the Silk Roads.[103]

*

Many are unconvinced by the Belt and Road Initiative, its declared aims and its proposed outcomes – while some also note that it is important to differentiate between the near $1tr that has been promised to projects and the amounts that have actually been committed and paid out, while conceding that even these are to be counted in the hundreds of billions of dollars.[104] To start with, there are the environmental concerns that go hand in hand with major construction projects, the extraction of minerals and the intensification of transportation networks – which are poorly understood, little studied yet likely to be of major significance.[105] Then there is the alarm that local elites have used the opportunity to line their own pockets, while burdening the wider population with debts that they cannot hope to pay back.[106]

It is also difficult to get a sense of exactly what the Belt and Road Initiative even is. It is 'breathtakingly ambiguous', notes Jonathan Hillman, a leading scholar on the subject, who also stresses mismatches between official plans and announcements and the project activities on the ground. 'There is always a risk of imposing order where, by design, it does not exist,' notes Hillman, who also draws attention to duplications and inefficiencies, and to the scattergun funding of projects that have little overlap, let alone forming part of a coherent master-plan.[107]

The ambition and ubiquity of the Belt and Road initiative on the one hand, and the apparent contradictions involved in assessing its purpose and aims, has perplexed many commentators, who have noted the lack of commercial logic behind many individual projects and have questioned the feasibility of the initiative as a whole. Is the scheme 'more public relations smoke than investment fire', Harvard's Joseph Nye wondered, before suggesting that Chinese motivations revolve less around helping raise standards of living in China or in neighbouring countries and more around the desire to find investments that produce better returns than low-yield US government bonds – of which Beijing owns more than $1 tr.[108]

And yet, Chinese officials themselves recognise that 80 per cent of the money ploughed into Pakistan, half that invested into Myanmar and a full third that is expended in Central Asia will probably be lost.[109] Not surprisingly, this has led to discussions about what China's long-term aims are with the Belt and Road Initiative and how most usefully to understand decisions to invest in schemes that are either commercially unviable, overoptimistic, one-sided – or all three.

Others have criticised the fact that, rather than being a 'win-win' scenario, the initiative enables Chinese companies to do well, not alongside others, but at their expense. As some have pointed out, 89 per cent of Chinese-funded Belt and Road projects have Chinese contractors.[110] 'It's about selling their stuff,' said a European Union official, who asked to remain anonymous, during the Beijing Forum of 2017 – when the French embassy issued a statement complaining about the lack of transparency and about the lack of attention paid to 'open, rules-based public tenders' for construction projects along the Silk Roads.[111]

There are also concerns about the fact that many of the countries that have received large loans are notorious for their bad business practices – as well as for their treatment of those who oppose the government or stand in the way of influential decision-makers. The US approach in Africa of 'incentivising good governance to meet long-term security and development goals', said Rex Tillerson, at the time secretary of state, 'stands in direct contrast to China's approach, which encourages dependency using opaque contracts, predatory loan practices, and corrupt deals that mire nations in debt'. There is no question, he added, that 'Chinese investment does have the potential to address Africa's infrastructure gap, but its approach has led to mounting debt and few, if any, jobs in most countries'.[112]

Criticisms like this have brought stinging responses. An article published in Zimbabwe's independent *Newsday* newspaper about Beijing's willingness to turn a blind eye to excessive debt levels, poor business practice and government corruption led to the Chinese embassy in Harare issuing a statement that attacked the 'slander' of the article and noted that 'China and Zimbabwe are good friends, good partners and good brothers who have stood together through thick and thin'. The Chinese government simply wanted to support the Zanu-PF government that was 'elected by the Zimbabwean people and recognised by countries across Africa and the world'. Surely, the fact that China 'conducts friendly exchanges and win-win cooperation with the Zimbabwean counterpart [should be] beyond criticism'?[113]

As it happens, when Robert Mugabe was finally removed from power after thirty-seven years of dictatorship, during which time he accumulated a fortune that US diplomats estimated to be worth more than $1bn, to say nothing of a swathe of human-rights abuses that scarred Zimbabwe, or of the doctorate awarded to his wife just two months after enrolment in a Ph.D. course, many specialists thought that the key role had been played by Beijing.[114]

But China has been careful to court friendships in a more progressive way too, pledging to support agricultural development projects, committing funds to emergency food-aid programmes and providing money to help establish an African Standby Force to assuage crises in the region.[115] The creation of a scheme to award 30,000 scholarships to African students has naturally been both popular and taken as a sign of China's long-term commitment to building ties. In less than fifteen years, the number of African students studying in China has grown twenty-six times – with the result that more anglophone students from across Africa now take courses in China than they do in either the UK or the US.[116]

*

Such steps have convinced some that it is time to look beyond 'aid' from the US, which, rather than being an expression of 'altruistic charity', is a mask for the exploitation of the local populations – and a way of passing subsidies to US corporations.[117] The release of documents that show how the US urged Belgium to withdraw its United Nations peace-keeping force from Rwanda in the 1990s to stop the United States being drawn into violence hardly casts the west's behaviour in even the recent past in a good light, to say nothing of the age of empire of a century ago, when European states controlled 90 per cent of Africa. According to one leading commentator, the US decision 'all but guaranteed the crisis in Rwanda would spin out of control'.[118] The resulting loss of 800,000 lives and the displacement of some 4 million people shows how hard it is to retain credibility while talking of providing leadership – and why criticisms of the US role in Africa, as elsewhere, are not just based on hyperbole but also on fact.[119]

This sits alongside rising criticisms of the rules-based international order, considered in the west as the cornerstone of global stability. In other parts of the world, it is now increasingly referred to as a western 'club' whose benefits 'such as market access, aid and investment, and the provision of a security umbrella [are] offered selectively and conditionally' by developed nations, while keeping China, India and others outside or connected only at the margins. Some developing countries were summarily excluded in a system that locks in advantages for the rich, at the expense of the poor – while enabling the former to pontificate to the latter.[120] Such voices are extreme and relatively rare; but they are growing in number and volume, and result from the perception, real or otherwise, that China is opening its doors at a time when those elsewhere are being closed.

Nevertheless, it is also true to say that many are all too aware that with the golden rays of Chinese attention can come a shadow. Beneficiaries of loans also note, for example, that opportunities do not cut both ways. It is important, said President Kenyatta of Kenya, to see how to enable 'Kenyan goods to penetrate the Chinese market'. With a new $3.6bn railway line to pay for, it is not surprising that leaders like Kenyatta are pushing to get access to markets that can help fuel domestic growth. If Beijing's 'win-win strategy is going to work,' said the Kenyan president in an interview with the *Financial Times*, 'it must mean that, just as Africa opens up to China, China must also open up to Africa'.[121]

Such concerns go hand in hand with worries about the indebtedness incurred by the governments of many countries whose capacity to meet their obligations and manage repayments is often questionable. Kenya is a case in point, where the cost of the new railway and a proposed inner-city expressway threatens to raise the country's debt from 40 to nearly 60 per cent of GDP.[122] Cases like this, such as a single agreement made between the government of Congo and a Chinese consortium regarding mines in the Kolwezi region of the country, which was worth more than the entire annual budget of the Congo in the year it was signed, have not surprisingly caught the attention of specialists.[123] The fact that things in this particular project in Congo have not gone to plan has led some to warn that 'the Belt and Road bubble is starting to burst'.[124]

*

Levels of debt are so acute, meanwhile, in eight countries (including Pakistan, Kyrgyzstan, Tajikistan, Laos and

Mongolia), that some observers have warned about the consequences if, as and when debt repayments cannot be met.[125] Christine Lagarde, managing director of the IMF, noted the potential benefits of large-scale projects, but also gave a diplomatically worded warning while in Beijing in the spring of 2018: 'Ventures can also lead to a problematic increase in debt, potentially limiting other spending as debt service rises and creating balance of payments challenges.'[126] She meant that countries could end with a sovereign default – and be at the mercy of their creditors.

The fiscal pressures that can exacerbate the anxieties of already weak economies can be a serious concern in terms of major infrastructure developments. While there clearly can be long-term benefits in improving local and regional connections, upgrading transport networks and energy supplies, the pain of getting these wrong can be serious. In 2011 Tajikistan's government ceded several hundred square kilometres of land to China in exchange for forgiveness of debts that it could not service.[127] Many have seen this as part of a sign of Beijing's ability and willingness to use its muscle to engineer outcomes that are heavily skewed in its own favour.[128]

Examples of future opportunities to do so are abundant elsewhere. The $7bn cost of the railway line being built to link Kunming with Vientiane represents more than 60 per cent of the GDP of Laos, leading to warnings that the level of debt is so heavy as to be all but unserviceable.[129] What this means in practice was set out in a front-page newspaper story in Angola, a country that has seen almost 4,000 km of new railway track laid down and dozens of stations built or rebuilt by Chinese contractors. As of 31 December 2017, said an editorial in *Expansão*, if the debt was averaged out between the whole population, Angolans effectively owed China $754 each – a considerable sum in a country where annual per capita income is only $6,200.[130] It is an even starker story in Kyrgyzstan, where the state debt is the equivalent of $703 per citizen (as against barely $1,000 annual per capita income).[131]

The same country provides a useful example of what happens when things go wrong with the case of the $386m upgrade to the Bishkek thermal power plants in Kyrgyzstan. In January 2018, the plant broke down following a major investment, leaving some 200,000 homes without heating for five days at a time when temperatures in the Central Asian republic had dropped to almost -30°C. This has created a national scandal in the country, centring on how the contract was awarded, who was responsible for the failings and questions about whether loans from China might create more problems than they solve.[132]

Another case comes with the deep-water port at Hambantota in Sri Lanka, built at a cost of $1.3bn, but whose usage proved to be far lower than the projections to justify the investment. In the summer of 2017, a ninety-nine-year lease was granted to a Chinese company in lieu of debt – a solution that created a political storm in the country, provoked concern in India at China's strategic, commercial and military expansion into the Indian Ocean, and sent an obvious signal to others about the consequences of a project failing to deliver its projected results.[133] Borrowing money from a lender who may have an interest in utilising the asset on which the loan is secured inevitably brings risks that need to be assessed carefully.

In the case of Sri Lanka, the fallout over Hambantota extended to the major new international airport at Mattala that was built in tandem – where bright projections about passenger use failed to materialise. Sri Lankan Airlines, the country's own national carrier, stopped flying to the airport less than two years after it opened for commercial flights due to lack of demand; the only other airline that operated scheduled flights, Dubai's flydubai, suspended operations in the early summer of 2018, raising questions about the future of the airport – and about the repayment of debts estimated to run to over $200m.[134] Discussions between the Indian and Sri Lankan governments to form a joint venture have been primarily motivated by the former's concern about the airport falling into China's hands.[135]

*

India's anxieties are in part based on long-term rivalry with China, and on the legacy of the war that broke out between the two countries in 1962. These have long made for a tetchy relationship, which has become more complicated in recent years. The Indian government pointedly did not send a delegation to the Beijing Forum in May 2017 and has regularly stressed 'serious reservations' about the Belt and Road Initiative.[136]

'No country can accept a project that ignores its core concerns on sovereignty and territorial integrity,' said a statement released by the Indian ministry of external affairs timed to coincide with a major Belt and Road Forum in Beijing in 2017. Driving concerns were plans to upgrade transport links in Kashmir, which India sees as a challenge to its sovereignty and a threat to its national security. But these were not the only criticism of China's plans. 'Connectivity initiatives must be based on universally recognised international norms,' continued the statement, namely 'good governance, rule of law, openness, transparency and equality'.[137] China's plans are 'little more than a colonial enterprise', opined a columnist in one leading Indian newspaper.[138] Nonsense, replied a commentator in the Chinese press. China had never been a colonial power. 'If it hasn't been in the past, why should it be now?'[139]

Underpinning Indian concerns is the amount of investment into Pakistan, with whom India's relations are even more strained than with China. The fact that one spur of the proposed upgrade to transportation links runs through the disputed region of Kashmir has caused considerable alarm in New Delhi. 'The CPEC [China–Pakistan Economic Corridor] passes through

Indian-claimed territory,' said India's ambassador Gautam Bambawale in an interview with China's *Global Times*, 'and hence violates our territorial integrity. This is a major problem for us.'[140]

That is one source of concern, but so too is the fact that Pakistan's close ties with Beijing pose a threat in themselves, given India's fractious history with both neighbours over the last seventy years; that Pakistan's economy may grow substantially as a result of major investment from China presents challenges of its own, not least the prospect of an intensification of already highly competitive political, military and economic rivalry. Indeed, some believe the impact of the China–Pakistan Economic Corridor may be worth an uplift of as much as 8 per cent annually to Pakistan's GDP – billions of dollars, in other words.[141]

Matters with China's plans came to a head in 2017 and threatened to escalate into something very serious indeed. India reacted quickly to Chinese contractors building a new road up to the Doklam Plateau in the Himalayas at the meeting point between the north-eastern Indian state of Sikkim with Bhutan and China. The plateau lies close to the Siliguri Corridor, known as the 'Chicken's Neck', that connects the north-eastern states to the rest of India. As such it is part of what some call a 'terrifyingly vulnerable artery in India's geography'.[142]

In the summer of 2017, as most of the world focused on the Twitter account of the US president and the circus surrounding Brexit, the threat of the two most populous countries on earth going to war was not just a possibility, it looked like becoming a fact: a stand-off between soldiers sent to the front line eventually spilled over and led to both sides engaging directly in hand-to-hand combat by the Line of Actual Control (LAC). Some expected the worst. 'We could be in a full-scale war with China within a month', said the Indian-born British economist Lord Desai.[143]

In fact, cooler heads prevailed and an uneasy truce was agreed. But the threat of escalation was clear from comments made by the chief of the Indian General Staff, General Bipin Ravat, who at the height of the Doklam dispute stated the Indian armed forces needed to be upgraded and put on a war footing. Although he recognised that 'not even a single bullet has been fired on the Indo-China border' and that there were ways of defusing the situation, there should be no doubt, he said, that India was 'fully ready for a two-and-a-half front war'. He meant that the army was ready to simultaneously engage with China and Pakistan, if needed, as well as being able to deal with civil disobedience and uprisings within India itself.[144]

It would be going too far to talk of a siege mentality developing in India when discussing relations with two of its neighbours with whom it often does not see eye to eye and whom it instinctively distrusts. But senior officers thinking, talking and preparing for large-scale action can sometimes create the context for self-fulfilling prophecies. This was the case just over a century ago, when those who went to war in 1914 did so thinking they were taking defensive action.[145]

The concerns of the Indian military are not only based on what is happening in Kashmir and the Himalayas, but also on the fact that the Indian Ocean is emerging as a contested space. In the summer of 2016 Pakistan announced that it would spend $5bn to buy eight modified diesel-electric attack submarines from China – most probably lighter export versions of the Type 039, but possibly even new Type 041 Yuan-class conventional attack submarines.[146] That is a concern for India, as is the fact that Pakistan has already conducted a test flight on the Babur-3, a modified-for-submarine version of the Babur-2 ground-launched nuclear-capable cruise missile.[147]

That is only part of the picture, however, because in addition to Pakistan's increasing capabilities and ambitions are those of China itself in the Indian Ocean. Although the government in Pakistan has insisted that Gwadar and its facilities are open only to commercial shipping and not to the Chinese navy, Indian defence chiefs have already started to think of how to deal with the situation if this changes in the future. The fact that there has been a minimum of eight Chinese naval vessels in the Indian Ocean at any one time – and on one occasion as many as fourteen on patrol – has also been noted at the highest levels in the Indian armed forces.[148]

It is not just the presence of Chinese warships that has become a concern. So too has an increasingly confrontational posture. An Indian navy spokesman was forced to deny that Chinese vessels that included missile destroyers had been threatened with a warning shot and 'war drill' in February 2018.[149] This was the second denial in a month that the two sides had come close to engaging each other.[150]

The challenges cut both ways. China has paid considerable attention to the Maldives as part of what one commentator has called a 'chain of military installations and economic projects aimed at projecting Chinese power in the Indian Ocean'.[151] When the chief justice and a former president of the Maldives were arrested, and a state of emergency declared in the spring of 2018, there were reports that India was preparing to send troops to restore order. These were met with a stark warning from Beijing: if India sent troops to the Maldives, 'China will take action to stop New Delhi. India should not underestimate China's opposition to unilateral military intervention.' India should exercise restraint. If it did not do so, there would be dire consequences. 'Unauthorised military intervention in Malé must be stopped.'[152]

Then there are the elevated fears of rising military confrontation as a result of missile development in India. The successful testing of pre-induction trials of the Agni-V Intercontinental Ballistic Missile (ICBM) from a road-mobile launcher in early 2018 raised alarm bells in Beijing, where it was described as 'a direct threat to China's security'. This was not surprising, given that Indian defence analysts themselves have noted that with a range of 'easily more than 5,500 km, the Agni-V clearly confers upon India the ability to hold all of China's Eastern Seaboard cities at risk from Peninsular India'. The fact that the need to develop 'a longer-ranged and heavier missile that will carry multiple independently targetable re-entry vehicles' in order to 'guarantee penetration against China's [anti-ballistic missile defence] system in the decades ahead', shows the stakes involved as a new world emerges.[153]

In March 2018 joint operations between the naval forces of twenty-three states, including India, Australia, Malaysia, Myanmar, New Zealand, Oman and Cambodia, brought a stern warning in the *Global Times*, a mouthpiece for the government in Beijing. These exercises will inflame tensions with China, the paper warned, and expand the potential for conflict from land to sea. It was likely that the participants would have China at the top of the agenda, with plans to create ties that would 'make China a target'. If there was 'any unreasonable provocation' during the exercises, China 'should be prepared for a military response'.[154]

Blunt warnings such as these underline the fragilities of the modern age. It does not take much to see that provocations, intentional or otherwise, can be easily misconstrued or acted upon in a way that escalates quickly. But nor does it take great insight to recognise that heavy-handed comments like these end up pushing rivals together by accentuating common interests, demonstrating that there is substance to concerns that Beijing is willing to use pressure – and force if necessary – to get its own way.

*

Working out how to cope with, respond to and understand China's expanding ambitions and presence is one reason why defence spending is rising in South and South East Asia and also in Oceania and the Pacific, where Chinese projects to build new airports, wharfs, facilities and to make a further series of investments in the Solomon Islands and Vanuatu have not just raised eyebrows in Australia but led to discussions about how best to respond to them.[155]

While some politicians have reverted to name-calling, such as Concetta Fierravanti-Wells, Australia's former international development minister, saying that China was funding expensive, 'useless buildings', 'roads to nowhere' and construction projects that build 'something for the heck of building it', more active steps have also been taken.[156] These include increasing aid to the region, the laying of expensive underwater cables (to prevent Chinese contractors doing so) and approving a $38bn deal to buy twelve new submarines from France.[157] Such steps – like the decision to spend $7bn on a small fleet of drones – were taken to try to compete with China in the future. 'It is very important,' said Christopher Pyne, the Australian defence industry minister, 'to know who is operating in our area and to be able to respond if necessary to any threats.'[158]

The extent of the concern can also be seen from the strategic defence policy statement released by the government of New Zealand in July 2018. 'New Zealand is navigating an increasingly complex and dynamic international security environment,' the document says. 'We will face compounding challenges of a scope and magnitude not previously seen in our neighbourhood.'[159] This is the prelude for a proposed new security agreement with Australia and a series of Pacific states, driven largely by the increasing Chinese activities in the region.[160]

*

Competition is even sharper and more immediate in Djibouti, where one of the many modern versions of the Great Game is being played out. Strategically located in the Horn of Africa, Djibouti sits at the chokepoint between the Gulf of Aden and the Red Sea (which connects to the Suez Canal), and sees 30 per cent of global shipping sail past each year. Djibouti has been home to a French military base since it gained independence from France in 1977 after more than a century as a colony, with the French garrison playing a role in the security of the country as well as performing anti-piracy patrols in the sea off East Africa. As recently as 2014 there were plans to cut the size of the force by half because of budget deficits in Paris.[161]

Since then, however, the region has become a honey-pot for other states, with Saudi Arabia proposing to build a base in Djibouti because 'we are one people who share the same values, and we have the same issues and problems'.[162] Turkey is also highly active nearby, as is clear from its embassy in Somalia, which is the largest Turkish diplomatic mission in the world.[163] Turkey too is building a military installation in the region, with plans to construct a base in Somalia well underway.[164]

This will be located not far from Japan's military establishment in Djibouti – which is in the process of being expanded.[165] Both will be close to a reinforced facility at Assab in the south of Eritrea that is being built by the United Arab Emirates; already operational, in addition to docking for corvettes and bigger naval craft, it can also accommodate attack aircraft and tanks.[166] Not too far up the coast, a new seaport at Suakin on the coast of Sudan is being built with $4bn of funding from Qatar – which will be the biggest port on the Red Sea, and will have military capabilities as well.[167]

The scramble for strategic position has drawn in all comers – including Russia, who are reportedly in discussions with Somaliland to establish a military base to include facilities capable of servicing two destroyers, four frigates and two submarine pens, as well as hosting a garrison. In return, Moscow will apparently set about helping the breakaway republic establish its independence from Somalia and be internationally recognised as a sovereign state.[168]

But for the US the region has become more than one of interest. It is now of pivotal importance for the military and for America's regional, international and global policies. The construction of a base in Djibouti was described in 2016 by Tom Kelly, then ambassador to the country, as 'the biggest active military construction project in the entire world ... It's number one of everything we're doing.'[169] Djibouti plays a key role for the US military mission not only in Africa, but also in Europe, Asia and globally. 'It's very, very important to us,' General Thomas D. Waldhauser told the House Armed Services Committee in the spring of 2018.[170]

It has also become important to China, which began construction of its own naval base in 2016. When the government of Djibouti terminated the contract of Dubai-based DP World, the operator of the Doraleh container terminal, in a move the company termed 'oppressive and cynical', it was widely believed that the reason for doing so was to hand control of the terminal to China, either as a reward for the loans, or perhaps in lieu of some of the debt repayments of a state that the IMF says faces a 'high risk of debt distress', which has increased significantly since 2014 as a result of 'large externally financed infrastructure projects' – almost all financed by China.[171]

While the Chinese military base is officially linked to providing 'better logistics and [to] safeguard Chinese peacekeeping forces in the Gulf of Aden, offshore Somalia and other humanitarian assistance tasks of the UN', satellite images of the building of a heavily fortified base just a few miles from the US military compound bear witness to a statement of intent.[172] Above all this includes what a defence white paper published by the State Council of China in 2015 called the 'long-standing task for China to safeguard its maritime rights and interests'.[173] As history shows, expanding economic and political interests go hand in hand with taking steps to protect them.

As such, while the fact that General Waldhauser noted that 'the consequences could be significant' if competition developed between the US and China for control of the shipping port in Djibouti, it seems inevitable that there will be similar rivalries elsewhere around the world. A senior adviser to the China Arms Control and Disarmament Association is quoted as saying that 'more overseas logistic bases will be built in the future to assist the PLA Navy [the Chinese navy] to conduct operations globally' – with the stated aim being to rival the US. 'There is no need to hide the ambition of the PLA Navy,' said Xu Guangyu; the purpose is 'to gain an ability like the US Navy so that it can conduct operations globally'.[174]

*

West Africa provides an example of just how – and where – this is happening. The tiny state of São Tomé e

Príncipe has relatively little going for it, at least according to the World Bank, which describes the country as one which has 'no single economic activity that serves as a driver for growth' – a polite way of saying that it is both sleepy and lacking in prospects.[175]

The country does have one thing going for it, however: a location that lends itself as a perfect potential strategic and economic hub for all of West Africa – not least since the small size of the island archipelago and its equally small population mean that it is less exposed to political fragilities than some of the many countries that it is well placed to service. Perhaps not surprisingly, then, it has been the subject not only of Chinese attention but of major investment, with a deep-water port under construction at an estimated cost of $800m.[176]

Although there is no military component to the development in São Tomé e Príncipe, winning friends in strategically important locations is useful – both now and in the future. The offer of additional collaboration, as well as well-chosen words by Wang Yi, the Chinese foreign minister, which note that 'China advocates that all countries, big or small, be on an equal footing', do much to improve relations and create a common narrative that is particularly appealing to countries that feel marginalised or excluded from the mainstream of international affairs.[177]

The approach can also bring more direct rewards. In the case of São Tomé e Príncipe that included the decision to rescind its recognition of Taiwan as an independent state, and the transference of allegiance to Beijing.[178] This finds a parallel with Panama, where Chinese companies with close ties to the government agreed to invest almost $1bn in upgrading port facilities that would help with ever-larger ships.[179] Not long after, Panama – one of a small and shrinking number of countries that recognised Taiwan – broke with Taipei and established diplomatic relations with Beijing.[180] The Dominican Republic, which will receive investment worth $3bn, did the same in May 2018, with the country's president announcing that 'there is a single China in the world, and Taiwan forms an inalienable part of Chinese territory'.[181]

El Salvador was the next to switch allegiance in the summer of 2018. 'We are convinced that this is a step in the right direction,' said the El Salvadorean president in a televised address.[182] The agreement reached with the Vatican over the appointment of Catholic bishops in China likewise would seem to have a context of Beijing seeking to draw support away from Taiwan – even if senior figures in Rome gave assurances that there were 'no diplomatic or political connotations' to the accord.[183]

Chinese sensitivities about Taiwan were clearly not helped by the fact that the island's president was the first world leader that Donald Trump decided to call after being elected president at the end of 2016 in an act described by the *Economist* as a bull entering a China shop.[184] Six months later, Trump took a different approach. President Xi 'is a friend of mine', he said, who was 'doing an amazing job as leader and I wouldn't want to do anything that comes in the way of that. So I would certainly want to speak to him first' before calling Taipei again.[185]

China's manoeuvres have extended to putting pressure on international airlines to amend the maps on their websites and inflight magazine to reflect Beijing's views of the status of Taiwan – dismissed by Trump's White House as 'Orwellian nonsense' and part of an attempt 'to impose Chinese political correctness on American companies and citizens'.[186] The question of the status of Taiwan is a highly delicate one, noted Yan Xuetong, one of the most influential and prominent foreign-policy experts: 'The core of the Cold War was about ideology, and only by preventing ideological tensions can we prevent a Cold War' between China and the US. It is therefore imperative to 'build effective prevention mechanisms' to avoid a crisis – or perhaps worse.[187]

'One of the biggest problems we will have to deal with,' said Yan, is 'Trump's unpredictability', because 'he makes decisions according to his own [whims and] there is little continuity between his decisions'.[188] Understanding this, and dealing with it correctly, requires both skill, patience and no little luck in being able to second-guess what the president will do next and if, when or why he will change his mind. Particularly worrying is the case of Taiwan. The status of this island, and how the US and China handle it, represents the 'biggest danger' to world peace in the next decade, said Yan.

The competition between Washington and Beijing has local consequences too. In September 2018, for example, the US recalled its ambassadors from El Salvador, Panama and the Dominican Republic for consultations over the recognition of Taiwan by the three states and to discuss how the US 'can support strong, independent, democratic states' in Central America and the Caribbean.[189] Put more bluntly, this meant working out what steps to take against those who had chosen to support China.

Countries like El Salvador would be sorry, the White House press secretary had already warned; China's economic inducements only facilitate 'economic dependency and domination, not partnership'.[190] Others are keen to take more direct measures – with four senators introducing the Taiwan Allies International Protection and Enhancement Initiative (TAIPEI) Act to allow the US to 'downgrade' relations and 'suspend or alter US foreign assistance' to any government that supports China over the status of Taiwan.[191]

Avoiding the escalation of rivalries and preventing them spilling over into a dangerous conclusion is of global significance. In that sense, the tensions and competition engendered by China's vision for the world fit into the wider question of how to assess or manage the rise of Beijing, which is seen by many as an economic, military and strategic threat – especially in the United States.

This has come as something as a surprise, as has the speed of China's emergence – forcing a series of second thoughts, reversals of opinion and attempts to correct imbalances. After many years of negotiation, China joined the World Trade Organisation (WTO) in 2001, giving it the ability to better ensure commercial exchange through its trade agreements, as well as providing a forum for resolving disputes. China's refusal to open up its own markets to outsiders was 'contrary to the fundamental principles of the WTO', reported the US Trade Representative, Robert Lighthizer, to Congress at the start of 2018. In retrospect, he said, 'the United States erred in supporting China's entry into the WTO on terms that have proven to be ineffective in securing China's embrace of an open, market-oriented trade regime'.[192]

These concerns are magnified by the large-scale theft of intellectual property (IP) by China and others, which one influential report claimed came at a cost of between $225-$600bn per year to the US economy.[193] According to a different study, Chinese cyberattacks have focused on 'massive theft of information and intellectual property to increase China's economic competitiveness and accelerate its efforts to dominate world markets in key advanced technologies'.[194]

The question of how best to understand and respond to China's rise is becoming an important (if not the dominant) challenge for US policy-makers. This was set out clearly in a speech delivered by US secretary of defence, James Mattis, at the US Naval War College in the summer of 2018. China, he told graduating students, harbours 'long-term designs to rewrite the existing global order'. Their attempts to do so, he said, were based on a return to the past. 'The Ming dynasty seems to be their model, albeit in a more muscular manner, demanding other nations become tribute states, kowtowing to Beijing; espousing One Belt, One Road, when this diverse world has many belts and roads ... and attempting to replicate on the international stage their authoritarian domestic model.'

There were three ways to deal this, said Mattis. By 'building a more lethal force'; by 'strengthening our military alliances and building new partnerships'; and by 'reforming and modernising the Department of Defense for greater performance, accountability and affordability'. The past taught a valuable lesson, he said: 'nations with allies thrive'. He did not explain why that did not apply to China's careful efforts to win friends around the world. Nor did he say why he was willing to learn from history at all, given he started his speech by enthusiastically quoting a recent statement by Donald Trump that 'the past does not have to define the future'.[195]

*

The escalating rivalry between the US and China and the implications this will have for global security were thrown into sharp relief by comments made by Lieutenant General Kenneth F. McKenzie Jr, joint staff director and one of the most senior officers in the American forces, when asked about the creation of artificial islands in the South China Sea. 'I would just tell you that the United States military has had a lot of experience in the western Pacific taking down small islands.' This, he said, was nothing more than 'a simple statement of historical fact'.[196]

General McKenzie's words were meant as a warning – and are best interpreted as a sign of the seriousness with which discussions are being held at the highest levels in the US military about how to deal with China. This is hardly surprising, given that US military assessments conclude that the Chinese military forces have 'rapidly expanded its overwater bomber operating areas' and have acquired the 'capability to strike US and allied forces and military bases in the western Pacific Ocean, including Guam'.[197] Perhaps not surprisingly, therefore, General McKenzie's bullish comments do not find echoes in the views given by Admiral Philip D. Davidson during recent nomination hearings for his appointment as commander, US Pacific Command, in April 2018. Admiral Davidson gave a series of written responses to the Senate Armed Services Committee that described the difficulties of adapting to a changing world – which included candid views of how things stand not in the future but in the present.

Admiral Davidson gave a frank assessment of China's capabilities, and the limitations of the options available to the US Navy. China was in the process of constructing a series of military bases in the South China Sea and beyond, he noted. 'Once occupied, China will be able to extend its influence thousands of miles to the south and project power deep into Oceania.' Its forces, furthermore, would 'easily overwhelm the military forces of any other South China Sea claimants'. His conclusion was as stark as it was clear: 'In short, China is now capable of controlling the South China Sea in all scenarios short of war with the United States.' Even in that event, he added, 'there is no guarantee that the US would win a future conflict with China'.[198]

This is despite major investment in naval technology that includes the construction of vessels like the USS *Zumwalt*, so sophisticated that one of the US Navy's most senior officers, Admiral Harry B. Harris, said that it would be Batman's choice of ship – if he had one. Built at a cost of $4.4bn, *Zumwalt* has the radar signature of a fishing vessel a twelfth of its actual size.[199] Nevertheless, China still raised concerns that a warship of this kind might be deployed close to the Korean peninsula – and therefore close to China.[200] Such worries are ill-placed, at least for now. For one thing, *Zumwalt* has suffered from a string of technical mishaps, including breaking down as it made its way through the Panama Canal.[201] But while it (and others in its class) may in due course become 'warships of unprecedented lethality', it does not look like that will happen soon. According to recent reports, the weapons systems either do not work well enough or not at all; and the cost of firing rocket-propelled shells is four times more than expected, at a cool $915,000 per round.[202]

Such reports do little to still growing fears within the US about the tide turning in China's favour, and help underpin a change in policy regarding the navy in particular. In 2017 an invitation was extended to China to take part in the Rim of the Pacific (RIMPAC) exercise, the largest multinational naval exercise in the world, which takes place every two years and which in 2016 involved forty-five surface ships, five submarines, more than 200 aircraft and 25,000 personnel.[203] Just weeks before this was due to start, James Mattis announced that 'as an initial response to China's continued militarisation of the South China Sea [the US has] disinvited the PLA Navy from the 2018 Rim of the Pacific (RIMPAC) Exercise'.[204]

*

Predicting how intense rivalry and geopolitical competition plays out or resolves is not easy. What is striking, however, is that mirroring the concern in the US about the rise of China is a very different perspective on the other side of the world. 'Western civilisation is built on a philosophical-theological tradition of binary antagonisms,' wrote Jiang Shigong, a prominent Chinese intellectual, in an essay that has been described as the 'authoritative statement of the new political orthodoxy under Xi Jinping'.[205]

For centuries, notes Jiang, 'Chinese culture was the envy of the west'. Since the time of the Opium Wars, however, 'China has experienced humiliation and misery'. The Chinese people, he states, 'who have long suffered in the modern age, have now made a great leap'. Dividing history into the eras of Mao Zedong, Deng Xiaoping and Xi Jinping, Jiang states that these correspond respectively to China 'standing up', 'becoming rich' and 'becoming strong'.

What is happening in China under Xi Jinping, both domestically and internationally, is the natural and logical culmination, in other words, of deep trends and a long process that Jiang ultimately traces back to 1921 and the foundation of the Communist Party. 'The great revival of the Chinese nation,' he concludes, 'is not only an economic and political revival. It is also the revival of political education … that will result in the great revival of Chinese civilisation.' The implications are clear: 'Chinese civilisation is spreading and extending itself into even more parts of the world.'[206] As far as visions go, it is hard to think of one that is more expansive and ambitious. The new Silk Roads are an integral part not only of China's economic and foreign policy, they are an integral part of how China sees the world – and how it is preparing for the future.

The Roads to Rivalry

Nostalgia can have an intoxicating and powerful effect. Looking back through rose-tinted spectacles can create false pasts that cherry-pick only the very best, while ignoring the worst and the mundane. While harking back to a previous golden age often triggers warm memories of supposedly better times, the process can be deceptive, misleading and wrong. In fact, today's world is better in almost every single way than the world of the past.

A child born today is not just statistically likely to live longer than their parents but longer than every single one of their ancestors. More children born today will grow up being able to read and write than at any time in history – both in sheer numbers (because global population is at its highest ever point), but also in percentage terms. Access to clean water and to medical care, to affordable and fast transportation, to energy and communication networks is not just high, but rising. There is much to celebrate and look forward to in the future.

That does not make coming to terms with change easier. It is not always easy to remain sanguine if one seems to be standing in the wrong place at the wrong time. That is the case in the United States, where the rise of China seems not only to pose systemic questions about America's future but also to cast a shadow that makes yearning for the supposed golden years of the twentieth century understandable. The sale of one major business after another, from hotels to aircraft-leasing companies, from biotech to General Electric's Appliance Business – once the jewel in the crown of GE, itself the totemic institution of corporate America – can be difficult to adjust to.[1]

Seeing big names fall to outside buyers armed with cash is a shock to the system – not least when expectations have rarely entertained the thought of buyers from parts of the world about which little is known and to which limited attention is paid. This runs true not only in the US but in Europe, where some of the most iconic names and brands – from Volvo to London taxis, from Warner Music to construction giant Strabag, have owners from abroad, mainly from the countries of the Silk Roads. A perfect example of this new and often strange world comes with the sale of the largest stake in the firm that quarries the Carrara marble in Italy that was used for the Pantheon in Rome, the Duomo in Siena, Marble Arch in London and the Peace Monument that stands in the grounds of the Capitol in Washington, DC. The principal shareholder is the bin Laden family – which in turn means that the marble that was used in the Freedom Tower in New York City comes from quarries now owned by the family of the man who masterminded the destruction of the Twin Towers that previously stood on the same site.[2]

Acquisitions like these have prompted considerable soul-searching and calls for government intervention to block sales. One typical example comes from an article written in the influential *Industry Week*, one of the oldest trade publications in the US. An article titled 'Should We Allow the Chinese to Buy Any Company They Want?' begins: 'We Americans blithely ignore the long-term effects of allowing foreign corporations to purchase the assets of our country in the form of companies, land, and resources. We are selling off our ability to produce wealth by allowing many American corporations to be purchased by foreign corporations.'[3]

Some go even further. 'A lot of Americans don't understand what's happening in China and how good their tech companies have become,' said Senator Mark Warner, who sits on the Senate Intelligence Committee. That Chinese hi-tech firms are globally competitive is bad enough. But for Warner, what was truly unforgivable was the fact that American companies 'have bastardised themselves so much to get into the Chinese market'; in fact, he said, US businesses were guilty of nothing less than 'prostituting themselves'.[4] As it subsequently turned out, these include Facebook, which has data-sharing partnerships with at least four major Chinese electronics businesses – all of which have close ties to the government in Beijing.[5]

The fact that this was not disclosed during high-profile hearings in Washington tells its own story about the steps corporations are willing to take in pursuit of opportunities – as a strongly worded statement from the bipartisan House of Representatives Energy and Commerce Committee explained.[6] That was issued before it emerged that Facebook had been sharing user data with four firms – Huawei, Lenovo, Oppo and TCL – that have been flagged as national security threats by US intelligence.[7]

The relentless search for profit is mirrored by Google's decision to develop a search engine, codenamed Dragonfly, to block websites and searches on topics to do with human rights, religion and other sensitive subjects, and that would be acceptable to the Chinese authorities – giving the company access to a huge market. Perhaps not surprisingly, this has led to considerable soul-searching within Google itself, a company that used to have the motto 'Don't be evil' enshrined within its code of conduct.[8] The dropping of the slogan in the early summer of 2018 is not just a sign of the times; it is a sign of the realities that go with putting the priorities of shareholders above those of others.[9]

The demonisation of China in various forms played an important role in the presidential election campaign. The Chinese 'want to take your throat out, they want to cut you apart', Donald Trump said in one interview.[10]

The Chinese 'have waged economic war against us', he said in a speech in Staten Island in April 2016. 'They're ripping us left and right. [The Chinese] abuse us beyond belief,' he said, finishing by claiming that 'in the history of the world, this is the greatest theft ever perpetrated by anyone or any country, what China has done to us'.[11]

This was an escalation of claims six months earlier, which called 'the money [that China] took out of the United States [is] the greatest theft in the history of our country'.[12] But such statements play well with a core part of the electorate: the economist Branko Milanović observed that 'the great winners' of the redistribution of global wealth 'have been the Asian poor and middle classes; the great losers, the lower middle classes of the rich world'.[13] Explaining the shift of the world's centre of gravity – and promising to do something about it – wins votes.

Given Trump's rhetoric – and key appointments in his administration, such as Peter Navarro (whose views are hinted at by the titles of his recent books *Death by China* and *The Coming China Wars*) – the only thing that came as a surprise was how long it took for a sweeping range of proposed tariffs to be announced on Chinese goods, including steel and aluminium. The explanation for the delay lay partly in the concern about the North Korean missile and nuclear programme, and the need to work carefully around antagonising Beijing as pressure was applied to try to bring Kim Jong-un to the negotiating table.

This was one reason why President Trump insisted on removing references to China in a speech announcing a year-long investigation into intellectual property violations – despite his senior advisors making clear that China was the main target of the inquiry. 'We're going to need their help for North Korea,' he told them.[14] As it was, over a year had passed after becoming president when Trump announced tariffs on more than 1,000 products, which would affect some $50–60bn of imports. The action, said Trump, would be the 'first of many'. Targeting China should have been done 'many, many years' ago. Besides, he added, doing so was 'probably one of the reasons I was elected. Probably the main reason.'[15]

A few days later, the president ordered a further slab of tariffs.[16] He did so despite being warned by powerful retailers that consumer prices in the US would rise as a result. Rather than helping American families, advised the CEOs of businesses like Costco, Gap and IKEA, tariffs 'would worsen and punish' them by resulting in 'higher prices on household basics like clothing, shoes, electronics and home goods'.[17] Too bad, said Peter Navarro. 'This is a historic event and President Trump should be applauded for his courage and vision on this.'[18]

Some commentators believe that Trump's actions are negotiating techniques whose ultimate aims are not to collapse global trade agreements but, rather, to bring a better deal for the United States. 'We view US trade actions targeting China more as an opening gambit for negotiations than the start of a trade war,' said Richard Turnill, chief strategist at the investment manager BlackRock.[19] After all, the president has openly mused about rejoining the Trans-Pacific Partnership trade agreement signed in 2016, which would have reduced trade barriers between Australia, Brunei, Canada, Chile, Japan, Malaysia, Mexico, New Zealand, Peru, Singapore, Vietnam and the United States.[20]

Gambits and gambles have consequences, however, especially when trumpeted with loud fanfare. Days after the president's announcement of a second wave of tariffs, Peter Navarro declared China's response to 'Mr Trump's legitimate defence of the American homeland has been a Great Wall of denial'.[21] This was not quite true, since the Chinese government had not responded with denial or silence at all, but instead had promptly issued a retaliatory list of tariffs that targeted American exports, many of which are produced in states won by Trump during the 2016 election, and which also happen to be areas represented by leading Republican politicians.[22]

The imposition of sweeping tariffs of more than $200bn that came into effect in September 2018 is bound to have an impact on 'our business, our customers, our suppliers and the US economy as a whole', wrote Walmart, the largest retailer in the country, in a letter to the US Trade Representative, warning that it would force prices up.[23] The introduction of tariffs on Chinese goods is rooted in the idea that trade deficits are detrimental. The Trump administration is seeking to rebalance the fact that the US imports $375bn more goods from China than it exports, and to force Chinese markets to open to US corporations and businesses. But as Gary Cohn, one of the president's most senior officials, tried to explain repeatedly at the White House, trade deficits are irrelevant and could even be seen in a positive light – as they effectively enable American consumers to buy the goods they want at the cheapest price.

The problem, according to some, is that while almost all economists agreed with this view, Peter Navarro did not. Cohn, a former Goldman Sachs banker, tried to use evidence and reason to show that tariffs make products more expensive, rather than less, and can prove counter-productive. 'If you just shut the fuck up', he reportedly said to the President and Navarro, 'you might learn something.'[24] They were not interested. Instead, a policy has taken root that sees that the best way to manage China is to put pressure on its economy – regardless of the impact on American consumers, taxpayers and voters.

*

Trump's negotiating technique of hoping to use apparent unpredictability to his advantage meant that, having initiated a trade war, he then tweeted messages declaring that he was 'very thankful' to Chinese President Xi, with whom he was sure to make 'make great progress', as negotiators from both sides met to try to move matters forward.[25]

Discussions were 'positive, pragmatic and constructive', said Chinese Vice Premier Liu He as a joint statement was released, which included an agreement that China would 'significantly increase purchases of United States goods and services' that would 'help growth and employment in the United States'. This would be done in order 'to meet the growing consumption needs of the Chinese people and the need for high-quality economic development' in China.[26] It was a solution designed to allow both sides to save face – and to enable each to claim they had found a good solution.

According to some, the likely impact of any tariffs is more presentational than substantive. 'The actual impact on growth is not very substantial, when you measure in terms of GDP,' said Christine Lagarde of the IMF, concerning the tariffs. The main worry is about 'the erosion of confidence' and perceptions of instability.[27] One of the issues is the perceived instability within the Trump administration and the impression that policies are the result of what the *Washington Post* has called the president 'operating on a tornado of impulses'. The sense of chaos is found throughout the White House. According to one anonymous insider, 'It's just like everybody wakes up every morning and does whatever is right in front of them, rather than working to a plan or in a coherent manner.'[28]

'We're in crazytown', were the reported words of John Kelly, the White House Chief of Staff for President Trump, summing up working conditions, before adding 'I don't even know why any of us are here.' Others noted that the way to prevent bad decisions was to take papers off the president's desk before he could see them in order to stop reactions that might be erratic, counter-productive and even dangerous. The fact that Trump turns on his own appointees, such as Attorney-General Jeff Sessions, whom he described as 'mentally retarded', or Wilbur Ross, Secretary of Commerce, to whom he said 'I don't trust you ... You're past your prime', perfectly illustrates the challenges facing policy-makers at the heart of government in the US.[29]

This could also be seen during the trade negotiations with China, when senior members of the US delegation were unable to get along and caused a public scene that raised eyebrows as well as basic concerns about the professionalism of those trusted with trying to defend American interests. According to the *New York Times*, midway through the negotiations, secretary of the treasury Steve Mnuchin and Peter Navarro, assistant to the treasury, 'stepped outside to engage in a profanity-laced shouting match' – hardly an encouraging sign for those hoping that choppy waters would be calmed.[30]

US rivalry with China goes beyond concerns with the rise of the latter in the South China Sea, in Africa or in more general political, economic or commercial terms. In fact, the question of China is a very existential threat to the United States. 'China inherently presents a fundamental challenge to American strategy,' said Henry Kissinger, before pondering how well this challenge would be dealt with. Not well, he suspected. 'We're not good at it, because we don't understand their history and culture.'[31]

How American policymakers think about China and about change in the world is articulated even more emphatically in a document, the *National Security Strategy of the United States of America*, that was released in December 2017. China is 'attempting to erode American security and prosperity' and wants to 'shape a world antithetical to US values and interests'. This must be stopped at all costs, says the document, and not just for the US's sake. 'America's values and influence, under-written by American power, make the world more free, secure, and prosperous,' it breezily proclaims.[32]

A parallel document, the *Summary of the 2018 National Defense Strategy of the United of America*, does not mince its words either when it comes to China. Beijing is pursuing a military modernisation programme that 'seeks Indo-Pacific regional hegemony in the near-term'. That pales compared to China's apparent wider aim: nothing less than 'the displacement of the United States to achieve global pre-eminence in the future'.[33]

At a Senate hearing, Dan Coats, director of national intelligence, talked about the Chinese and their supposed aim of global domination. 'They're doing it in a very smart way. They're doing it in a very effective way. They are looking beyond their own region.' Christopher Wray, director of the FBI, put this in context. The 'China threat,' he said, is 'not just a whole-of-government threat, but a whole-of-society threat'.[34] Neither commented on whether the US has a policy seeking to do things 'in a very smart way', and if not, why not? And neither set out proposals as to how best to engage with China or manage the relationship with Beijing constructively.

As some East Asia specialists have been at pains to point out, shrill caricatures of China are unhelpful, not least because they avoid trying to analyse and understand China or its motivations. For one thing, it is obvious that far from being a subversive power seeking to undermine the international liberal order – as the Soviet Union was – China is in fact conspicuous in the way that it works within institutions such as the UN, G20 and others, even if it often reluctantly and sometimes even ambiguously does so.[35]

In fact, and ironically, it is the US that is increasingly perceived as bending rules to its own will or breaking them altogether. In August 2018, President Trump threatened to withdraw from the World Trade Organisation (WTO), calling the agreement to create the body 'the single worst trade deal ever made'.[36] This followed the US withdrawal from the UN Human Rights Council two months earlier. The council was a 'cesspool of political bias', said the US ambassador to the UN, Nikki Haley. The UN body was 'hypocritical and self-serving', she said. 'It makes a mockery of human rights.'[37] Rather than try to reform from within, the decision taken in Washington was to withdraw from an internationally recognised forum – however flawed it might be – and to do so both loudly and bitterly.

This forms part of a much wider pattern of the US choosing to act unilaterally – something that provides cheap political capital for its rivals. After President Trump pulled out of the Iran nuclear deal (the JCPOA agreement), for example, Russia's foreign minister, Sergei Lavrov, noted that 'it is unfortunate that we note that Washington is once again seeking to revise previously agreed international accords' – including the Iran nuclear deal, the designation of Jerusalem as the capital of Israel 'and a whole array of other agreements'.[38] Theatrical actions, such as when one of Trump's closest advisers ripped up and spat on papers he pretended were copies of the JCPOA deal in public, while talking about regime change in Iran, may strike a positive note with some in the US; but they have a significant impact on America's reputation around the world, particularly when they form part of a pattern.[39]

This chorus about America's unreliability is becoming more and more common. The United States is responsible for instability in Syria, Iraq and Afghanistan, said the Iranian foreign minister, Mohammed Zarif. By contrast, he said, Iran had always sought stability and stood against upheavals that have done nothing but cause destruction and spread extremism.[40] 'The United States' attempts to impose its own policies on others is a growing danger,' said Iran's President Hassan Rouhani. Unilateral actions, he said, 'are not only against international rules and regulations, but also damage legitimate international trade'.[41]

President Putin has taken a similar line, talking about the destabilising effect of the recent decision-making by the US and the fact that this 'destroys the existing world order' – a bit rich given Russian intervention in Ukraine and purported attempts to influence voting in the US, UK and elsewhere. If it does not come as a surprise that he should talk in this way and accuse the US of causing instability, rather than accepting responsibility for doing the same, it is certainly remarkable to find President Macron of France agreeing with him. 'I share your point of view. I completely share your point of view, all your economic and financial reasoning,' Macron told President Putin at a meeting in St Petersburg in May 2018.[42]

Other leading voices also warn of the detrimental effects of US policies. Talking about the trade war instigated with China, Christine Lagarde said, 'The multilateral trade system has transformed our world over the past generation. But that system of rules and shared responsibility is now in danger of being torn apart. This would be an inexcusable, collective policy failure.' Tariffs, she added, 'not only lead to more expensive products and more limited choices, but they also prevent trade from playing its essential role in boosting productivity and spreading new technologies'.[43]

Or there is Turkey, a long-time NATO member, which has been threatened by President Trump and Vice President Pence because of the detention of Andrew Brunson, an evangelical Presbyterian Christian from North Carolina accused of being involved in the coup of 2016 that sought to temove President Erdoğan from office. If Brunson was not released immediately, said Trump, 'the United States will impose large sanctions on Turkey', before adding in a further tweet that 'this administration doesn't practice "strategic patience" with terrorists' – a reference to the government of President Erdoğan.[44] 'Release Pastor Andrew Brunson NOW,' warned Pence, 'or be prepared to face the consequences.'[45] The first of these were sanctions issued against Abdulhamit Gül, the Turkish justice minister, and Suleyman Soylu, the interior minister. The Turkish lira slumped to a record low a few days later after the Trump administration was reviewing Turkey's access to US markets.[46]

US actions against Turkey, a state that according to President Trump 'has been a problem for a long time', have had an impact on the world beyond, with currencies across the Caucasus sliding as a result, putting pressure on their economies too.[47] Concerns about the consequences of the crisis reached India, where the rupee fell to record lows agains the dollar – and had an impact on currencies all around the world.[48]

Cases like this explain why it is that others around the world are more sceptical about the wonders of the rules-based order – and see this either as a screen that masks the reality of how the powerful get and take what they want, or as systemetised hypocrisy that castigates the behaviour of others on the one hand – while seeking to enjoy the benefits on the other. As a Chinese spokesperson put it when asked separately about US behaviour: 'Who would believe that the rule-maker would make rules to serve others than itself?'[49]

But perhaps the starkest sign of the change in the way the US is perceived by its allies comes from the comments made by Donald Tusk, president of the European Council. 'What worries me most,' he said, 'is the fact that the rules-based international order is being challenged not by the usual suspects but by its main architect and guarantor, the US. We will not stop trying to convince President Trump that undermining this order makes no sense at all.'[50]

In fact, Tusk is quite wrong, for there are, of course, reasons why undermining the 'rules-based international order' makes sense from an American perspective. There should be no question that the US is within its rights to reconsider international agreements, alliance and trade deals, which have become uneven or even unfair, and threaten to amend them. For example, the fact that Germany (among many others) is not only falling but will continue to fall well short of its pledge to spend 2 per cent of its GDP on defence that it agreed at a NATO summit in 2014 raises obvious questions about why the US should carry the burden for an organisation that is under greater strain because of a host of threats and potential problems in North Africa, the Middle East, Russia, Ukraine and beyond.[51] The fact that spending by other NATO members on defence is so low means that US threats to refuse to carry the burden of others are not so much understandable as entirely logical.[52]

Striking better terms with China or with the European Union – which has also been threatened with the introduction of tariffs – is not an unreasonable aim in itself. The problem comes partly from the fact that so many agreements are being overturned at the same time, but the real issue concerns the way in which this is happening repeatedly and the way it is being done. 'We love the countries of the European Union,' Trump said at a rally in North Dakota. 'But the European Union was set up to take advantage of the United States. And, you know, we can't let that happen.'[53]

Asked on Fox News whether he would work with allies in Europe on the question of Chinese trade tariffs, the president was dismissive. 'I love those countries, Germany and all of the countries. Scotland – you know.' But, he said, 'they treat us very badly'. It was nothing personal, he said. 'My parents were born in the European Union,' he claimed, even though his father was born in New York City, and his mother was born in the UK forty-five years before the European Economic Community, the ultimate forebear of the EU, was founded. 'The European Union is possibly as bad as

China,' Trump said, 'just smaller, OK? It is terrible what they do to us.'[54]

The constant search for targets and opponents does little to make friends – and less to keep the ones the US has worked with so successfully for many generations. 'Don't say I never give you anything,' said Trump to German Chancellor Angela Merkel at the G7 meeting in Canada in June 2018 (to which the US president arrived late and left early), before tossing two sweets on to the table in anger. It is not clear what the German chancellor made of this Starburst outburst.[55]

Merkel was more vocal when she met Trump in July 2018 at a NATO summit. 'Germany is a captive of Russia,' said the president in an excoriating opening statement that seemed to have his own advisers squirming – although his press secretary said that their grimaces were not because of Trump's comments but because of their displeasure that they had been 'expecting a full breakfast and there were only pancakes and cheese'. Germany knew what it was to be a captive of Moscow, Merkel reminded the president. 'I've witnessed that myself,' she said in response to his comments, referring to the fact that she grew up in East Germany when it was a satellite of the Soviet Union.[56]

'The President has first and foremost his own interests at the top of his mind, as opposed to the government,' said one US diplomat, speaking anonymously after Trump spent ten days 'shitting on our NATO allies and kissing Putin's ass' – a reference to the fact that the president overruled US intelligence agencies in the summer of 2018 to claim that Russia had not been involved in rigging the presidential election, and seeming to agree to a 'tremendous' offer to allow Russian officials to interview American citizens, including a former US ambassador to Moscow, accused by the Kremlin of 'illegal actions'.[57] Although Trump later rejected the proposal, Susan Rice, a former national security advisor, said that the White House was effectively 'serving a hostile foreign power [and] not the American people'.[58]

Then there was the way President Trump dismissed Justin Trudeau, the mild-mannered prime minister of Canada, one of the US's closest allies as well as its neighbour, as 'very dishonest and weak' after Trudeau gave a press conference at the G7 meeting in 2018 where he said it was 'insulting' that the American president claimed that the introduction of trade tariffs that hurt Canada was connected to US national security.[59] That was positively genial compared to what Peter Navarro, director of the White House National Trade Council, had to say about Trudeau: 'There's a special place in hell,' he told Fox News, 'for any foreign leader that engages in bad-faith diplomacy with President Donald J. Trump and then tries to stab him in the back on the way out the door.'[60]

Full-blooded dismissals of allies are set alongside descriptions of others that are not just brutal, but also highly damaging to the reputation of a country once famed for its tolerance and willingness to give people a chance to work hard to fulfil their dreams. 'Why do we want

all these people from "shithole countries" coming here?'
Trump asked senators at a meeting in the Oval Office
at the start of 2018 about Haiti, El Salvador and some
parts of Africa.[61] Then there is the cutting of $25 million
of humanitarian funding to the East Jerusalem Hospital
Network that provides care treatments including neonatal
intensive care, children's dialysis, cardiac and eye surgeries,
primarily – but not only – to Palestinians. These cuts
were described as 'particularly vindictive' by a former
senior US official overseeing aid to the Palestinians, who
also warned that the withdrawal of funds might cause the
collapse of several hospitals.[62]

Or there is the acquiescence to marchers the previous
summer in Charlottesville, Virginia, who carried
placards declaring 'Jews are Satan's children', and proudly
held up swastikas, while others wore symbols such as
the Confederate flag, white supremacist logos and even
crusader imagery that hark back to supposedly better
times.[63] Instead of condemning the demonstrators,
Trump instead declared, 'You had many people in that
group other than neo-Nazis and white nationalists ...
The press has treated them absolutely unfairly.' In any
event, he added, 'you also had some very fine people
on both sides'.[64] This was all made worse when the
president shared inflammatory videos posted by the far-
right group Britain First a few months later.[65]

It is easy to get carried away by worrying what people
think. After all, today's newspapers are tomorrow's fish-
and-chip wrappers – that is to say, all gets forgotten in

due course. Besides, when it comes to the head of the IMF, United Nations agencies, European Union officials, Canadian politicians or foreigners, one could question the extent to which the president of and officials in the United States should care if others feel they have had their noses put out of joint and spend time complaining about it.

But some go further. According to one (anonymous) senior national security official, the chaos is not just not bad news, but actually a good thing. 'Permanent destabilization creates American advantage,' they told Jeffrey Goldberg, editor-in-chief of *The Atlantic*. Keeping all and sundry off-balance by necessity benefits the United States. Staying friends with people is less important, in other words, than getting things done.[66]

Another 'senior White House official with direct access to the president and his thinking' put it more directly when asked if there was a way of summing up the 'Trump doctrine'. Yes, they said. There is a way to sum it up. 'The Trump Doctrine is, "We're America, Bitch." That's the Trump Doctrine.'[67]

*

That sounds like a slogan rather than a plan. It also suggests a confidence that high-fives and rude hand gestures to others can be effective in the long run. One of the problems is that while it is all very well claiming to want to put 'America first', the reality of an interconnected global economy is more complex. For example, 20 per cent of Apple's revenue comes from mainland China, Hong Kong and Taiwan, which means that tariffs – or an enforced slowdown prompted by US economic policies – will have an impact on the company's bottom line, its shareholders and employees.[68] Or there is Alcoa, one of the world's largest aluminium producers. Headquartered in Pittsburgh, it informed the market in the summer of 2018 that the introduction of tariffs would cost it as much as $14 million per month – sending its shares down by almost 15 per cent.[69]

As Eric Zheng, Chairman of American Chamber of Commerce in Shanghai, put it, American businesses welcomed the fact that President Trump was trying to reset trade relations with Beijing and seeking to 'address long-standing inequities and level the playing field'. The problem, said Zheng, is that the way the administration is going about it 'is hurting the companies it should be helping' as a result of the imposition of tariffs.[70]

Many other of the world's largest companies, as well as young, promising start-ups, either have plans to expand in China, or are already doing so. Trade wars put pressure on their business models, their share prices and on those who have invested in their futures. Historically low interest rates, coupled with hefty corporate tax cuts, have concealed the dangers somewhat, but they are not that hard to see. The shares of General Motors and Fiat Chrysler slumped by 8 per cent and 16 per cent respectively, for example, in a single day after cutting forecasts either on the basis of increased metals costs, reduced expectations in China – or both.[71] 'We're America, Bitch' sounds better in the corridors of power in Washington than it does in the boardrooms of North America – or to pensioners whose savings have reduced in value in the process.

This can be shown too by the case for another of the US's biggest companies, Boeing. Boeing's corporate research suggests that Chinese airlines will buy more than 7,000 passenger jets in the next twenty years. That represents acquisitions worth $1.1tr.[72] Shutting the American door to exports from outside will naturally mean the door being slammed on US corporations elsewhere in the world and create opportunities for others in the process. That will in turn accelerate, rather than slow down, the progress of businesses outside the US, and serve as a catalyst that prompts them to innovate, invest – and win business.

In fact, American companies have done well from China's expanded international vision: the Belt and Road Initiative is 'a very big deal' for General Electric, said Rachel Duan, one of the company's most senior executives – not surprisingly, since it won business worth $2.3bn in 2016 alone. The New Silk Roads will continue to be. As Duan admitted, 'We have a laser focus on winning' more contracts along the new Silk Roads. Other US corporations, like Caterpillar and Honeywell, take similar views.[73] Targeting China with tariffs and an economic slowdown could serve to make life more rather than less difficult for giant corporations that compete in global morliets for global customers.

The reality that 'We're America, Bitch' can be counter-productive comes from the sanctions imposed in the spring of 2018 by the US on five entities and nineteen individuals because 'the [Trump] administration is confronting and countering malign Russian cyber activity, including their attempted interference in US elections, destructive cyber-attacks, and intrusions targeting critical infrastructure'.[74] This had the side effect of leading to a surge in metal prices, with prices of alumina, a key raw material for producing aluminium, surging by more than 80 per cent – and leaving 450 workers fearing for their jobs at the Aughinish alumina refinery in Ireland (owned by Rusal, one of the firms sanctioned).[75] That means raised prices around the world, including, of course, in the USA – which imports 90 per cent of the aluminium it uses in domestic manufacturing.[76]

Steps taken against Russia likewise degrade US intelligence capabilities with regard to assessing the Kremlin's actions, not least regarding potential interventions in elections held in the United States. As it later emerged, detailed reports about likely efforts to influence the presidential election in 2016 were received from a series of informants in Russia. These have fallen silent, probably because of higher levels of counterintelligence from Moscow because of the rising antagonism between the two states – and because of President Trump's willingness to overlook, excuse or deny Moscow's involvement in 2016.[77]

One of the ironies of the sanctions imposed on Russia in 2017, followed by further rounds in 2018, has been a sharp spike in the price of oil – which rose by 30 per cent in twelve months. This not only put an additional burden on American pockets filling up at the pump, it served to boost government revenues from hydrocarbons in Moscow – where higher prices are a boon for an economy that gets 50 per cent of its revenues from the exploitation and export of fossil fuels. The introduction of sanctions on Iran in the spring of 2018 was a godsend to oil exporters such as Russia and Iran – where one senior figure taunted Trump that his 'frequent and indecent tweets' had added at least $10 to the price of oil per barrel.[78] All this, of course, means higher prices at petrol stations and higher energy costs around the world, including in the US. Putting America first is not as easy as it sounds.[79]

*

The same is the case when trying to work through a response to China's Belt and Road Initiative. When asked about the initiative by the Senate Armed Services Committee in October 2017, Defense Secretary Mattis declared: 'In a globalised world, there are many belts and roads, and no one nation should put itself in a position of dictating "one belt, one road"'.[80] That may well be so. But as the prime minister of Cambodia, Hun Sen, put it when asked about the Belt and Road Initiative a few months earlier, 'Other countries have lots of ideas but no money. But for China, when it comes with an idea, it also comes with the money.'[81]

This sentiment is echoed elsewhere, for example in Pakistan, where the minister of commerce, Khurram Dastgir Khan, gave a direct answer when asked about China. 'China,' he said, 'is the only game in town.'[82] Senior figures in the US have recognised this issue. 'We have watched the activities and actions of others,' noted Rex Tillerson, then secretary of state, 'in particular China, and the financing mechanisms it brings to many … countries [along the Silk Roads], which result in saddling them with enormous levels of debt'. Belatedly, he had come to realise 'It's important that we begin to develop some means of countering that with alternative financing measures, financing structure.'[83] In a fast-changing world, being slow off the mark does not just mean being at a disadvantage; it means showing a lack of initiative – and a lack of leadership.

This was what General Waldhauser was pleading for when talking about Africa. All the leaders of the states in Africa he had met 'want US involvement. They all want US leadership. And it doesn't have to be large. It doesn't have to be grand. But they want to know that they have our support. They want to have our leadership. And they want to have a relationship with us. They really do.'[84]

Being slow off the mark also means having to deal with fait accomplis, which are difficult if not impossible to reverse. Failure to stop China's expansion in the South China Sea, said Michael Collins, deputy assistant director of the CIA's East Asia Mission Center, meant that the US was effectively dealing with 'the Crimea of the East' – a reference to the annexation of the Black Sea peninsula by Russia in 2014. It is hard to stop a ship that has sailed.[85]

But another problem is that 'permanent destabilisation' might indeed create 'American advantage' in some cases and in some situations. But it does not win friends. And, perhaps more tellingly, it can also help crystallise new alliances and new blocks that turn out to be challenging and difficult to deal with – by pushing others to find common ground and solutions that are mutually beneficial.

*

In the case of the new, emerging world, and in particular with a rising China, the US has decided to bet the house on India. This had seemed likely even before Trump's election. At a time when the then presidential candidate was talking about how China was damaging the American economy, he also made clear that he saw India very differently. 'I am a big fan of Hindu. I am a big fan of India. Big, big fan,' he said while on the campaign trail. 'If I'm elected president,' he added, 'the Indian and Hindu community will have a true friend in the White House. That I can guarantee you.'[86]

The desire to create a new bulwark in Asia was expressed equally forcefully by Vice President Mike Pence in the summer of 2017. US strategy in Afghanistan and beyond, wrote Pence, should be based on 'a stronger strategic partnership with India – the world's largest democracy and a key security and economic partner'.[87] Secretary Mattis was even more explicit: 'What we have now,' he told one Senate hearing, 'is a strategic convergence, a generational opportunity, between the two largest democracies in the world [US and India] to work together based on those shared interests of peace, of prosperity, of stability in the region.' India was playing a 'bigger role in the world', he said, 'and that role, from our perspective, is a wholly positive one right now'. It was obvious, he said. 'We are natural partners, India and the United States.'[88]

History is not on the side of this glossy view, given that India was a leading member of the Non-Aligned movement during the Cold War and had close relations with the Soviet Union, which not only supplied all three Indian armed forces with the bulk of their weapons, but did so on generous credit terms and even allowed co-production of the MiG fighter jets in India.[89] In four years in the 1980s the Soviet Union delivered more than $7.5bn of weapons to India – an eye-watering sum at the time.[90] Even now, Russia is by far the largest supplier of arms to India. According to the Stockholm International Peace Research Institute, Russia accounted for almost two-thirds of all Indian arms purchases between 2013 and 2017.[91] The acquisition of a controlling stake in the Indian assets of Essar Oil for $12.9bn in 2017 is mirrored by Indian investment in Russian producers, oil fields and the first imports of liquefied natural gas, and provides other important ties between the two countries.[92] Delhi has looked to Moscow for support and partnership, in other words, rather than Washington, not just for years but for generations.

US attempts to curry favour with Delhi explain why Secretary Mattis weighed in heavily on the rights and wrongs of the Belt and Road Initiative when challenged in Congress. The plans involve 'going through disputed territory', he said, and, 'I think that in itself shows the vulnerability of trying to establish that sort of a dictate.'[93] It made sense, in other words, for US and India to work together, given they have a mutual rival in common.

Briefings by the State Department talk in similar terms. Although China is not mentioned directly, it does not take much to see that the US's aim is to balance out Beijing's influence and power. 'It is our policy,' stated one senior official, 'to ensure that India ... does become over time a more influential player' in the 'Indo-Pacific region'. This aim was explicitly linked to America's idealised vision of global affairs. 'It in our interest, the US interest, as well as the interest of the region, that India plays an increasingly weighty role in the region.'[94]

The assumptions of a natural alignment between the US and India are clear from the comments of Admiral Harry B. Harris, then commander of US Pacific Command, who told the annual Raisina Dialogue conference in New Delhi that 'American and Indian navy vessels steaming together will become a common and welcome sight throughout Indo-Asian Pacific waters as we work together to maintain the freedom of the seas for all nations'.[95]

There certainly are mutual interests in so far as it serves India to keep options open. Military strategists in Delhi set considerable store too by co-operating with Taiwan, whose close attention to Chinese military deployments is eagerly followed in India. 'We are dependent on Taiwan because they are watching the Chinese,' said one senior source, adding that Indian officers regularly visit Taiwan 'on study leave'.[96]

The problem here is that while India seems a perfect partner for the US in Asia, it is by no means clear that the Indian government feels the same way. For one thing, there are close ties to Russia, which has been careful to court Prime Minister Modi at every opportunity – to good effect, to judge from the announcement of a slew of agreements ranging from the sale of military hardware, to nuclear reactors in Goa in October 2016. Russia is 'an old friend of India', said Modi – which, he added, is better than two new friends.[97] There was considerable criticism in India after Admiral Harris's remarks, including a statement released by the minister of defence, Manohar Parrikar, declaring that 'no talks have been held with the United States on conduct of any joint naval patrols. Further,' he went on, '[the] Indian navy has never carried out joint patrols with another country.'[98]

Then there are the problems of a tetchy commercial relationship between India and the US. On the one hand, India is seen as an ideal partner, but on the other as a rival – and one that is dealt with scornfully. It was time for India to stop using the United States as a 'piggy bank that everybody is robbing', said Trump in the summer of 2018. Calling Prime Minister Narendra Modi 'a beautiful man' might appeal to the Indian leader's ego, but most Indians hearing Trump talk like this and threaten to slap taxes on 'thousands and thousands' of Indian products are unlikely to think more sympathetically about the US than if the president had not said anything at all – especially in the context of how Trump talks about America and how he talks about the rest of the world.[99]

The threat of being priced or shut out of American markets is one reason why Delhi has tried to keep Washington happy – for example, offering to buy aircraft and step up imports of oil and gas from the United States. Following the American refusal to allow India an exemption from steel and aluminium tariffs, the government in Delhi imposed new duties on walnuts and almonds, a step that was not insignificant given that around half of all US almond exports are bought by India, but one calculated as a gesture to respond but not to antagonise.[100] The economic muscles of the United States are so strong that fighting back needs to be done carefully and cautiously.

Nevertheless, there are important benefits to aligning with the US – as is clear from the signing of the landmark Communications Compatability and Security Agreement (COMCASA) that will allow for closer cooperation across a range of defence topics, give India access to sensitive equipment and nudge India into an 'Asian NATO' along with Japan and Australia. All stand to gain from better ties, especially when it comes to the question of China.[101]

And yet, despite its rivalry with China, India is reluctant to be unnecessarily antagonistic towards its powerful neighbour, seeking to develop a constructive narrative rather than sharpen antagonisms for the sake of it. In India's case, moreover, there are obvious advantages in trying to keep relations with China – and indeed with other countries – as pragmatic as possible. A summit in Wuhan that in the spring of 2018 witnessed important statements of solidarity between president Xi and Prime Minister Modi alongside diplomatic niceties saw the Indian leader received with particular distinction. It was striking that, rather than emphasise difference, not least over the Doklam frontier dispute and over maritime issues, Modi was keen to underline the leading role that both countries had played in world history. The two had much in common, he said. Not surprisingly so, given that 'India and China acted as engines for global economic growth for 1600 years out of the past 2000 years'.[102] The leaders also talked at the summit about how to work more closely together – with projects in Afghanistan mooted as possible initial scenarios for collaboration.[103]

Cooperation has continued since the Wuhan meeting. During the meeting of the Shanghai Cooperation Organisation held in Qingdao in June 2018, for example, it was announced that China had agreed to provide hydrological data on the Brahmaputra River in flood season to India – a step that is helpful both to predict floodwaters and to be able to anticipate shortages well in advance. An agreement under which China commits to importing non-basmati rice, and tentative plans for military cooperation provide more examples of early-stage collaboration between the world's two most populous countries.[104]

If that muddies the waters as far as US hopes for India go, then so too does the decision by President Trump to withdraw from the nuclear agreement on Iran. Few were surprised by the announcement that the president would take this action, given the fact that it falls into a pattern of systematically disparaging, denigrating or dismantling almost every step taken in both international and domestic affairs by his predecessor in the White House, Barack Obama. The determination to talk about liberating the Iranian people and effecting regime change showed that more effort could be usefully expended studying even recent history by those in or within shouting distance of the Oval Office.[105]

The fact that Rudy Giuliani, one of Trump's closest confidants, talks brazenly about how the French and Russian revolutions should serve as templates for contemporary Iran without seeming to recognise the brutality, violence and disruption that both caused in the short term – or that they led to the emergence of megalomaniac despots – is not exactly promising. His advocacy of martyrdom as a route for those wishing to change Iran and offering support to those 'willing to pay with their blood' shows an extraordinary blindness from a man who was Mayor of New York during its bleakest hour, when it was attacked by men willing to kill themselves for their beliefs on 11 September 2001.[106]

Withdrawing from the JCPOA in May 2018, Trump claimed that 'a constructive deal could easily have been struck at the time [of the Obama presidency], but it wasn't. At the heart of the Iran deal was a giant fiction that a murderous regime desired only a peaceful nuclear energy program.' Despite assurances to the contrary from the International Atomic Energy Agency, Trump said that he had 'definitive proof that this Iranian promise was a lie'. The agreement was 'poorly negotiated', he said. 'It didn't bring calm, it didn't bring peace, and it never will.' It was important to scrap the agreement, he went on, to help Iranians themselves. 'The future of Iran belongs to its people,' he said. 'They are the rightful heirs to a rich culture and an ancient land. And they deserve a nation that does justice to their dreams, honour to their history, and glory to God.'[107]

To enable that to happen, said Mike Pompeo, secretary of state, two weeks later, 'we will apply unprecedented financial pressure on the Iranian regime'.[108] The effects were almost immediate, with the Tehran bazaar effectively shutting down because traders could not import goods to sell – and also because of the difficulties of properly pricing what merchandise they did have available in the face of rampant inflation and economic uncertainty.[109] The collapse in the value of the rial was one immediate result of US policy; street protests in many cities across Iran in the summer of 2018 was another.[110] The sacking of the minister of the economy, the arrest of dozens of 'economic saboteurs' and the remarkable televised grilling of President Rouhani provide further evidence of the strain that US measures have placed on the country.[111]

*

In an effort to buy time, Iran issued a suit at the International Court of Justice in The Hague seeking to suspend the US sanctions, describing these as 'naked aggression' whose aim was nothing less than the 'economic strangulation' of the country.[112] The US response was to declare that it did not matter what verdict the court reaches; it had no jurisdiction to rule over the dispute.[113] If Iran wants a new agreement with the US, there were twelve demands it had to meet; if it did so, Washington would drop 'every one of our sanctions', 're-establish full diplomatic and commercial relationships with Iran' and even allow the country access to 'advanced technology'.[114]

The problem is that the list of demands is reminiscent of those included in the ultimatum issued to Serbia in the build-up to war in 1914 – that is to say, a sweeping series of requirements that are designed to be not so much humiliating as impossible to achieve. In any event, assuming that the approach causing Iran to break will produce an outcome that is positive for the country's people, for the region or for the US is unclear. As Chinese Premier Li Keqiang warned, perhaps the greatest risk of the was precisely that there would be unforeseeable consequences locally, regionally and potentially beyond.[115] So while the US might be behind the decision by the authorities in Iraq not to pay Iran $1.5bn for energy supplies, as some Iraqi politicians have claimed, the result – street protests and riots in Basra and the south of the country after Iran stopped supplying electricity – may serve not just to make life difficult in one country, but bring about the implosion and collapse of another.[116]

As it is, the US approach has been a catalyst for an alignment within Iran, with the head of the Islamic Revolutionary Guards Corps writing to President Rouhani after the latter issued fiery words about Trump's actions. 'I will kiss your hand,' said Major General Qasem Soleimani, 'for your timely, prudent and correct statement' – sentiments shared by the hard-line *Vatan-e*

Emrooz newspaper, which likewise praised the angry rhetoric of the Iranian president.[117] As could have been predicted, pressure from outside usually serves to unite, rather than divide.

But the pressure applied to Iran also demonstrates the dangers of focusing on one country and neither seeing the bigger picture, nor recognising or understanding the consequences of what decisions made in one place have on others. The sanctions on Tehran introduced after the US decision to withdraw from the JCPOA have also created opportunities for Tehran and Moscow to draw closer – one reason for the reconciliation over the legal status of the Caspian Sea in the summer of 2018. 'Iran is not a country that one can bully,' said the Russian ambassador to Iran, Levan Dzagaryan. The only way to work with Iran is through diplomacy, engagement and persuasion, he added. From Moscow's point of view, he went on, US sanctions against Iran are 'illegal'. Threats from Washington would have no impact on Moscow's relations with Tehran, said the ambassador.[118]

The alignment between Russia and Iran has led to the proposals of future collaborative projects – such as plans to link Crimea, annexed by Russia in 1914, with Iran via new train lines and the Volga-Don canal, which are more expressions of hope than reality given their cost and limited economic sense.[119] They are part of a wider enthusiasm to cooperate and reassure, of which enthusiastic reporting by institutions like the Oriental Institute of the Russian Academy of Sciences is another element. Iran has always been the 'back door' to Russia, according to one article that explains what would happen if Tehran was attacked by the US. 'War with Iran might well be the end of America as a world power', would result in Saudi oil supplies being stopped 'for all time' and lead to the ruin of Israel for good measure.[120]

'America should know that peace with Iran is the mother of all peace,' said President Rouhani soon after, 'and war with Iran is the mother of all wars.' Hostile policies would only result in regret, he added.[121] This brought an immediate response from President Trump. 'NEVER, EVER THREATEN THE UNITED STATES AGAIN,' he tweeted in capital letters for emphasis, 'OR YOU WILL SUFFER CONSEQUENCES THE LIKES OF WHICH FEW THROUGHOUT HISTORY HAVE EVER SUFFERED BEFORE.'[122] The warning, presumably a reference to a nuclear strike, was re-emphasised by US national security advisor John Bolton shortly after. 'If Iran does anything at all to the negative,' he said, 'they will pay a price few countries have ever paid.'[123] These were the threats of a nightclub owner, said Major General Soleimani, a nod at Trump's business interests in casinos. Perhaps it would be better for the president to reflect on the US's track record in Afghanistan and elsewhere before expecting Iran to back down.[124]

While the prospect of an escalation of animosities, barbed comments and threats is a real one, in the meantime the war of words promises to be highly problematic for

India. Delhi has worked hard to establish good relations with Tehran, both to build trade links – particularly in the energy sector – but also as a counterbalance to India's long-standing rivalry with Pakistan.

The declaration that any company doing business with Iran would face sanctions is a source of considerable alarm in India, which has been in discussion about laying a new deep-water pipeline from southern Iran and increasing sales of gas and oil to help fuel the growing Indian economy. Given that India currently receives around a third of its oil from Iran, US sanctions have significant implications for hundreds of millions of people living in India – designated as the US's principal ally in South if not all of Asia. 'Why would any business, why would the shareholders of any business, want to do business with the world's central banker of international terrorism?' asked National Security Advisor Bolton when pressed about the purpose of sanctions.[125] Those trying to heat a stove or switch on a light in Mumbai would be able to answer that question.

The US has adopted an uncompromising line on Iran, with no exceptions. 'We're not granting waivers,' said a senior US State Department official when discussing what the sanctions will mean for India. The United States expects and demands that India's oil imports from Iran 'go to zero, without question'.[126] Little thought seems to have gone into how India will replace supplies, or what the logical price rises will do to economic growth – or to the millions of poor for whom even small inflationary pressures can be difficult to absorb.

It is not just India's oil supply that is in question. In 2016, after the JCPOA was agreed in the first place, India committed to invest $500m in expanding the port of Chabahar, partly as a response to the Chinese-built and funded port at Gwadar, but also as a collaboration that the Iranian supreme leader, Ayatollah Khamenei, said could 'prepare the ground for deep, long-term and useful cooperation' between India and Iran.[127] In addition to the port is the proposed $16bn investment in a free-trade zone that is itself part of a wider plan to connect India to rail and road networks into Iran and Afghanistan and open up opportunities for the future.[128] Work on some of these new networks has begun – and some phases are complete.[129] What happens next is anyone's guess.

As well as putting Indian investment at risk, the threat to those doing business with or in Iran also threatens to compromise others. Chabahar had already proved not just a viable but highly competitive route to market for goods and products from Afghanistan, opening up a new one that took business away from Karachi.[130] Quite how the US now squares the circle is difficult to predict. 'We know the port has to happen and the US is going to work with India to do that,' said Nikki Haley on a visit to India in the summer of 2018. India has been 'a great partner with us in Afghanistan', she said, 'and really trying to assist the US'. What that means for Chabahar and for India is unclear. 'We realise we're threading a needle,' said Haley, in something of an understatement.[131]

*

The move against Iran opens can after can of worms. The development of Chabahar offered the chance for resource-rich Central Asian republics, such as Uzbekistan, to be able to export quickly and cheaply – something that has been complicated if not curtailed by sanctions against Iran.[132] Then there is the issue of Turkey, which has been a long-term US ally, but is now drifting in another direction. 'Iran is a good neighbour and we have economic ties,' said Turkish Foreign Minister Mevlüt Çavuşoğlu. 'We are not going to cut off our trade ties with Iran because other countries told us so.'[133] The Turkish minister of economy, Nihat Zeybekci, went further: 'The stronger Iran gets in this region,' he said, 'the stronger Turkey becomes as well, and the stronger Turkey becomes, the stronger Iran gets as well.'[134]

Efforts to weaken Iran therefore have a negative effect on other states too. 'I am sorry,' Turkish President Erdoğan told US President Barack Obama last time sanctions were imposed, 'but we are purchasing natural gas from Iran.' How else will we get 'natural gas if I cannot buy it?'[135] Iran is 'one of the most important strategic partners for us', said the Turkish leader, refusing to join anti-Iranian sanctions.[136]

The risks of getting on the wrong side of the US government are enough for some to leave nothing to chance. Such is the concern at Nike that three days before the start of the FIFA World Cup in June 2018, the sports apparel company announced that 'US sanctions mean that, as a US company, Nike cannot supply shoes to players in the Iranian national team at this time'. If a sportswear company is too afraid of repercussions for supplying twenty-two pairs of boots to the Iranian football team, it is perhaps not surprising that others feel equally concerned.[137]

These include Total, the French oil explorer, which had signed a deal to develop Iran's South Pars, the world's largest gas field, with estimated exploitation costs of $5bn.[138] This is now unlikely to go ahead. Then there are Boeing and Airbus, the world's two largest aviation companies, which signed business agreements worth a total of $39bn to supply commercial aircraft to Iran at the end of 2016 – and whose contracts will also presumably not be fulfilled, something that will affect workers and shareholders of the businesses alike.[139]

The obvious beneficiary, ironically, is of course China. According to Ministry of Commerce spokesman Gao Feng, Beijing is unconcerned by American sanctions and will continue to carry on business as usual with Tehran, regardless of Washington's threats and actions.[140] That is not surprising, both in the context of China offering a geopolitical alternative to the US, but also because of the opportunities created for Chinese companies. A contract that had been awarded to Swiss company Stadler Rail to provide 1,000 underground railway carriages will not proceed in light of US sanctions on any corporation doing business with or in Iran. The contract, said Stadler's head of sales, 'will probably be snapped up by the Chinese'. This was not surprising, commented Philippe Welti, former Swiss ambassador to Tehran: 'China jumps into every vacuum that opens.'[141]

Sanctions – or the fears of sanctions – were part of the reason for Exxon's withdrawal from a joint venture with Russia's Rosneft, after it was made clear that those close to President Putin would have their lives made difficult by the US and by EU authorities. The decision was directly linked to the fact that 'in the latter half of 2017, the United States codified and expanded sanctions against Russia'.[142] According to estimates, this meant walking away from plans to invest as much as $500bn in exploration projects in the Russian Arctic.[143]

Apart from the effect that these measures have on American jobs and the American economy, the strong-arm tactics and threats by the US have ruffled feathers among old friends. There was shock in Germany when, on his first day in Berlin as ambassador, Richard Grenell warned that 'German companies doing business in Iran should wind down operations immediately'.[144] If they did not do so, he said, there would be consequences that would hit German businesses hard.[145] This forced the minister of the economy, Peter Altmaier, to make a sanguine admission that there was nothing he could do through legal means 'to protect German companies from the decisions of the American government'.[146]

This has in turn led to an extraordinary sequence of events, which has included the president of the European Commission seeking to activate a so-called blocking statute that bans European companies from complying with the US sanctions against Iran. 'We have the duty, the Commission and the European Union, to protect our European businesses,' said Juncker. 'We must act now, and we will act now,' he added.[147]

The blocking statute, which came into effect on 7 August 2018, formally forbids companies based in the EU from cancelling business ties with Iran – under the threat of punishment. In what can only be described as surrealist politics and economics, European businesses face the choice of being fined if they do business with Iran by the US – and being fined by the European Union if they do not. It is hard to think of a more appropriate way to show how the west has lost its way. The fact that President Macron of France felt compelled to tweet that Donald Trump found himself isolated and alone amidst a group of nations that historically had always stuck together after the G7 summit in Quebec in June 2018 shows just how difficult the countries that have led the world for the last 300 years are finding it to adapt to the changing world of the twenty-first century.[148]

*

It is tempting to think that what we are seeing revolves around the temperament and eccentricity of a single US president with an unusual and emphatic doctrine, and such self-confidence that he can declare when asked about his summit with North Korea's Kim Jong-un about how he would know how the meeting would develop that 'I think within the first minute I'll know. Just my touch, my feel. That's what I do.'[149]

But, in fact, there is something more profound at stake – of which Trump himself is a symptom, rather than a cause. Leaving to one side the current incumbent in the White House, it is striking to note just how few true allies the US has around the world, and how even long-term partners questions its basic reliability. The isolation of the US is a matter of deep concern for experienced old hands like former Deputy Secretary of State Strobe Talbott, who has warned that American isolationism is not just foolish, but against US national interests.[150] Making alliances is an art, and a lengthy, slow process that brings long-term rewards. But building, maintaining and cultivating such relationships takes time and requires investment. To paraphrase Oscar Wilde, jettisoning one might seem like a misfortune; getting rid of them all at the same time looks like carelessness.

The Roads to the Future

The ability to prepare for the future looks questionable. In Europe, the energy, resources and focus of politicians, policy-makers and bureaucrats are almost exclusively committed to one question: Europe itself. There is no little irony in the extended period of introversion at a time when connections are being forged all over the rest of the world – in a classic case of fiddling while Rome burns.

In the course of 2017 alone, the Foreign Service officer corps at the State Department lost 60 per cent of its career ambassadors – its most experienced, knowledgeable and connected country experts.[1] This gap extended right up to the very highest echelons. Before Tillerson's sacking in early 2018, eight of the ten most senior positions in the State Department were formally vacant, as were thirty-eight ambassadorships.[2] Of 626 top jobs in the executive branch of the US government as a whole, not only were some 40 per cent unfilled a year after Trump's inauguration, but there was not even a candidate taking part in the appointment process.[3]

Perhaps, not surprisingly in the circumstances, the most natural path is to follow the course of least resistance. Thus, Saudi Arabia has become the pillar of US policy in the Middle East – despite the fact that the country's goverment is currently being pursued through the courts by families of victims of the 9/11 atrocity.[4] One reason for this is the oil wealth of Saudi, but another is the prodigious amount of money that the country spends on weapons, much of it bought from the United States. During President Obama's time in office, the US sold an astonishing $112bn of armaments to Saudi alone over the course of eight years, including one deal for over $60bn in 2009.[5]

The depth of Saudi pockets for weapons-buying, but also the importance of Iran in American foreign-policy thinking explains why Trump's first trip abroad as president was to Riyadh. This was a statement of intent and a sign of a major re-orientation in thinking of how to deal with Tehran.

So far, Trump's success in emulating the arms-selling of his predecessor has proved illusory. Despite his much-heralded business background and eye for the deal, and despite announcing a package of $110 billion of weapons sales during his visit to Riyadh, the sales of hardware were not finalised. This was one reason why Trump upbraided the Saudi crown prince when the latter visited Washington in the spring of 2018, telling Mohammad bin Salman that he should have increased his spending and that sums of several hundred million dollars 'are peanuts to you'.[6]

Saudi Arabia is 'a very great friend', Trump said when receiving the crown prince, because it is 'a big purchaser of equipment and lots of other things'.[7] This explains why Saudi had been singled out for special treatment, as is clear from the fact that when Mike Pompeo was appointed CIA director in 2017 he lost no time in telling his hosts in Riyadh that his first overseas trip was to Saudi Arabia, just as President Trump's had been.[8]

Trump's visit to Riyadh in 2017 had certainly been memorable. Indeed, said the president later, it was 'one of the most incredible two-day meetings that I've ever seen – that anybody has ever seen'. Those who saw Trump, secretary of state Rex Tillerson and his then chief strategist Steve Bannon attend exhibitions of sword-dancing and hop about uncomfortably as they took part in festivities alongside their Saudi hosts would agree.[9]

Trump's alignment with Saudi has consequences for proposed arms sales elsewhere in the region. In 2017, visiting Qatar, the president had addressed the Gulf state's leader and told him, 'We are friends. We've been now for a long time indirectly, haven't we? And our relationship is extremely good. We have some very serious discussions right now going on. And one of the things that we will discuss is the purchase of lots of beautiful military equipment because nobody makes it like the United States. And for us that means jobs and, frankly, great security back here, which we want.'[10]

That is a problem in the context of a major falling-out between Qatar and Saudi Arabia and its neighbours, which has seen a land blockade imposed on the gas-rich state. Relations have become so bad that Riyadh is planning to 'change the geography of the region', according to one senior Saudi official, by digging a canal to cut off Qatar from the mainland – and not only to build military installations along it, but also use it as a dump for atomic waste.[11]

This has prompted the Qataris to intensify political, military and economic ties with Turkey, which has aspirations of its own across the region, and has also led to a remarkable rapprochement with Iran – restoring diplomatic relations and significantly boosting trade links.[12] That complicates matters for the US. As many US administrations have found, sitting on the fence can be very difficult. 'You have been a great friend to the US', Treasury Secretary Steve Mnuchin told the Qatari Foreign Minister, Sheikh Mohammed bin Abdulrahman al-Thani in the summer of 2018.[13]

So when Trump calls Saudi Arabia 'a very great friend' when receiving the crown prince at the White House in March 2018, many across the Middle East were listening carefully, trying to read the tea leaves. Trump kept to what he knows best – sales. Saudi, he said, could be relied on to buy massive amounts of weapons, and would be bound to buy them from the US. 'We make the best equipment in the world,' he said. 'There's nobody even close.'[14]

Moscow might disagree – especially given that it signed a major deal to sell state-of-the-art military hardware to Saudi Arabia at the end of 2017. The multibillion-dollar agreement involved the sale of Russia's much-feared S-400 air defence system, but also Kornet-EM anti-tank guided missile systems, an unguided thermobaric rocket system, automatic grenade launchers and Kalashnikov AK-103 assault rifles.[15] As President Putin told listeners to his annual 'question and answer' session on Russian TV and radio, there was no better showcase for Russian weapons than the battlefield – as 'no amount of military exercise could compare with the use of force in combat conditions'. Being involved on the ground in Syria, therefore, provided a 'priceless' opportunity to test new weaponry and prove them to potential buyers.[16]

Washington's assumption that Saudi Arabia's antipathy to Iran and its substantial purchases of American weapons means that it will only look to the US is also put into context by high-level discussions between Moscow and Riyadh about a long-term alliance that could result in higher prices – and therefore better outcomes – for both oil-rich countries if output is controlled carefully. 'We are working,' said Mohammad bin Salman, to find a 'ten to twenty-year agreement' with Moscow. Discussions were well advanced, he added. 'We have agreement on the big picture but not on the detail.'[17] Not yet, that is.

*

Betting on Saudi when the latter has common interests with Russia is only part of the risk that the US is taking. It also has to contend with Moscow chipping away elsewhere. Turkey, for example, was once a cornerstone of NATO's Cold War strategy, thanks to its position relative to Russia, the Middle East and Central Asia. Erdoğan has been assiduously courted and steered away from the US and Europe. That has partly been done through cooperation in Syria and through the improvement of commercial ties.[18] But it has also involved offering Turkey its advanced S-400 anti-aircraft missile system – to the delight of a defiant President Erdoğan. 'Nobody has the right to discuss the Turkish republic's independence principles,' he said, or any 'decisions about its defence industry'.[19]

This set off alarm bells in the US, where General Joseph Dunford, chair of the Joint Chiefs, was forced to release a statement to deal with 'a media report that was incorrect'. Despite speculation to the contrary, he said, Turkey had 'not bought the S-400 air defence system from Russia. That would be a concern, were they to do that; but they have not done that.' The importance of this statement can be seen from the fact that it was picked up by Chinese news agencies.[20]

Five months later, Turkey agreed to buy the S-400 system in a deal worth a reported $2.5bn – posing questions about Turkish membership of NATO, and indeed about NATO itself.[21] Mike Pompeo, the US secretary of state, tried to impress the implications on his Turkish counterpart, Mevlüt Çavuşoğlu. The fact that a measure was introduced in the US Senate just a few hours earlier to block the sale of a fleet of Lockheed Martin's F-35 joint strike fighters did not help calm the waters. Attempts to put pressure on Turkey would not be tolerated, Çavuşoğlu said.[22] This was music to Russian ears: the Turks, said the Kremlin, would be more than welcome to buy Su-57 fighter jets instead.[23]

Likewise, with the US issuing sanctions against senior Turkish government ministers and threatening further punitive measures over the detention of an American pastor, Beijing has been quick to offer to improve ties and deliver 'fruitful results' from increased cooperation with Ankara.[24] This was articulated clearly in a meeting between Presidents Xi and Erdoğan at the BRICS meeting in July 2018, where both resolved to improve relations and to 'take care of each other's core interests'. Perhaps not surprisingly, the Chinese leader noted that China and Turkey were 'natural partners in the joint construction of the Belt and Road [project]'.[25]

They are also natural partners because 'the raging dispute between Ankara and Washington shows no sign of easing'. A lengthy editorial in China's *Global Times* set out how the timing was right for China and Turkey to explore 'new opportunities to deepen cooperation'. It was important to prepare the ground, said the article, because the perception of Turkey in China is poor and many are indifferent to the 'hand of friendship' that is now being extended. Support for the US during the Korean War and inconsistent purchasing of the HQ-9 missile gave the impression that the Turks were 'playing tricks with China'. What was 'most unacceptable', however, was support for separatists in Xinjiang and 'irresponsible remarks on the ethnic policy' of this region. China offered a potential for a new partnership at a time when Turkey's already strained economy had been put under further pressure by US policies.[26] Problems in Ankara have opened the door for Beijing.

There is more at stake than the sale of hardware, more significant implications than simply the fact that there is competition that can strike to take advantage of opportunities as and when they present themselves. For in the rivalry and jostling for position that is now being played out along the Silk Roads between the Eastern Mediterranean and the Pacific, as well as in Africa and elsewhere, decisions have to be taken. As a result of the Countering America's Adversaries Through Sanctions Act, US arms sales are prohibited to any nation that buys Russian weapons. This means that if Saudi Arabia, Turkey and others can be persuaded by Moscow to switch allegiances, then they fall decisively out of Washington's orbit.

It is a major problem, conceded US Secretary of Defense James Mattis. The United States is in the process of paralysing itself, he told Congress. 'In the dynamics of today,' he said, 'issues can shift countries very, very quickly.' It was bad enough that the US was boxed in by its own rules. The fact that 'every day Russia is in a position basically to checkmate us with what they're doing' made it even worse. 'It's urgent,' he said.[27]

Russia may have limited economic capabilities at its disposal, but it has the diplomatic nous and political savvy to recognise the world is changing – and to adapt to it. That is one reason for the way that President Putin has taken the initiative to play a role in Syrian peace talks, where Russia, alongside Iran and Turkey, present themselves as stabilising forces – in contrast to the United States. The US-led interventions in Iraq and Afghanistan resulted in nothing but 'destructions and [the] expansion of extremism', said the Iranian foreign minister, Mohammed Zarif.[28] Airstrikes by US, French and British forces were violations of international law, stated Sergei Lavrov, Russia's foreign minister.[29] The west, he added, behave as though they still 'decide all the affairs in our world. Fortunately,' he said, 'their time has passed.'[30] This is part of a wider pattern of Moscow trying to present itself as a reliable and calming force, as well as an independent international arbiter.[31]

The presentation of Russia, Turkey and Iran as pacific and seeking to find peaceful ways to reach settlements comes as a surprise to those who have followed the annexation of Crimea, the presence of Russian troops in Ukraine, the attempted assassination of a former intelligence officer in the UK and claims by the British MP Bob Seely that Russia is using 'active measures practised by the KGB during the Cold War' to undermine the stability of the British political system.[32] A report by the House of Commons Foreign Affairs Committee in the early summer of 2018 not only found that the 'use of London as a base for the corrupt assets of Kremlin-connected individuals' was so important that it 'has implications for our national security', but that 'combating it should be a major UK foreign policy priority'.[33]

Turkey is hardly static either in its aims and actions. Nostalgia for the Ottoman Empire has given way to ideas about how to restore Turkey to its glorious past, a time when cities from Sarajevo to Damascus, Benghazi to Erzurum lay within a multicultural, multi-ethnic state whose successes have been overshadowed by more recent history.[34] 'The republic of Turkey,' said President Erdoğan in a speech in 2017, is 'a continuation of the Ottomans' – even if the borders have changed.[35] As the wild popularity of soap operas set in the Ottoman Empire show, rekindling the past is very much part of the present-day story of Turkey's role in the world.[36] So too is military intervention in Syria and Iraq, an increasingly muscular position adopted in relations with neighbouring Greece – and its defiant choice of words to Washington. 'We are not tied from our stomachs [by an umbilical cord] to the US' ran front-page headlines in five pro-government newspapers on the same day – a clear sign that pressure from Washington has annoyed Ankara.[37]

And then there is Iran, whose adventures in Iraq and Syria and whose support for Houthi rebels in Yemen, alongside assistance to Hamas and Hezbollah in the Middle East, are not necessarily the most obvious credentials for a country wishing to describe itself as one that is keen to protect the international order. Tehran's claims to work within parameters that look above all for negotiated settlements and avoid the use of force except as a last resort, while committing troops to military action in other states and also being involved in proxy wars, underline how important it is to focus on actions rather than words.

*

It is revealing, nevertheless, that China, Russia, Turkey and Iran are attuned to the fact that the world is changing. It is striking too to note how many states in Asia have not just understood this but have been actively trying to work out how to prepare for the future. Almost all have developed blueprints setting out the opportunities and challenges in the short and medium term, along with analysis of how best to cope with these.

The Belt and Road Initiative falls into this category. But so too does Saudi Arabia's Vision 2030 plan, the Eurasian Economic Union of Russia, Belarus, Kazakhstan, Armenia and Kyrgyzstan, the Bright Road initiative of Kazakhstan, the Two Corridors, One Economic Circle initiative of Vietnam, the Middle Corridor initiative of Turkey, the Development Road initiative of Mongolia and the development plans of Laos, Cambodia and Myanmar. Then there is the array of plans developed by India, such as the Act the East policy, the Trilateral Highway project, the Go West strategy and the Neighbourhood First plan.[38]

Conspicuously absent from this list is the European Union. Although President Xi included Britain's Northern Powerhouse project as an example of how states around the world are seeking to boost connections via investments in infrastructure, the reality is rather different.[39] Announced just a few months after the Belt and Road was launched, Northern Powerhouse progress has been more modest. While China's strategy has captured the imagination and committed hundreds of billions of dollars to the roads, railways, ports and energy plants, many of which are now up and running, the Northern Powerhouse's main achievement so far has been the opening of the new southern entrance at Leeds railway station.[40]

Compared with the Silk Roads and Asia, Europe is not so much moving at a different speed as in a different direction. Where the story in Asia is about increasing connections, improving collaboration and deepening cooperation, in Europe the story is about separation, the re-erection of barriers and 'taking back control'. Brexit provides a good example of this, but so do rising anti-EU movements in Italy, Germany, Poland, Hungary and elsewhere – and the support by hundreds of thousands of people for independence in Scotland and Catalonia.

These pressures lead to a sadness in some parts for a world that seems to be melting away in front of our eyes. 'The European Union,' said the Archbishop of Canterbury in the summer of 2018, 'has brought peace, prosperity, compassion for the poor and weak, purpose for the aspirational and hope for all its people.' It has been, he said, 'the greatest dream realised for human beings since the fall of the Western Roman Empire' – a comment that not only betrays profound Eurocentrism but a lack of historical perspective, both about world history and also about the EU itself.[41] Nevertheless, it is symptomatic of the melancholy that accompanies the setting of the sun in a part of the world that has enjoyed the benefits of centuries basking in its warm rays.

*

Europe's stuttering offers opportunities to others. China, for example, has been quick to recognise that economic investments create political advantages. Many expected a robust stance to be adopted by the EU over the dispute in the South China Sea, especially following remarks by Donald Tusk, president of the European Council, at a G7 meeting in Japan, shortly before the ruling of the Permanent Court of Arbitration was released, about the need not only to 'defend the common values that we share' but also of taking 'a clear and tough stance' over China's maritime claims.[42]

In fact, China worked hard behind the scenes to ensure that the EU did not do so, using its ties with Greece,

Hungary and Croatia to ensure that the statement released by Brussels did not 'support' or 'welcome' the decision of the tribunal, but merely 'acknowledged it'.[43] This was testimony to the efforts that China has put into cultivating new friends not only in Asia and Africa but in Europe too, where the 16+1 Initiative provides a forum for discussion between Beijing and eleven EU members in Central and Eastern Europe (including the Baltic States, Bulgaria, Croatia, Hungary and Poland) – as well as five Balkan states (Albania, Bosnia and Herzegovina, Montenegro, Macedonia and Serbia).

The countries that are part of this initiative are turning towards China because of the potential for Chinese investment, but also, as the Hungarian Prime Minister Viktor Orbán said in October 2016, because 'the world economy's centre of gravity is shifting from west to east; while there is still some denial of this in the western world, that denial does not seem to be reasonable'. The world is changing, he said, with the global economy's 'centre of gravity shifting from the Atlantic region to the Pacific region. This is not my opinion – this is a fact.'[44]

For others, though, the turn to the east is also about the paralysis of Europe and the EU. Europe 'is withdrawing – or rather not keeping its promise about making the Balkans part of the European Union,' said the prime minister of the former Yugoslav Republic of Macedonia, Gjorge Ivanov. The EU's failure served as a call to others 'to come and fill in that space'. That opened the door to China – and also to Russia. What a shame, said Ivanov, that the EU seems to have forgotten important lessons from history.[45]

While such mournful pleas mask the significant attention and resources that the EU and indeed the US have paid to the Balkans, the fact that multiple attempts to influence elections, to pressure senior clergy and even to overthrow local governments seem to lead back to Moscow tells its own story about the competition for hearts, minds and wallets in this region.[46] Likewise, the fact that Johannes Hahn, the EU Commissioner for European Neighbourhood and Enlargement, has warned about China's growing interest in the Balkans speaks volumes about the fact that the world is becoming more complicated.[47]

Some recognise that not having a plan of action can have consequences. 'If we do not succeed for example in developing a single strategy towards China,' said Sigmar Gabriel, the German foreign minister in 2017, then China will succeed in dividing Europe.[48] This drew a stinging response from the Chinese Foreign Ministry. 'We are shocked by these statements,' said a spokeswoman, before adding, 'we hope that he can clarify what he means by "one Europe" and whether there is a consensus on "one Europe" among EU members' – which captured perfectly the divisions within Europe about the lack of a common direction of travel.[49]

That was put well by Gabriel in subsequent speeches where he talked about change in the world, and about Europe's failure to adapt. 'China currently seems to be the only country in the world with any sort of genuinely global, geostrategic concept,' he said in February 2018. This was a matter of fact, he added, noting that 'China is entitled to develop such a concept'. The problem, said Gabriel, was that Europe and the west had no coherent ideas, no plans, no response and, seemingly, no ideas. 'What we can blame ourselves for,' he said, 'is the fact that we, as the "west", do not have our own strategy for finding a new balance between worldwide interests, one that is based on conciliation and common added value and not on the zero-sum game that is the unilateral pursuit of interests.'[50]

Gabriel's successor as foreign minister, Heiko Maas, has tried to find a way to articulate the dangers of isolationism. He called for countries like Germany that 'are too small to be able to call the shots on their own on the global stage', to find ways to work together In a speech in Tokyo in July 2018, he warned of the consequences of President Trump's willingness to use '280-character tweets' to undermine 'alliances that have developed over decades'. This, coupled with the challenges of Russia and China, made it vital to 'think about new paths'. Germany should work with Japan – a country, incidentally, that has very active aid and infrastructure programmes of its own along the Silk Roads – to form the 'heart of an alliance of multilateralists' to work together to promote stability and to fill 'the vacuum that has continued to emerge following the withdrawal of others from many parts of the world'.[51]

Beijing is attuned to such demands, and has been at pains not only to anticipate but even echo them. 'We need to uphold multilateralism,' Premier Li Keqiang told a meeting of the 16+1 countries from Central and Eastern Europe and the Balkans. 'We need to uphold free trade ... and work together to prevent a slowdown of the global economic recovery.' The European Union, he added, 'is a very important force for peace and stability and prosperity. It is an indispensible force in the world.'[52]

*

China's rise – combined with a clear-eyed understanding of what it wants and needs in the present and future – has also led to doors opening elsewhere, such as in the Middle East, for example, where Beijing has been both assiduous and successful in courting Riyadh. The potential sale of a stake in Aramco, the Saudi oil company that is privately owned but would become the biggest in the world if it floats on the open market, has drawn China's attention – as have logistics facilities, infrastructure projects and smaller producers in the kingdom. China and Arab countries, said Foreign Minister Wang Yi, are 'natural partners in Belt and Road cooperation'. The mantra of the Silk Roads supersedes all division: all should follow the 'Silk Road spirit of peace and cooperation, opennesss and inclusiveness, mutual learning and mutual benefit and seek greater synergy' in pursuit of 'national renewal'.[53]

This is part of a wider charm offensive, where comments by Foreign Minister Wang that China 'will always side with Arab countries and safeguard their just rights and interests as well as peace and stability in the Middle East' are music to Saudi ears – even if it belies the fact that most Chinese loans and investment in the region have so far gone to Saudi's arch-enemy, Iran.[54]

A close relationship with Saudi Arabia does not preclude Beijing deepening its ties with Tehran. When the US withdrawal from the JCPOA was announced, for example, Chinese businesses had already made plans to take the place of western major oil companies, including signing an option to acquire stakes such as those held by Total, in the event that sanctions were reintroduced and western businesses forced out of Iran.[55]

But Beijing has been shrewd in creating and repeating a narrative that seeks to unite, rather than divide elsewhere. Just a week after hosting King Salman of Saudi Arabia, President Xi received a visit from Israeli Prime Minister Netanyahu, and shortly after that Palestine's President Abbas. It was China's hope, he said, that 'Palestine and Israel can achieve peace as soon as possible and live and work in peace'.[56] Such comments are always welcome; but they will not play a role in bringing peace to the Middle East.

All peoples in the region should work together and 'in a just manner to avoid regional disputes'. This could be done, said Xi, if 'we treat each other frankly, not fear differences, not avoid problems, and have ample discussion on each aspect of foreign policy and development strategy'. To show it is prepared to put its money where its mouth is, Beijing promptly pledged $20bn of loans for 'projects that will produce good employment opportunities and positive social impact in Arab States that have reconstruction needs'.[57] A further $100m of aid was promised 'to revive economic growth'.[58]

This was part of a series of initiatives, said an official at China's Ministry of Foreign Affairs, 'among which many measures are very forward-looking, innovative and pioneering' that are part of the Belt and Road masterplan.[59] Such comments and actions sit in direct contrast to the words and actions of the US, which has chosen to take sides – and a very different tack.[60] While Beijing has been busy trying to find partners in all places at all times, it is striking then to see how few friends the US and the west have along the Silk Roads.

*

The consistency of China's message sits in sharp contrast to that emanating from Washington, which is haphazard, erratic and contradictory. 'We want all nations, every nation, to be able to protect their sovereignty from coercion from other states,' said Mike Pompeo in the summer of 2018. 'We want the peaceful resolution of territorial and maritime disputes,' he said. 'Where

America goes, we seek partnership, not domination,' in comments clearly directed at China – which he did not mention by name. 'We believe in strategic partnerships, not strategic dependency.'[61]

That is news to most around the world, where the US has earned a reputation, sometimes unfairly, for shooting first and asking questions second. But as historians learn, controlling the narrative is important in itself – that is to say, being able to showcase and demonstrate the benefits of cooperation, being able to show how 'win-win' is possible and benefits all, taking care to make actions and words align when it comes to international affairs and, of course, also being ready and able to counter criticisms and arguments of rivals. And in this, the US has slipped a long way behind a highly competitive field.

*

A case in point comes with Pakistan, a country that has been singled out and publicly humiliated, for example, partly as punishment for being too close to China, partly as a sacrifice on the altar of the US's idealised grand alliance with India, and partly as a result of the deteriorating situation in Afghanistan. In his first tweet of 2018, Trump stated that the US 'has foolishly given Pakistan more than 33 billion dollars in aid over the last 15 years, and they have given us nothing but lies & deceit, thinking of our leaders as fools'.[62] It was time to change tack in Afghanistan, said John Bolton, now national security advisor. 'The big issue,' he said, 'wasn't land-war tactics. The big issue is Pakistan.'[63]

It was disgraceful, said Pakistan's foreign minister at that time, Khawaja Asif, that the US should turn his country into a 'whipping boy' rather than confront its own failures in Afghanistan and elsewhere.[64] US statements and actions such as suspending more than $1bn of security aid have naturally served to push Pakistan and China closer together at a time when the latter has been busy promoting a common vision for the future, cheap finance, technical capacity and support.[65]

The relationship looks likely to deepen, despite widespread fears that Pakistan will need to seek a bailout from the IMF for as much as $12bn as a result of spiralling public debt – at least some related to infrastructure expenditure financed by China – but also because of a range of other factors, including a weakening currency. 'Make no mistake,' said Mike Pompeo. 'We will be watching what the IMF does. There's no rationale for IMF tax dollars, and associated with that, American dollars that are part of the IMF funding, for those to go to bail out Chinese bondholders or China itself.'[66]

This went down badly in Pakistan, where resistance to a potential bailout was seen as another case of Washington trying to prevent the country's growth and ruin its future.[67] Far from pushing back against Beijing, said Imran Khan, leader of the PTI party that won the most seats in the 2018 election, the opposite would be the case. He told the Chinese ambassador, 'after the

PTI assumes office it will fully cooperate with China and promote the persistent development and deepening of the bilateral relations'.[68] As it happened, China immediately made a credit line of $2bn available – a demonstration that waving a carrot can be more attractive and as effective as wielding a stick.[69]

Perhaps the single most important question mark hanging over the Belt and Road not only in Pakistan but elsewhere too is precisely how China deals with situations where major projects run into trouble or when restructuring of loans is necessary. Understanding how decisions get made in such circumstances and assessing how and why Beijing behaves when it is asked or expected to come up with a different medicine from that proposed by the US or by institutions that may well be more transparent – but can also have less flexibility when it comes to renegotiation or debt forgiveness – will shape reactions to the initiative as a whole, as well as its progress and success.

In the case of Pakistan, at least, the shift in US policy has not only pushed the country closer to China – partly as a last resort – but it has also strengthened the hand of Russia in the region. Moscow already has close ties with India, where the government was reported to be yet another considering buying Russia's S-400 system.[70] Its links with Pakistan, though, look set to improve too with deals announced that Islamabad would buy SU-35 fighters and T-90 tanks from Russia. Joint military exercises, intelligence sharing and criticisms of US policies in Afghanistan have provided further common ground – as does a propose $10bn offshore gas pipeline deal that again serves to benefit both sides.[71]

While the idea that 'permanent destabilization creates American advantage' might sound convincing to policymakers in Washington, it has consequences. Announcements that children of illegal immigrants will be separated from their parents and held in a 'separate refugee facility' in tented cities at military posts in Texas does not so much make America look determined and bold as unkind and cruel.[72] Reports of mothers being in tears after their children were taken for a shower and then not brought back shocked the world.[73]

The revelations that DNA tests needed to reunite children with their parents – after some had been forcibly injected with drugs, leaving them unable to walk, afraid of people and wanting to sleep constantly did enormous damage to the US abroad.[74] Such revelations are all but unbelievable in a country that has long been regarded as a beacon of hope, a bastion of decency and the defender of freedom and justice.

Part of this must stem from a brain drain and systemic failure in Washington. The decision to cut the budget of the State Department has reduced expertise and empathy. At a time when the US could and should be doing all it can to highlight the positive role it has played in global security and trade, to build friendships and offer a vision of the future that is hopeful, inclusive and collaborative, it is turning its back on history. Tariffs are not reserved for competitors and rivals – but also for former friends and allies, who stand to suffer most.[75] 'The question is no longer whether or not there will be a trade war,' said French Finance Minister Bruno Le Maire in the summer of 2018. 'The war has already started.'[76]

US policy towards Russia has also proved to be chaotic, if not counterproductive. According to the National Security Strategy document, Russia – like China – is viewed formally as 'wanting to shape a world antithetical to US values and interests' and being determined 'to restore its great power status'. It 'aims to weaken US influence in the world and divide us from our allies and partners'.[77] In the spring of 2018 a series of sanctions was announced targeting several high-profile oligarchs as well as leading officials in the Russian government. Citing intervention in Ukraine and Syria, along with 'malign activity' that included 'attempting to subvert western democracies, and malicious cyber activities', the tough line was intended to send a strong message to President Putin and his inner circle.[78] 'Nobody has been tougher on Russia than I have,' said Trump at a press conference announcing the sanctions.[79]

In fact, as elsewhere, US actions have had the opposite effect to those intended. Diplomatic and political pressure on Russia has already served to push Moscow closer to Beijing – perhaps more closely that the former is comfortable with, as Chinese imports of energy resources have become disproportionately important to the Russian economy.[80] In 2017, for example, even though total oil exports rose fractionally, Russian oil shipments to China went up by 40 per cent.[81] In the same year, in a sign of the strengthening of commercial ties between the two countries, Chinese investment in Russia rose by nearly three quarters.[82]

The close relationship paid dividends after US airstrikes in Syria in April 2018, which, as well as seeking to target assets connected with Assad's regime, were also intended as a show of force and a warning to Russia, which has troops on the ground offering support to the discredited Syrian leader. The airstrikes were promptly condemned by Beijing, with a Chinese Foreign Ministry spokesperson saying that their government considered that the strikes 'violated the principles and basic norms of international law'.[83]

More striking, however, were the comments made by General Wei Fenghe, the newly appointed defence minister in China, who was sent to Moscow in a display of solidarity. In remarkably candid language, General Wei remarked, 'I am visiting Russia ... to show the world a high level of development of our bilateral relations and firm determination of our armed forces to strengthen strategic cooperation.' His visit had a more immediate purpose, however: 'The Chinese side has come to Moscow to show Americans the close ties between the armed forces of China and Russia ... we have come to support you.'[84]

This is part of a narrative that emphasises friendship and common interests. 'President Putin and I have built good working relations and a close personal friendship,' said President Xi before a state visit to Moscow in July 2017. It was not just important to note that China and Russia 'are each other's most trustworthy strategic partners', he said. So too was it worth noting that China–Russia relations are at their 'best time in history'.[85]

This can be seen from the enormous Vostok-18 military drills that took place in the summer of 2018 – the biggest war games orchestrated by Moscow since 1981. Chinese and Russian forces have taken part in joint exercises regularly in the past, but the Vostok-18 exercises, to which Beijing committed thirty fighter jets and helicopters, nine hundred pieces of military equipment and more than three thousand personnel, are on a new scale altogether. If that is striking, then so too is the fact that the drills are designed to practice against foreign invasions, while also simulating the use of nuclear weapons. Perhaps not surprisingly, US officials have expressed unease about the operations and have asked Russia 'to take steps to share information' to avoid any 'potential misunderstanding.'[86] Two of Washington's main competitors are working more and more closely together.

For the US, this is part of a nightmare scenario. 'Russia and China are cosying up to each other and it's a lethal combination if they're together,' said one official involved in the meeting between Presidents Trump and

Putin in Helsinki in 2018. Henry Kissinger was among those advising Trump to work together with Russia to 'box in' China – a concept that Richard Haase, president of the Council on Foreign Relations, admitted had obvious merits on paper but was impractical, if not impossible in practice, given Moscow's current trajectory.[87] For Washington, the options are either unrealistic, unavailable or unpalatable.

One gloomy recent report set out clearly that 'the partnership between China and Russia has matured and broadened ... with serious negative consequences for US interests', strengthening significantly in recent years. 'The current outlook', notes the author, 'is bleak, offering no easy fixes for the US.'[88]

Then there is the underwhelming response to the Belt and Road Initiative that was worked on for months before being unveiled by Secretary of State Mike Pompeo at a speech designed as a statement of intent for an 'economic approach to the Indo-Pacific as a truly whole-of-government mission'. The Indo-Pacific, said Pompeo, 'which stretches from the United States west coast to the west coast of India, is a subject of great importance to American foreign policy'. It is, he went on, 'one of the greatest engines' of the global economy.[89]

As such, and to show how much the United States wanted to help play a role in the region, he was delighted to announce '$113m in new initiatives'. While the precise amount of Chinese investment and financing along the new Silk Roads is a matter of considerable discussion amongst specialists, all would agree that the amount promised by Pompeo is miniscule to the point of irrelevant. To put it into perspective, the sum promised by the US was marginally more than Jared Kushner and Ivanka Trump, the president's son-in-law and daughter, personally received in outside earnings in 2017.[90] A tidy sum indeed for a young couple, but almost meaningless in the scale of international relations and large-scale, transformational infrastructure projects.

*

For others, a new world is being born. It is a world of increasing connections, greater cooperation and widening collaboration. None of those are easy or straightforward to get right, and it is important to recognise that rivalry, competition and tensions can be hidden by glossy statements of superficial friendships – such as the agreed statement made by the leaders of Russia, China, Kazakhstan, Uzbekistan, Tajikistan, Kyrgyzstan and India, which noted that events like the FIFA World Cup, the International Wushu (martial arts) competition in Chongqing and the International Yoga Day taking place in 2018 'will contribute to stronger friendship, mutual understanding and peace'.[91] That seems optimistic, to put it mildly.

Yet co-operation between states is often not straightforward – because of strategic rivalries, competition for resources and personality clashes between leaders who might be described as charismatic visionaries by their supporters and as having autocratic instincts by their critics. One example comes with the high-profile case of an ethnic Kazakh Chinese citizen who crossed illegally from China into Kazakhstan to join her family, and whose trial effectively forced the decision over whether agreeing to Beijing's demands for deportation or risk angering the latter and providing asylum was the lesser of two evils.[92]

A similar example of the fragility of how difficult the practicalities are of co-operation in the new world that is emerging comes with the case of Russia's relations with Turkey. On one level, both are aligned in their disposition towards the west at a time when both countries have been experiencing bumpy relationships with the EU and with the US. The fact that Vladimir Putin offered Recep Tayyip Erdoğan support during the attempts to remove him from office in 2016 helped improve ties, not least since the Russian leader either tipped off his Turkish counterpart before the coup, or managed to convince media outlets afterwards that he had done so.[93] The importance of bilateral trade also provides considerable common ground between the two.[94]

But there are important areas where Russia and Turkey have aims that are not so much divergent as positively at odds. Following the Russian annexation of Crimea, Erdoğan urged NATO to take action. 'The

Black Sea,' he told Jens Stoltenberg, NATO secretary-general, 'has almost become a Russian lake. If we don't act now, history will not forgive us.'[95] His alarm was not surprising, not least since Putin had long been triumphantly celebrating the fact that Russia had turned Crimea into 'a fortress both by land and by sea' that would never fall.[96] This is not how Erdoğan sees it. 'We neither did, nor will we, recognise the annexation of the Crimean peninsula by Russia,' he declared during a visit to Kyiv in October 2017.[97]

Concern about Russian ambitions, meanwhile, led to changes in the most recent update to Kazakhstan's Military Doctrine, which explicitly discusses the threat that Russia poses to the country's territorial integrity and sovereignty – hardly an indication of the expectation that relations between the countries will be smooth and easy in the coming years.[98]

Not surprisingly, while happy to talk about cooperation with their neighbour in public, the Kazakhs have also been keen to keep their options open and to find a balance that prevents Russian – or Chinese – attentions from becoming overwhelming. This is one reason why Kazakhstan has agreed to provide support to US operations in Afghanistan in order to maintain good links with Washington.[99] This had already caught Moscow's eye. So when the government of Nursultan Nazarbayev allowed the US military to use two ports on the Caspian Sea to transport materials in June 2018, the Kazakh foreign minister, Kairat Abdrakhmanov, was given a dressing-down by his Russian opposite number, Sergei Lavrov, who reportedly subjected him to an almighty grilling about how and why the decision was made to be so accommodating to the United States. There was no commercial or logistical sense to reaching this agreement with the US; clearly the Kazakhs were up to something – not least since they had not informed Moscow what it was.[100] There was no question of American military bases being built in the Caspian, protested Abrdakhmanov, who said in an interview to calm the situation that people who claimed otherwise did not know what they were talking about.[101]

China's efforts to build a brave new world are also not as popular as they might first seem. Land purchases in Siberia have prompted a rash of headlines in the local press not only about the effect of price rises and the influx of outsiders, but warning that the Chinese had territorial intentions over Lake Baikal and the surrounding area.[102] Such anxieties were hardly calmed by statements on tourism websites in China that the region had once been under Chinese control.[103]

The changing world is also not easy to navigate. In an unusual turnaround, land reform was put on hold in Kazakhstan in the summer of 2016 after unrest triggered by Chinese buyers acquiring leases for large areas of farmland, and proposed changes to the land code. Local farmers were concerned that they would not be able to compete with better-resourced rivals, while others voiced their unease that the country's prime land was being parcelled off without thought of what the long-term consequences would be.[104]

The complexities that stem from the hard-line US approach to Iran provide another useful reminder of the realities that accompany a world on the move. If Trump implements his threat to squeeze Iran's oil exports, said President Rouhani, 'Tehran is prepared to escalate against the US to impose direct costs for global oil markets.'[105] If Iran is not allowed to ship its oil through the Gulf, said Mohammad Bahgeri, chief of staff of the Iranian armed forces, 'there will be no security for others, either, and no crude will be exported from this region'.[106]

The threat to disrupting shipments through the Gulf has in turn been countered by major exercises by the US Navy across the region to ensure stability and security 'anywhere, anytime'. The US 5th Fleet, supported by F-35B jets ('the world's most advanced fighter aircraft') will 'ensure the freedom of navigation and the free flow of commerce'.[107]

This may not be all plain sailing. After all, specialists have long been concerned about military cooperation between Iran and North Korea and the striking similarities of their ballistic missile programmes, and especially the reliance that Tehran has on technologies developed by the regime of Kim Jong-un – although there have also been instances of advancements made in Iran being shared with North Korea. Of particular concern in this context are the capabilities of the Ghadir-class submarine, which include the potential to launch cruise missiles against surface shipping as well as land-based targets.[108]

Fear of an escalation with Iran, or even a restriction in the passage of hydrocarbons through the Gulf, should set alarm bells off in London and elsewhere. With 30 per cent of all seaborne-traded crude oil and liquefied natural gas passing through the Strait of Hormuz, any disruption would have both a direct hit on the UK – which imports considerable quantities from Gulf countries – and a heavy indirect hit as a result of the impact of slowdowns in related economies that would follow.[109] While some argue that many nations would be keen to resolve a dispute as quickly as possible, countless examples from the past can point to the fact that optimism that arguments can be brought to a swift conclusion is often, if not usually, misplaced.[110]

Rouhani's comments about a potential blockade also brought a strongly worded response – from Beijing. Chinese Assistant Foreign Minister Chen Xiaodong said that Iran 'should do more to benefit peace and stability in the region, and jointly protect peace and stability there'. The country should spend less time issuing threats and more time focusing on 'being a good neighbour and co-existing peacefully'. It is not hard to understand the context for these comments: China also relies heavily on oil from the Middle East and North Africa, which accounts for nearly 50% of its imports.[111] Any dislocation in supply as a result of Iran's efforts to respond to US sanctions will have an immediate impact on China itself. Hence Chen's advice that 'all sides' agree 'to meet each other halfway and give consideration to each other's concerns'.[112]

*

These examples illustrate the difficulties of managing situations where interests do not overlap. So too does the decision by Rosneft, an oil company with close ties to the Kremlin, to drill in a block in the South China Sea that lies within what Vietnam claims to be its territorial waters, but lies within the waterways about which China is so sensitive. Rosneft's action met with a stern rebuke from Beijing: no state or corporation should 'carry out exploration activity in the maritime area under China's sovereignty', unless it had obtained prior permission from Beijing.[113]

Russia and China may often claim to see eye to eye and do indeed often have mutual interests that overlap. But common aims are not uniform. The fact that the Russian 29th Army's 3rd Missile Brigade, stationed in the east of the country close to the Chinese border, has been issued with the road-mobile 9K720 Iskander-M missile system, which is capable of delivering nuclear payloads, shows that it is important to look beyond well-chosen words about the friendship between Moscow and Beijing.[114] After all, it is more normal to deploy such firepower near to enemies and potential enemies, rather than within striking distance of firm and reliable friends.[115]

And then, of course, there are the concerns about China's economic robustness in the face of a rapid growth and change. This has in part 'been maintained by an exceptional degree of credit growth', according to a recent Bank of England report that seeks to assess the impact on the UK of potential turbulence in financial markets. The credit boom in China is 'one of the largest ever recorded', the report notes, adding that 'similar credit booms have typically preceded crises in other countries'.

There have been signs of the problems that come from rapid expansion fuelled by loans, with large corporations like HNA Group seeking to dispose of assets at speed, China Energy Reserve and Chemicals Group defaulting on a $350m bond, and, in July 2018, US investment firm Elliott Management Group taking control of AC Milan from its owner, Li Yonghong, after he failed to keep up with an ambitious repayment schedule.[116]

The challenges are not lost on policy-makers in China, where Zhou Xiaochuan, the governor of the Central Bank, has spoken not only about the need for reform, but also of the risks facing the economy. These could be 'hidden, complicated, sudden, contagious and dangerous', he wrote in an article on the People's Bank of China – in which he reminded readers that Xi Jinping had repeatedly emphasized that 'financial security is an important part of national security'.[117]

Then there are problems around several Belt and Road projects, such as in Malaysia, where three of the largest infrastructure projects with a combined value of more than $20bn were suspended because of cost concerns and the allegations of corruption at a Malaysian state investment fund – as were three pipeline projects worth almost $3bn.[118] Overcommitment to projects like the Orange Line metro in Lahore, coupled with rising government deficits, have led to sobering assessments about whether major adjustments will be needed for Pakistan's budget in the coming months and year, and about if, when and how loans will be restructured.[119] The previous government 'did a bad job negotiating with China' said Abdul Razak Dawood, a senior politician in Islamabad. 'They didn't do their homework correctly and didn't negotiate correctly, so they gave away a lot,' he said, promising to review all the agreements and renegotiate them if necessary.[120]

In Tonga, the burden of keeping up with repayments has led the Prime Minister, Akalisi Pohiva, to declare that his nation is suffering from 'debt distress'.[121] Then there is Myanmar, where plans to invest $7.3bn in a port on the Bay of Bengal have been scaled back by more than 80%, to avoid similar problems.[122] While examples like these have led some to say that Belt and Road problems are proliferating, the fact that around 85 per cent of all projects have proceeded without difficulty tells its own story.[123]

Nonetheless, in the circumstances, it is not surprising that Beijing has set out to explain the virtues and benefits of the Belt and Road Initiative. The initiative 'originates from China, but belongs to the world', said a feature in Xinhua, the Chinese state news agency. By putting ideas into practice, it 'has become the world's biggest international cooperation platform and the most popular international public product'. It was helping to illuminate 'the dreams of millions of people' and to unify the hopes of 'every country and their citizens'.[124]

The Belt and Road Initiative, said President Xi, benefits all by creating a community 'with a shared future for humanity'. This was clear from the fact that China's trade with Belt and Road countries now exceeded $5tr, while helping to play an important role in 'peace and development'. Implicitly acknowledging criticisms, Xi noted that the initiative was not a 'geopolitical or military alliance', nor a 'China club', but rather an open and inclusive process designed to improve global development patterns, global governance and economic cooperation.[125]

This has been followed through with signs that Beijing both recognises the problems of debt burden – and is prepared and willing to help resolve it, at least in some cases. In September 2018, it was announced that loans that had been given to 'Africa's least developed countries' would be exempted and forgiven.[126] Although no specific information was given about which debts and which countries this referred to, the fact that the Ethiopian prime minister, Abiy Ahmed, announced a few days later that China had agreed to restructure some of Ethiopia's debts – including a $4bn loan to build a new railway linking Addis Ababa with the coast to allow payback over thirty years, rather than ten – provided an example of how it is not impossible for lender and recipient to renegotiate terms that are mutually acceptable.[127]

Announcing a further round of grants, interest-free loans, credit lines and development financing worth $60bn for African nations, Xi responded to accusations that too many poorly thought-through schemes had received funding. Resources, he said, 'are not to be spent on vanity projects, but in places where they are needed the most'. These investments 'must give Chinese and African people tangible benefits and successes that can be seen, that can be felt'.[128]

Evaluating China's motivations, actions and their outcomes not just in Africa or along the Silk Roads but around the globe is the perhaps the single most important challenge for policy makers in every country around the world today. Much depends on what decisions are made if, when and where individual investments and loans do not go to plan. Just as it is possible to talk of win-win when things go well, it is also reasonable to see that it becomes a 'lose-lose' scenario when they do not.

*

The risks to the global economy in the event of a slowdown, correction or crash in China are obvious, given that China is 'deeply embedded in global supply chains', says the Bank of England report. There would be potential benefits – for example, a sharp reduction in some commodity prices like coal, steel and copper, as well as a fall in oil prices, leading to lower prices in the UK.[129] Assessments like these presumably lie behind the aggressive stance on tariffs being adopted by the United States against China, with steps taken to put pressure on the economy to both weaken Beijing but strengthen consumers in the US at the same time. It also explains the robust attempt by China not only to issue economic countermeasures but to warn of the dangers of playing a game the consequences of which are hard to predict. The United States is 'attacking the global supply chain', said Ministry of Commerce spokesman Gao Feng, when asked about the introduction of yet more tariffs. 'The American government is firing shots at the whole world and at itself too.'[130]

In Britain's case, as the Bank of England's report makes clear, the prospect of lower prices in the event of a major financial crisis in China is only one side of the story. In fact, the UK would be hit particularly badly by a financial crisis in China – far more so than any other country in Europe, because the exposure of the UK's banks is 'greater than the US, Euro area, Japan and Korea combined'. Modelling exercises about the possible implications on the UK's economy have caused the Bank to raise its views on the potential spillover impact by 50 per cent. A major correction in China, perhaps triggered by decisions made in the US, would have a serious impact on the United Kingdom.[131]

The stakes are high – and all but overlooked at a time when the only topic of discussion about the economy by leading advocates of Brexit in the UK is about the prospect of new free-trade deals that will easily materialise when Britain stops being what some refer to as 'a colony' of the European Union.[132] There seems little or no recognition of the fact that while 'the will of the people' to leave the European Union was expressed in 2016, the world has changed dramatically since then. Challenges have appeared that were not just not known about at the time of the referendum, and indeed in some cases did not even exist. As such, perhaps the biggest problem about Brexit is not the question of whether leaving the European Union is right for the UK; it is whether it is right to do so at a time of such profound geopolitical and economic fragility. There are real dangers in concentrating only on matters that are of parachial importance when so many other more significant and challenging problems require and demand attention.

*

The rapid development of new technologies is also a significant difficulty to address, in terms of trying to predict the impact these will have in the coming years – and working out how to prepare accordingly for a world where artificial intelligence (AI), robotics, machine learning, Blockchain, Ethereum and more will change the way we live, love, work and communicate.

Then there are cryptocurrencies like Bitcoin, which, while exciting for digital pioneers, seem most obviously of interest to those who seek to keep their transactions secure and away from prying eyes – including those who deal in illicit substances or goods, or who prefer to keep potentially taxable revenue away from the authorities. Ironically, the impact of decentralised digital currencies might prove more important for states seeking to continue to engage in trade in the face of pressures – such as sanctions – where the dominance of the dollar, euro and the yen in international transactions makes large-scale trade in other currencies impractical, inconvenient or impossible.

This would seem a logical step for countries like Iran, which is faced with trying to deal with a blanket ban on all its international commerce – and which has been exploring ways to do business in non-dollar-denominated currencies.[133] In fact, the German Foreign Minister, Heiko Maas, has suggested that Europe needs to find a way to overcome the existing financial-clearing system, in order to help Iran and presumably others too in the future. New payment channels should be set up, he said, including a European Monetary Fund and an independent SWIFT system to allow inter-bank transfers.[134] Inevitably, new technologies will be part of these solutions – and counter-technologies too. But hearing a senior European politician discussing finding ways to undermine and subvert US policy is almost as momentous as the Fourth Industrial Revolution itself.

As was the case in previous revolutions, the connection with the development (and funding) of new technologies is closely linked with military applications and with attempts to deliver tactical advantages that are decisive on the battlefield. As such, while being able to pay for a Chicken Zinger burger in Kentucky Fried Chicken outlets in China using facial technology is exciting, the fact that the same tools can be used by state security agencies for surveillance and security is undoubtedly more significant.[135]

The government in Beijing is pouring money and resources into artificial intelligence, building new technology parks across the country, such as a new $2.1bn campus in the Mentougou district of the capital, or in the former imperial capital of Xi'an.[136] According to one authoritative report, in 2016 China accounted for only 11.3 per cent of global funding going to start-ups in AI; that figure had risen to almost 50 per cent the following year. 'China is aggressively executing a thoroughly designed vision for AI,' the report notes, adding that 'in some areas of AI, China is clearly beating the US'.[137]

While some elements of the 'futuristic artificial intelligence plan' involve smart agriculture, intelligent logistics and new employment opportunities, others are closely linked to defence and even foreign policy. China should 'break new ground in major country diplomacy', said President Xi at the Central Conference on Work Relating to Foreign Affairs in Beijing in the summer of 2018. This includes working out how to form a 'clear understanding of China's status and role in the evolving world' and to help 'formulate principles and policies of China's external work in a scientific way, though cool-headed analysis of international phenomena'.[138] According to reports, considerable effort is going into producing artificial-intelligence systems that help analyse and respond to changes in global geopolitics – and provide a competitive advantage over other states. 'AI can think many steps ahead of a human,' said a researcher at the Institute of Automation at the Chinese Academy of Sciences. 'It can think deeply in many possible scenarios and come up with the best strategy.'[139]

This is just one area where resources are being expended – as they are, presumably, in other states, too. Another example, however, comes from the development of new military technology, such as in November 2015, when the China Academy of Aerospace Aerodynamics unveiled a new version of its CH-class drone.[140] Previous generations of this unmanned aerial vehicle (UAV) were cheaper versions of US equivalents that proved popular with buyers in the Middle East and Africa.[141]

The new UAV, however, is in a different league thanks to its ability to identify its own targets autonomously and engage them.[142] This opens up a new world of problems for military strategists, who will be faced with new and untested scenarios in the event that an unmanned autonomous weapons system attacks without direct instruction, or if an unmanned asset is disabled, compromised or hacked and used against its operators. Needless to say, the uncertainties of how to respond to such scenarios offers possibilities too in cases where it becomes difficult or even impossible to verify claims and counter-claims.

'I fear our seventy-year-long holiday from history may be over,' said General Sir Nick Carter, chief of the defence staff in the British Army, in a lecture in the summer of 2018. We are living in an era of 'constant competition', he said, marked by difficult questions 'about the evolving character of warfare'. It was vital to recognise that 'energy, cash, corrupt business practices, cyber-attacks, assassination, fake news, propaganda – and good old-fashioned military intimidation' are being used as weapons. 'What constitutes a weapon,' he warned, 'no longer has to go "bang".' And in this new era, it was a matter of fact that 'our state-based competitors have become masters at exploiting the seams between peace and war'.[143]

Technological innovation produces an array of benefits, ranging from lower financial costs as opposed to maintaining large forces (including the costs of training and equipping), improved and enhanced performance and, of course, lower levels of political risk to leaders who are averse to images of fallen sons and daughters being brought home from wars that are become less and less popular in proportion to how long they go on. They also reduce time and expense required for training. According to the Chinese state media reports, a CH-5 drone could be operated by an undergraduate with a basic knowledge of aviation after only one or two days' training.[144]

The Russian military is likewise investing heavily in new technologies to transform its armed forces, developing robots that are capable of mounting operations to evacuate wounded soldiers from the battlefield and to diagnose and treat casualties. Researchers are also working on biomorphic robots like the four-legged Lynx, which will be equipped with a machine gun and anti-tank guided missiles and will be able to operate in conditions including on ice and in sand that would test, challenge and tire human soldiers. Unmanned mine-clearance vehicles, robot nurses capable of operating in the extreme cold, as well as a remotely operated version of Russia's T-14 Armata tank are also in development.[145] This fearsome tank is already the envy of many outside Russia. 'Without hyperbole,' said a British Ministry of Defence report, 'Armata represents the most revolutionary step change in tank design in the last half century.'[146]

Not surprisingly, it is difficult to verify claims of exactly what is being worked on or how efficient or effective new unmanned weapons systems are – or how expensive they are to develop. But there can be no doubt that this is an area of particular interest to countries like Russia, which hosted its third Military Scientific Conference in May 2018 on 'The Robotisation of the Armed Forces of the Russian Federation'.[147]

The intensification of military competition is moving fast and is a source of considerable concern. The US Air Force recognises, for example, that it is a matter of time before either China or Russia, or both, will develop the software and hardware needed to crack the 'stealth' technology that has long given the US a significant air-power advantage.[148] Then there are concerns about the development of 'carrier-killer' missiles that are capable of turning aircraft carriers from advanced, fearsome warfare platforms into expensive sitting ducks.[149]

Staying ahead of the competition is also fast extending to a new era of a space race. Progress made by Indian scientists in ballistics has led to announcements that a manned mission will take place by 2022.[150] This sits alongside China's growing program of manned and unmanned launches, which now includes a major new facility being built in Patagonia in southern Argentina that will help with expeditions to the far side of the moon.[151] Initiatives such as these have sparked a response in Washington. Significant funds will be committed to US space programs, announced President Trump recently. These need to produce results: 'It is not enough to have American presence in space,' he said. 'We must have American dominance in space'.[152]

Increasing efforts towards restricting access to IT to China and Russia, also to Iran, is an important element of the US's attempts to respond to the fact that it is facing new and rapidly moving competition. Punitive measures against Chinese mobile and IT technology companies like ZTE – which was issued with a $1bn fine (plus another $400m in escrow), and a ten-year ban on buying American-made components – are an opening salvo of efforts to slow down, if not restrict, the pace of innovation that looks increasingly like a threat to US national security.[153]

But in an interconnected world, things are not so simple. For example, Space-X, which deploys US military satellites, uses RD-180 rockets made by Energomash in Russia – and raises the question of how Washington will deal with the gap if, as seems likely, purchases such as and including these will be blocked as part of wider sanctions against Moscow.[154] And in any event, as a recent report to US Congress notes, Russia has customers for its technology and expertise elsewhere, not least in China. If, as seems likely, necessity is the mother of invention, then it may well prove that attempts to strangle technological developments by starving other states of components and knowledge will only serve to accelerate them.

Some can see the writing on the wall. There are many industries where China is making rapid advances – like aeronautics, high-speed rail and new energy vehicles, noted US trade representative Robert Lighthizer. These industries should be targeted, he said, for trade tariffs. It didn't take a genius (or spies) to work out that 'these are things that if China dominates the world, it's bad for America'.[155] China's rise needs to countered if the US is to continue to thrive.

This was articulated forcefully in confirmation hearings for the appointment of the first director of Pentagon Research, Engineering, in the early summer of 2018. The nominee, Lisa Porter, did not mince her words. 'We need to change the culture at the Pentagon,' she said. There should be no doubting the scale of the challenge facing the United States. The Department of Defense is 'too big, too slow', she said.[156]

The US faces 'difficult intelligence gaps', said Gina Haspel, Director of the CIA, in a speech in the autumn of 2018, because of 'the intelligence community's justifiably heavy emphasis on counter-terrorism'. The time had come, she said, to be 'sharpening our focus on nation-state rivals'.[157] The problem is that 'the United States and allied leaders remain preoccupied with troubles at home' and close to home – and have woken up late in the day to the realities of a changing world. Big changes are needed for the US, and the West, to stay in the game.[158]

*

These are difficult and dangerous times. On the one hand is a US administration that seeks to reshape the world to its own interests, using the stick, rather than the carrot; on the other, a Chinese government that talks of mutual benefits, of enhancing cooperation and of using incentives to weave together peoples, countries and cultures in a 'win-win' scenario – while at the same time raising fears for many of an empire being built by design or by default.

This dichotomy is shaping the twenty-first century. 'We are moving away from a state in which international norms are led by western liberalism to a state where international norms are no longer respected,' notes Yan Xuetong, who argues that the turbulence is part of a period of transition from a unipolar to a bipolar world. 'Strategic relationships,' he states, 'have also become quite clearly a matter of other nations choosing between the United States and China.'[159]

It is a view echoed by Henry Kissinger. 'We are in a very, very grave period,' he told the *Financial Times*. A divided Atlantic, he said, would turn Europe into 'an appendage of Eurasia', forced to look not west but east to a China whose aim is to be 'the principal advisor to all humanity'.[160] China's leadership ambitions extend to political philosophy too. The country's progress over the last four decades has 'enabled the world to develop a "whole new understanding of socialism"', said a recent article in the Chinese press, 'and proved that the western model of modernisation is not the sole pattern but only one of many choices.'[161] The triumph of liberal democracy is on hold, if not over.

Some are resigned to the trade-off of freedoms in return for 'getting things done', as Clare Foges, a columnist with *The Times* of London, put it in a column in which she praised dictatorial leaders like Trump, Erdoğan and Putin. 'Strongmen may be tyrannical and unpleasant, yet on the credit side of the ledger they truly believe they can transform their nations.'[162] This encapsulates perfectly how the west has lost its bearings and is losing its way in a changing world.

The rise of this new world is taking place before us, driven by shifts in power that are so profound that it is hard to see how they can be stopped, slowed down or held back, except by the forces of conflict, disease and climate change that have played such important roles in the past in shaping world history and redirecting and reshaping the present and the future.

In a speech delivered at the Davos summit in 2017, the Chinese president, Xi Jinping, talked about the need for nations to work with rather than against each other. 'Our real enemy,' he said, 'is not the neighbouring country; it is hunger, poverty, ignorance, superstition and prejudice.' It could not be right, he said, that 'the richest 1 per cent of the world's population own more wealth than the remaining 99 per cent … [while] for many families, to have warm houses, enough food and secure jobs is still a distant dream'. Moreover, he concluded, 'when encountering difficulties, we should not complain about ourselves, blame others, lose confidence or run away from responsibilities. We should join hands and rise to the challenge. History is created by the brave. Let us boost confidence, take actions and march arm-in-arm toward a bright future.' This epitomises the efforts by China to articulate a role of global leadership that is appealing to all.[163]

It is, moreover, a message that is articulated consistently from Beijing. President Trump is 'opening fire on the entire world', said a Chinese government spokesman in July in the face of yet more trade barriers being erected. 'China will stand with the rest of the world in resolutely opposing protectionism, which is backward, antiquated and inefficient, and unilateralism, which turns back the wheels of history.'[164] China offers solidarity, common interests and mutual benefits, in other words; the United States does not.

The reality is more complex. The countries that lie between the Baltic and the Gulf, between the eastern Mediterranean and the Pacific Ocean, are deeply flawed. Most have poor records on human rights, limited freedom of expression in matters of faith, conscience and sexuality, and control of the media to dictate what does and what does not appear in the press. Criticising the government, the president or their intimates often results in time in prison, or in some cases, death.[165] In most cases, since my original book was published, these have either not improved or have got worse.

Well-chosen words by some world leaders should not be any more distracting than those that are poorly chosen by others. What matters is trying to see the wood for the trees, to try to understand the rhythms of global change that are destabilising and worrying for some, but creating a world of hope and promise for tomorrow. Along the Silk Roads there is a great deal that is imperfect and a great deal that can, should and needs to be improved in the future.

It is also important to recognise the fragilities that come with the transference of the economic centre of gravity and with the uncertainty of a period of transition. The Chinese army is suffering from 'peace disease', according to a recent front-page article in the *People's Liberation Army Daily* newspaper, because it has not fought a war for so long. New training techniques are needed, said the paper, to ensure that China is able to fight and win a confrontation with an enemy.[166] Such comments make for sobering reading. So too does the fact that Chinese bombers are 'likely training for strikes against US and allied targets', according to the recent assessments of the Department of Defense.[167]

It is sometimes hard to believe that scenarios develop that lead to military confrontation, not least since logic dictates that disputes and rivalries are much better settled at the negotiating table than on the battlefield. But one of the lessons that history teaches is that no generation has a monopoly on peace, nor unique abilities to reduce tensions, nor the skill to defuse situations that are escalating.

In the short term, sanctions on Iran have a significance that goes beyond Tehran and the regime change that seems to be an article of faith in Washington despite all the evidence to the contrary as to how states fare when brought to breaking point. In fact, the implications of US policy towards Iran are most serious when it comes to China. It seems that the efforts to impose a stranglehold over Tehran will have a serious impact on China – though whether this is intentional or not is unclear. 'Our goal is to increase pressure on the Iranian regime by reducing to zero its revenue from crude oil sales', said Brian Hook, director of policy planning at the US State Department. 'We are prepared to use secondary sanctions on other governments that continue this trade with Iran.' This includes China, which imports over a quarter of Iran's oil, and which is already having to respond to trade tariffs that are more problematic for the Chinese economy than they are for the US.[168] As such, additional pressure on Beijing threatens to raise the stakes further still. Even though China has dismissed US demands to cut imports, it is little wonder that articles have begun to appear in the press in China that talk of 'mountains to climb and treacherous waters to wade across'.[169]

The Chinese people should not be fearful, for China has spent time developing a 'comprehensive understanding of the trade war', said one article in *People's Daily*, the government mouthpiece. This meant that the leadership could 'handle [the challenges] with calmness'. Nevertheless, few should doubt that 'the US wants to profit from its economic and trade relations with China', and at the same time, 'wants more to contain China's development'.[170]

'We are looking forward to a more beautiful counter-attack [in response to the tariffs]', said the *Global Times*, with the anonymous author promising that China 'will keep increasing the pain felt by the US'.[171] These comments are designed to placate the middle classes, who stand to suffer from the trade war. With a stock market slide of 25% in the months following the escalation by Washington, coupled with a marked weakening of the yuan, some commentators have noted that one challenge facing the leadership will be to placate public opinion. As one Beijing financier reputedly put it, 'the sword of Damocles' hangs 'over the Chinese financial system'.[172]

For some, though, the situation requires more drastic action. In a remarkable essay published in July 2018 entitled 'Our current fears and our expectations' (我们当下的恐惧与期待), Xu Zhangrun, a leading professor at Tsinghua University, issued a challenge for the country's direction of travel – and to its leadership. Civil society had not evolved for decades, Xu wrote, leading to a lack of political maturity of its citizens that was not just unfortunate but regressive. Huge financial resources had been built up from the 'blood and sweat of the workers', only for this to be spent on supporting failed states like North Korea and Venezuela and making enormous investments in other countries – and giving aid to states in the Middle East that are 'literally oozing with riches.' What China needs, he said, is 'a clear vision for the nation's future'.[173]

Dissent is not easy in states where control of the media and even of private correspondence is carefully regulated. Statements like Xu's are unusual, both in terms of the content but also in terms of the expression of such forceful opinions. They serve as a useful reminder though that just because voices cannot always be easily heard does not mean that they do not exist. It can be tempting to think that in states where freedoms are curtailed that all agree with the policies of those in positions of authority. That is rarely the case.

In fact, the rumour mills are busy whirring in Beijing, trying to keep up with events, seeking to make sense of what China is having to contend with in a changing global situation and how to best respond to it. Part of this is shaped by working out how to apply 'Xi Jinping Thought', a fourteen-point manifesto that was added formally to the country's constitution – alongside 'Marxism-Leninism, Mao Zedong Thought and Deng Xiaoping Theory' – in March 2018 at the National People's Congress. One of the key elements to this is creating an international community with a shared future, based on collaboration and cooperation. That is not easy when others either do not want to share a future or want to advance a different vision altogether.[174] Perhaps it is no surprise that the top 'hot research topic' of 2017 in China was reported to be research on Xi Jinpging thought.[175] It is not just other parts of the world that are at a crossroads and are looking to see what may, or may not, lie ahead.

*

Finding ways to work together is neither easy nor a given. But the nations in Asia have much in common.

As Xi said in Astana in 2013, however, while the peoples of the Silk Roads are of 'different races, beliefs and cultural backgrounds', they are 'fully capable of sharing peace and development', as history shows. This is not a new world being born; it is the old world being reborn.

We are already living in the Asian century. The shift of global GDP from the developed economies of the west to those of the east has been breathtaking in both scale and speed. According to some estimates, thanks to sharp rises in oil prices, the countries of the Middle East (and North Africa) will earn more than $210bn more in 2018–19 than in they did in the previous twelve months – a windfall of enviable proportions.[176] That change has led to a series of obvious growing pains in Asia, ranging from environmental damage to an almost insatiable appetite for infrastructure investment. It has also led to challenges in how states engage, cooperate and in some cases compete with each other.

What is striking, however, as new connections forge and old links are renewed, is that the west is in danger of becoming less and less relevant. When the west does engage and play a role, it is invariably to intervene or interfere in ways that create more problems than they solve – or to place obstacles and restrictions in place that limit the growth and prospects of others. The age of the west shaping the world in its image is long gone – although that seems to have been lost on those who think that managing the fates of others is appropriate and even possible.

'China, Russia [and] Iran ... are forces of instability,' said John Sullivan, US deputy secretary of state, when launching a human rights report in April 2018. These states are 'morally reprehensible and undermine our interests'. Such comments sit uncomfortably alongside reports that even before the election of Donald Trump as president, he was being sounded out by influential figures in the Middle East – including the crown prince of Abu Dhabi and the Israeli ambassador to the US – to strike a deal with Russia and Vladimir Putin. Essentially, this amounted to a trade: in return for forcing Iran to withdrawal from Syria, Moscow would be rewarded with the ending of sanctions and recognition of Crimea. 'We're going to have to see,' said Trump when asked if he would change the US position on Russia's intervention in Ukraine.[177]

*

Forces of instability, it seems, are in the eye of the beholder. When branding other states as destabilising, it is easy to take a rose-tinted view of – or even forget – the impact that US intervention in Iraq and Afghanistan has had in the last fifteen years – to say nothing of decades going back to the middle of the twentieth century. The belief that it is other states that cause problems poses questions about which lessons from history, if any, are learned in Washington. Trading Ukraine for Syria is one thing; being blind to the irony of accusing others of being disruptive is another.

From the perspective of the US, then, something seems to have gone badly wrong with the spine of the Silk Roads, where China, Russia and Iran – three of the largest and most important states in the world – are deemed to pose a direct threat to the US and a threat to global stability.[178] Two others, Turkey and Pakistan, are seen to be cancerous problems that can only be dealt with aggressively, while the experiences with Syria, Iraq and Afghanistan provide salutary lessons on how interventions do not often go to plan.

One of the challenges as a historian or as an observer of contemporary affairs is to see the bigger picture. Identifying the ways in which the world is connected and assessing how the dots join up not only allows for a better understanding of what is going on around us, but provides a platform for a more accurate vantage point too. Assessing how the different pieces of the global geopolitical puzzle are connected to each other also helps to better explain the fragilities and dangers – as well as the opportunities for cooperation and collaboration – that can help frame better decision-making too.

The King of Zhao in north-eastern China, who ruled nearly 2,500 years ago, declared that, 'A talent for following the ways of yesterday is not sufficient to improve the world of today.' Those words of wisdom are as apt today as they were then. Understanding what is driving change is the first step to being able to prepare and adapt to it. Trying to slow down or stop that change is an illusion. What is not, though, is the fact that the

Silk Roads are rising. They will continue to do so. How they develop, evolve and change will shape the world of the future, for good and for bad. Because the Silk Roads have always done just that.

Notes

INTRODUCTION

1 Ferdinand von Richthofen, 'Über die zentralasiatischen Seidenstrassen bis zum 2. Jahrhundert. n. Chr.', *Verhandlungen der Gesellschaft für Erdkunde zu Berlin* 4 (1877), pp. 96–122.

2 Yuqi Li, Michael J. Storozum, Xin Wang and Wu Guo, 'Early irrigation and agropastoralism at Mohuchahangoukou (MGK), Xinjiang, China', in *Archaeological Research in Asia* 12 (2017), 23–32.

3 'Spy satellites are revealing Afghanistan's lost empires', *Science* 358.6369 (2017).

4 See, for example, Kathryn Franklin and Emily Hammer, 'Untangling Palimpsest Landscapes in Conflict Zones: a "Remote Survey", in Spin Boldak, Southeast Afghanistan', *Journal of Field Archaeology* 43.3 (2018), pp. 58–73.

5 Taylor R. Hermes et al., 'Urban and nomadic isotopic niches reveal dietary connectivities along Central Asia's Silk Roads', *Scientific Reports* 8.5177 (2018).

6 Paola Pollegiono et al., 'Ancient Humans Influenced the Current Spatial Genetic Structure of Common Walnut Populations in Asia', *Plos One* 10.1371 (2015), pp. 1–16.

7 Ranajit Das, Paul Wexler, Mehdi Piroonznia and Eran Elhaik, 'Localizing Ashkenazic Jews to Primeval Villages in the Ancient Iranian Lands of Ashkenaz', *Genome Biology and Evolution* 8.4 (2016), pp. 1132–49.

8 Alexander F. More et al., 'Next-generation ice core technology reveals true minimum natural levels of lead (Pb) in the atmosphere: Insights from the Black Death', *GeoHealth* 1 (2017), pp. 211–19.

9 State Department, Memorandum of Conversation, Byroade to Matthews, 'Proposal to Organize a Coup d'état in Iran', 26 November

1952, General Records of the Department of State 1950–54, Central Decimal File 788.00/11-2652.

10 Strategic Air Command, 'Atomic Weapons Requirements Study for 1959' in W. Burr (ed.), *National Security Archive Electronic Briefing Book No. 538.*

11 BBC News, 'Turkey sentences 25 journalists to jail for coup links', 9 March 2018.

12 Nergis Demirkaya, 'Hükümetin 2023 planı: 5 yılda 228 yeni cezaevi', *Gazete Duvar*, 10 December 2017.

13 https://news.nike.com/news/kobe-x-silk-shoe-inspired-by-kobe-bryant-s-personal-connections-to-asia-and-europe

14 https://www.hermes.com/uk/en/product/poivre-samarcande-eau-de-toilette-V38168/

15 Kevin G. Hall and Ben Wieder, 'Trump dreamed of his name on towers across former Soviet Union', McClatchy DC Bureau, 28 June 2017; Adam Davidson, 'Trump's business of corruption', *New Yorker*, 21 August 2017.

16 Turkmenistan.gov.tm, '2018 год: Туркменистан – сердце Великого Шёлкового пути', 2 January 2018.

17 *BP Statistical Review of World Energy June 2017*, pp. 12, 26.

18 US Department of Agriculture, *Grain: World Markets and Trade*, July 2018.

19 US Geological Survey, *Mineral Commodity Summaries 2017*, p. 151; p. 135.

20 UN Office on Drugs and Crime, *Afghanistan Opium Survey 2007* (Islamabad), p. v.

21 Alfred W. McCoy, *In the Shadows of the American Century: The Rise and Decline of US Global Power* (London, 2017), p. 111.

22 UN Office on Drugs and Crime, *Afghanistan Opium Survey 2017. Challenges to sustainable development, peace and security* (2018), p. 4; for the value of the markets, see UNODC, Drug Trafficking at https://www.unodc.org/unodc/en/drug-trafficking/index.html

23 Andrew Gilmour, 'Imprisoned, threatened, silenced: human rights workers across Asia are in danger', *Guardian*, 18 May 2018. See also Freedom House, *Freedom of the Press 2017* (April, 2017)

24 Asian Development Bank, *Asia 2050. Realizing the Asian Century* (2011), p. 3.

25 PricewaterhouseCoopers, *The World in 2050. Will the shift in global economic power continue?* (2015), p. 11.

26 George Magnus, *Red Flags: Why Xi's China is in Jeopardy* (London, 2018), p. 117.

27 International Monetary Fund, Press release, 'People's Republic of China: 2017 Article IV Consultation', 8 August 2017.

THE ROADS TO THE EAST

1 'The President's News Conference with President Boris Yeltsin of Russia in Vancouver', 4 April 1993', in Public Papers of the President of the United States, William J. Clinton, January 20 to July 31, 1993, p. 393.

2 https://www.nobelprize.org/nobel_prizes/peace/laureates/1993/press. html

3 Agence France-Presse, 'Forgiveness gesture in accepting Nobel prize', 9 December 2013.

4 Joint Statement of the Democratic People's Republic of Korea and the United States of America, New York, June 11, 1993, at http://nautilus. org/wp-content/uploads/2011/12/CanKor_VTK_1993_06_11_joint_ statement_dprk_usa.pdf

5 United Nations Peacemaker, 'Agreement on the Maintenance of Peace along the Line of Actual Control in the India–China Border, 7 September 1993'.

6 Geremie Barmé, 'Red Eclipse', in *Red Rising, Red Eclipse. China Story Yearbook 2012* https://www.thechinastory.org/yearbooks/yearbook-2012/; J. Gewirtz, *Unlikely Partners; Chinese Reformers, Western Economists, and the Making of Global China* (Cambridge, Mass., 2017), pp. 245ff.

7 Fareed Zakaria, 'Give South Korea a gold medal', *Washington Post*, 8 February 2018.

8 Infosys, *Navigate Your Next. Annual Report 2017–18*, 13 April 2018.

9 S. V. Krishnamachari, 'How Rs 950 invested in Infosys in 1993 IPO is now worth over Rs 50 lakh', *International Business Times*, 9 June 2017.

10 For more information Qatar Airways, see https://www.qatarairways. com/en/about-qatar-airways.html

11 Kurt Hofmann, 'Qatar Airways increases stake in IAG to 20%', *Air Transport World*, 1 August 2016; *The Economist*, 'Why Qatar Airways has bought 9.6% of Cathay Pacific', 7 November 2017.

12 *Gulf Times*, 'Qatar Airways signs MoU to buy 25% stake in Moscow's Vnukovo Airport', 4 April 2018.

13 Paul Routledge and Simon Hoggart, 'Major hits out at Cabinet', *Guardian*, 25 July 1993.

14 FIFA, 'History of Football – The Origins' http://www.fifa.com/about-fifa/who-we-are/the-game/index.html

15 *Independent*, 'Arsenal fans' group set to urge Alisher Usmanov not to sell his shares to Stan Kroenke', 4 October 2017.

16 Cinzia Sicca and Alison Yarrington, *The Lustrous Trade. Material Culture and the History of Sculpture in England and Italy, c.1700–1860* (London, 2001).

17 Charles Thompson, *The Travels of the Late Charles Thompson*, 3 vols (Reading, 1744), 1, p. 67.

18 World Bank, 'From local to global: China's role in global poverty reduction and the future of development', 7 December 2017.

19 Niall Ferguson and Xiang Xu, 'Make Chimerica Great Again', *Hoover Institution Economic Working Paper* 18105, 3 May 2018, p. 11.

20 Julien Girault, 'Hu Keqin; "Nous prenons un soin extrême de nos terres", en France', *Le Point*, 23 February 2018.

21 Sylvia Wu, 'China Wine Imports: Australia and Georgia taking a leap', *Decanter*, 5 February 2018.

22 Adam Sage, 'Bordeaux whines as rich Chinese give lucky names to old châteaux', *The Times*, 23 November 2017; Natalie Wang, 'Bordeaux wary of rich Chinese changing estates' names', *The Drinks Business*, 30 November 2017.

23 IATA, *20 Year Passenger Forecast Update*, 24 October 2017.

24 Aaron Chong, 'Boeing sees demand for 500,000 new pilots in Asia-Pacific', *FlightGlobal*, 7 December 2016.

25 Australian and International Pilots Association, 'Australian pilots land $750,000 in China', 28 December 2017.

26 Richard Weiss, 'Pilot Shortage Forces World's Biggest Long-Haul Airline to Cut Flights', Bloomberg, 11 April 2018.

27 Wolfgang Georg Arlt, *China's Outbound Tourism* (London, 2006), p. 19.

28 United Nations World Tourism Organisation, Press release, 'Strong outbound tourism demand from both traditional and emerging markets in 2017', 23 April 2018.

29 CLSA, *Chinese outbound tourists – new 2017 report*, 19 July 2017. For estimates of Chinese passport holders, see, for example, Goldman Sachs, *The Asian Consumer. The Chinese Tourist Boom, November 2015*.

30 The Donkey Sanctuary, *Under the Skin. The emerging trade in donkey skins and its implications for donkey welfare and livelihoods* (January 2017).

31 BBC News, 'Niger bans the export of donkeys after Asian demand', 6 September 2016; Media Group Tajikistan Asia Plus, 'Donkey market booms in Tajikistan', 4 January 2017.

32 Kimon de Greef, 'Rush for Donkey Skins in China Draws Wildlife Traffickers', *National Geographic*, 22 September 2017.

33 Filipa Sá, 'The Effect of Foreign Investors on Local Housing Markets: Evidence from the UK', *CEPR Discussion Paper No DP11658* (2016), pp. 1–43.

34 Emanuele Midolo, 'Russian investors: Welcome to Londongrad', *Propertyweek*, 13 April 2018.

35 Yuan Yang and Emily Feng, 'China's buyers defy the law to satisfy thirst for foreign homes', *Financial Times*, 13 March 2018.

36 Esha Vaish and Dasha Afansieva, 'Hong Kong property investors go trophy hunting in London despite Brexit', Reuters, 21 August 2017.

37 Matt Sheehan, 'How Chinese Real Estate Money is Transforming the San Francisco Bay Area', MacroPolo, 22 August 2017; Paul Vieira, Rachel Pannett and Dominique Fong, 'Western Cities Want to Slow Flood of Chinese Home Buying. Nothing Works', *Wall Street Journal*, 6 June 2018.

38 Dinçer Gökçe, 'Kiler, Sapphire'de 47 daire birden sattı', *Hürriyet*, 21 February 2017.

39 Faseeh Mangi, '135 Million Millennials Drive World's Fastest Retail Market', Bloomberg, 28 September 2017.

40 Euromonitor International, 10 Facts about India, 12 January 2014. For income distribution to the top earners, see L. Chancel and T. Piketty, 'Indian income inequality, 1922–2015: From British Raj to Billionaire Raj?', World Inequality Database Working Paper Series No. 2017/11.

41 Boston Consulting Group, *The New Indian: The Many Facets of a Changing Customer* (March, 2017).

42 Bain & Co., *Luxury Goods Worldwide Market Study, Fall–Winter 2017*, 22 December 2017; Yiling Pan, 'Luxury Spending to Double in China Over Next 10 Years, Says McKinsey', *Jing Daily*, 15 June 2017.

43 CPP Luxury, 'Prada Group opens seven stores in Xi'an China', 25 May 2018.

44 Astrid Wendlandt, 'Chanel snaps up four companies to secure high-end silk supplies', Reuters, 22 July 2016; Yiling Pan, 'China Wants Fewer Burberry and BV Handbags, More Chanel and Hermès', *Jing Daily*, 23 April 2018.

45 Angelica LaVito, 'Starbucks is opening a store in China every 15 hours', *South China Morning Post*, 6 December 2017.

46 Cleofe Maceda, 'UAE's residents' luxury goods spending to reach more than $8 billion in 2017', *Gulf News*, 20 November 2017.

47 Associated Press, 'China's new baby policy lifts stocks, sinks condom maker', 30 October 2015.

48 Credit Suisse, *Spotlighting China's new two child policy*, 30 October 2015.

49 CLSA, *Chinese Outbound Tourism – New 2017 Report* (2017).

50 World Bank, GDP Growth (annual percentage) at https://data. worldbank.org/indicator/NY.GDP.MKTP.KD.ZG

51 Wouter Baan, Lan Luan, Felix Poh, Daniel Zipser, 'Double-clicking on the Chinese consumer. 2017 China Consumer Report', McKinsey & Company, 2017.

52 Bangalore Water Supply and Sewerage Board, *Bengaluru Water Supply and Sewerage Project (Phase 3) in the State of Karnataka, India. Final Report* (2017); *Times of India*, 'Water Crisis: Is Bengaluru heading for Day Zero?', 13 February 2018.

53 For Russia, see Orlando Figes, *A People's Tragedy: The Russian Revolution 1891–1924* (London, 1996), pp. 84ff, esp. pp. 111–15; for Turkey, Michael M. Gunter, 'Political Instability in Turkey During the 1970s', *Conflict Quarterly* 9.1 (1989), pp. 63–77; Sabri Sayari, 'Political Violence and Terrorism in Turkey, 1976–80: A Retrospective Analysis', *Terrorism and Political Violence* 22.2 (2010), pp. 198–215.

54 See, for example, Ronak Patel and Frederick Burkle, 'Rapid Urbanization and the Growing Threat of Violence and Conflict: A 21st Century Crisis', *Prehospital and Disaster Medicine* 27.2 (2012), pp. 194–7.

55 UN Habitat, *Urbanization and Development. Emerging Futures. World Cities Report 2016* (2016), p. 5.

56 *The New Arab*, 'Saudi Arabia welcomes Ramadan with a spate of arrests', 19 May 2018; Chris Gelardi, 'Saudi Authorities Arrest Women's Rights Activists Ahead of Lifting Driving Ban', *Global Citizen*, 21 May 2018.

57 Abdullah bin Zayed al Hahyan, 'In the Middle East, momentum for women must pick up speed', *Globe and Mail*, 30 May 2018; *Al-Jazeera*, 'UAE rights activist Ahmed Mansoor sentenced to 10 years in prison', 30 May 2018.

58 State Council of China, 'China looks to regulate city growth', 22 February 2016.

59 Adam Schreck, 'Isolation by the West fuels a tech start-up boom in Iran', *Phys Org*, 5 June 2017.

60 Techrasa Press Release, 'Silk Roads Start-up Announces Irnas' Top 10 Start-ups', 5 November 2017.

61 For a useful infographic, see https://www.statista.com/chart/10012/fintech-adoption-rates/

62 Don Weinland and Sherry Fe Ju, 'China's Ant Financial shows cashless is king', *Financial Times*, 13 April 2018.

63 Shrutika Verma, 'Paytm valuation pegged at $10 billion after secondary share sale', *Livemint*, 23 January 2018.

64 See for example Indikator.ru, 'Предприниматели стали меньше финансировать науку', 2 November 2017.

65 United States Senate Committee on Armed Services, 'Advance Policy Questions for Lieutenant General Paul Nakasone, ISA Nominee for Commander, US Cyber Command', 1 March 2018.

66 Pavel Kantyshev, 'Путин предложил госкомпаниям закупать российский софт', *Vedemosti*, 30 March 2016.

67 US Computer Emergency Readiness Team, Alert (TA18-106A), 'Russian State-Sponsored Cyber Actors Targeting Network Infrastructure Devices', 16 April 2018.

68 See, for example, Sergei Brilev, 'Хочется плакать': вирус атаковал Минздрав, МЧС, МВД, РЖД, 'Сбербанк' и 'Мегафон', *Vesti.ru*, 13 May 2017.

69 *RIA Novosti*, 'Клименко объяснил слова главы Роскомнадзора о "блокировке Facebook"', 26 September 2017.

70 Donie O'Sullivan, Drew Griffin and Curt Devine, 'Russian company had access to Facebook user data through apps', CNN Tech, 11 July 2018.

71 Interfax, 'Роскомнадзор будет блокировать инструменты для обхода запрета на Telegram по запросу', 16 April 2018.

72 See Ella George, 'Purges and Paranoia', *London Review of Books* 40.10 (2018), pp. 22–32; *Turkish Minute*, 'Turkish govt ready to block "abnormal" social media messages on election day', 26 May 2018.

73 Sarah Zheng, 'Beijing tries to pull the plug on VPNs in internet "clean-up", *South China Morning Post*, 13 July 2017.

74 See, for example, Peter Frankopan, *The Silk Roads: A New History of the World* (London, 2015), pp. 202ff.

75 Madeleine Albright, 'Will We Stop Trump Before It's Too Late', *New York Times*, 8 April 2018.

THE ROADS TO THE HEART OF THE WORLD

1 Jason Blevins, 'Donald Trump, in Grand Junction, says he will "drain the swamp in Washington, D.C.", *Denver Post*, 18 October 2016.

2 *Time*, 'Here's Donald Trump's Presidential Announcement Speech', 16 June 2015.

3 Jonathan Swan, 'Trump calls for "hell of a lot worse than waterboarding"', *The Hill*, 6 February 2016.

4 Rishi Iyengar, 'Read Donald Trump's Speech on Immigration', *Time*, 1 September 2016.

5 Univision, 'Former Mexican President to Donald Trump "I'm not going to pay for that fucking wall"', 25 February 2016.

6 Cassandra Vinograd and Alexandra Jaffe, 'Donald Trump in Indiana Says China is "Raping" America', CNBC, 2 May 2016.

7 *Good Morning America*, Interview, ABC, 3 November 2015.

8 Donald Trump, *Great Again: How to Fix Our Crippled America* (New York, 2015), p. 43.

9 White House, 'The Inaugural Address', 20 January 2017.

10 For the budget, https://www.whitehouse.gov/wp-content/uploads/2017/11/2018_blueprint.pdf. For America First, Sarah Churchwell, *Behold, America: A History of America First and the American Dream* (London, 2018).

11 White House, Presidential Memorandum Regarding Withdrawal of the United States from the Trans-Pacific Partnership Negotiations and Agreement, 23 January 2017.

12 White House, Statement by President Trump on the Paris Climate Accord, 1 June 2017.

13 White House, 'Executive Order Protecting the Nation from Foreign Terrorist Entry into the United States', 27 January 2017.

14 White House, 'Remarks by President Trump on the Policy of the United States Towards Cuba', 16 June 2017.

15 Shawn Donnan, 'Is there political method in Donald Trump's trade madness?', *Financial Times*, 23 March 2018.

16 http://www.europarl.europa.eu/resources/library/media/20180411RES01553/20180411RES01553.pdf

17 Reuters, 'EU is not at war with Poland, says EU's Juncker', 17 January 2018.

18 Agence France-Presse, 'Italy threatens EU funding in migrant row', 25 August 2018.

19 Anushka Asthana and Rowena Mason, 'Michael Gove attacks David Cameron over EU "scaremongering"', *Guardian*, 4 June 2016.

20 BBC News, 'UK "better off" out of EU – Michael Gove', 20 February 2016.

21 *The Herald*, 'Boris Johnson: EU tariffs would be "insane" if UK backs Brexit', 21 June 2016.

22 BBC News, 'Liam Fox warning of customs union "sellout"', 27 February 2018; Chloe Farand, 'UK government post-Brexit plans to create Africa free-trade zone are being internally branded "Empire 2.0"', *Independent*, 6 March 2017.

23 UK Prime Minister's Office, press release, 'PM; UK should become the global leader in free trade', 4 September 2016.

24 Association of Southeast Asian Nations, http://asean.org/?static_
post=rcep-regional-comprehensive-economic-partnership; Yasuyuki
Sawada, quoted in Asian Development Bank, *International
Financing Review Asia. Special Report: Growing up Fast* (2018), p. 9.

25 Turkmenistan.ru, 'В Туркменистане открыт новый
железнодорожный мост Туркменабат – Фараб', 7 March 2017.

26 *AKIPress*, 'CTSO to help Tajikistan to reinforce its border with
Afghanistan', 11 June 2018; *Novosti Radio Azattyk*, 'Состоялась
первая встреча глав оборонных ведомств Кыргызстана и Узбекиста
на',13 June 2018.

27 Dana Omirgazy, 'Shymkent hosts first Kazakh-Uzbek business forum',
Astana Times, 25 May 2018.

28 Uzbekistan National News Agency, press release, 'The Year of
Uzbekistan in Kazakhstan and the Year of Kazakhstan in Uzbekistan
will be held', 16 September 2017.

29 Uzbekistan National News Agency, Press release, 'Uzbekistan and
Kazakhstan: dynamic development of cooperation based on friendship
and brotherhood', 2 March 2018.

30 *AzerNews*, 'Trade turnover between Uzbekistan and Tajikistan
doubles', 22 June 2018.

31 Tasnim News Agency, 'Grounds Paved for Long-Lasting Cooperation
between Iran, Azerbaijan: Official', 4 June 2018.

32 *Pahjwok Afghan News*, 'Afghanistan, Tajikistan sign two co-operation
accords', 24 June 2018.

33 Simon Parani, *Let's not exaggerate: Southern Gas Corridor prospects to
2030*, Oxford Institute for Energy Studies Paper NG 135 (July 2018).

34 Fawad Yousafzai, 'Work on CASA-1000 power project in full
swing: Tajik diplomant', *The Nation*, 19 July 2018.

35 *Dispatch News Desk*, 'Kyrgyzstan keen to improve bilateral trade with
Pakistan: Envoy', 10 May 2018.

36 TASS, 'ЕАЭС и Иран завершают подготовку соглашения о зоне
свободной торговли', 9 April 2018.

37 Nicholas Trickett, 'Reforming Customs, Uzbekistan Nods Towards the
Eurasian Economic Union', *The Diplomat*, 26 April 2018.

38 United Nations Office on Drugs and Crime, 'President of Uzbekistan
calls to develop reliable mechanisms of co-operation in Central Asia at
the international conference in Samarkand', 10 November 2017.

39 See, for example, Raikhan Tashtemkhanova, Zhanar Medeubayeva,
Aizhan Serikbayeva and Madina Igimbayeva, 'Territorial and
Border Issues in Central Asia: Analysis of the Reasons, Current
State and Perspectives', *The Anthropologist* 22.3 (2015), pp. 518–25;

International Crisis Group, 'Central Asia: Border Disputes and Conflict Potential', *Asia Report* 33 (2002).

40 For the draft agreement, see Kommersant, 'Море для своих Пять стран договорились о разделе Каспия', 23 June 2018.

41 Bruce Pannier, 'A landmark Caspian agreement – and what It resolves', *Qishloq Ovozi*, 9 August 2018.

42 Interfax, 'Kyrgyzstan, Uzbekistan agree to swap land on border', 14 August 2018.

43 *Astana Times*, 'Kazakhstan resolves all Central Asian border issues, announces Kazakh President', 20 April 2018.

44 Virpi Stucki, Kai Wegerich, Muhammad Mizanur Rahaman and Olli Varis, *Water and Security in Central Asia. Solving a Rubik's Cube* (New York, 2014); Suzanne Jensen, Z. Mazhitova and Rolf Zetterström, 'Environmental pollution and child health in the Aral Sea region in Kazakhstan', *Science of the Total Environment* 206.2–3 (1997), pp. 187–93.

45 *Fergana Informationnov agentstvo*, 'Соляная буря превысила допустимую концентрацию пыли на северо-западе Узбекистана в шесть раз', 27 May 2018; *RIA Novosti*, 'Белая пыль неизвестного происхождения накрыла столицу Туркмении', 28 May 2018.

46 Matt Warren, 'Once Written Off for Dead, the Aral Sea Is Now Full of Life', *National Geographic*, 16 March 2018.

47 United Nations Office for the Coordination of Humanitarian Affairs, 'Drought grips large parts of Afghanistan', 6 June 2018.

48 Ben Farmer and Akhtat Makoli, 'Afghanistan faces worst drought in decades, as UN warns 1.4 million people need help', 22 July 2018.

49 Igor Severskiy, 'Water related problems of Central Asia: some results of the (GIWA) international water assessment program', *Ambio* 33 (2004), pp. 52–62.

50 Albek Zhupankhan, Kamshat Tussupova and Ronny. Berndtsson, 'Water in Kazakhstan, a key Central Asian water management', *Hydrological Sciences Journal* 63.5 (2018), pp. 752–62.

51 F. M. Shakil 'New Indian dam threatens to parch Pakistan', *Asia Times*, 28 May 2018.

52 Khalid Mustafa, 'India out to damage Pakistan's water interests on Kabul river', *The News*, 5 June 2016; Jehangir Khattak, 'Pakistan's unfolding water disaster', *Daily Times*, 2 June 2018; Nirupama Subramanian, 'In Kishanganga dam security, more than Pakistan shelling, sabotage a concern', *Indian Express*, 23 May 2018.

53 Hongkai Gaa et al, 'Modelling glacier variation and its impact on water resource in the Urumqi Glacier No. 1 in Central Asia', *Science of the Total Environment*, 844 (2018), 1160–70.

54 Babak Dehghanpisheh, 'Water crisis spurs protests in Iran', Reuters, 29 March 2018; Shashank Bengali and Ramin Mostaghim, 'A long-simmering factor in Iran protests: climate change', *LA Times*, 17 January 2018.

55 Khamenei.ir, 'Persian New Year 1397; Support for Iranian Products', 20 March 2018.

56 Trend News Agency, 'Water shortage hits Iran's hydroelectric power plants', 4 June 2018.

57 Tasnim News Agency, 'Afghanistan Committed to Supplying Iran's Water Share, Zarif Says', 6 May 2018.

58 Address by HE Mr Shavkat Mirziyoyev, President of the Republic of Uzbekistan at the General Debate of the 72nd Session of the United Nations General Assembly, 19 September 2017. For the full text, see https://gadebate.un.org/sites/default/files/gastatements/72/uz_en.pdf

59 Human Rights Watch Report, 'Uzbekistan: A Year in to New Presidency, Cautious Hope for Change', 25 October 2017; Human Rights Watch Report, 'Time to Seek Hard Commitments on Uzbekistan's Human Rights Record', 9 May 2018.

60 Committee to Protect Journalists, 'Uzbekistan releases remaining jailed journalists', 7 May 2018.

61 Freedom House, *Uzbekistan: the Year After*, August 2017.

62 Andrew Higgins, 'As Authoritarianism Spreads, Uzbekistan Goes the Other Way', *New York Times*, 1 April 2018; Editorial Board, 'A Hopeful Moment for Uzbekistan', *New York Times*, 13 April 2018.

63 Human Rights Watch, 'US: Focus on Rights as Uzbek Leader Visits', 15 May 2018.

64 Luca Anceschi, 'Modernising authoritarianism in Uzbekistan', *Open Democracy*, 9 July 2018.

65 Trend News Agency, 'Ashgabat and Dushanbe hold talks on consular issues', 20 April 2018.

66 *Turkmen Petroleum*, '"Узбекнефтегаз" о планах работы на морских шельфах в Азербайджане и Туркменистане', 27 June 2017.

67 Anadolu Agency, 'Train service linking Baku–Tbilisi–Kars launched', 30 October 2017; Reuters, 'First freight train from China arrives in Iran in "Silk Road" boost': media,16 February 2016; Xinhua, 'First China–Britain freight train reaches London', 18 January 2017.

68 Mehr News Agency, 'Iran–Kazakhstan transit potentials complementary: Press. Rouhani', 12 August 2018.

69 Ministry of Foreign Affairs of the Russian Federation, 'Foreign Minister Sergey Lavrov's remarks and answers', 7 April 2016.

70 *Financial Express*, 'India–Iran–Russia resume talks on activating key trade corridor', 7 April 2018.

71 P. Stoban, 'India Gears Up to Enter the Eurasian Integration Path', Institute for Defence Studies and Analyses, 7 June 2017.

72 Cited by Mohsen Shariantinia, 'Sanctions threaten Iran's dream of becoming Eurasian transport hub', 20 July 2018.

73 *Times of Oman*, 'You could soon travel visa-free to Kazakhstan from Oman', 8 May 2018.

74 Kamila Aliyeva, 'Five Nations agree to create Lapis Lazuli transport corridor', *AzerNews*, 15 November 2017.

75 *Dispatch Daily News*, 'Turkmenistan will build Ashgabat–Turkmenabat Autobahn', 19 June 2018.

76 *Eurasianet*, 'Turkmenistan's new $1.5 billion port: Show over substance', 3 May 2018.

77 *Туркменистан сегодня*, 'Морская гавань Туркменбаши отмечена международными наградами', 2 May 2018.

78 Turkmenistan.ru, 'Ashgabat enters Guinness Book of World Records as most white-marble city', 26 May 2013. For a summary of all the world records, see https://www.turkmenistan-kultur.at/oesterreich739-guinness-book.html

79 Apa, 'Azərbaycan, İran və Rusiya elektroenergetika sistemlərinin birləşdirilməsi üzrə işçi qrup yaradacaq', 26 April 2018.

80 Rashid Shirinov, 'Azerbaijan, Iran sign agreement on electricity sale', *AzerNews*, 13 April 2018.

81 *Tehran Times*, 'Rail freight transport in Iran up 55%', 14 August 2017

82 *Iran Daily*, 'Iran's transit revenues up by 20%', 10 April 2018.

83 Anadolu Agency, 'Turkey, Kazakhstan look to boost ties "in all areas"', 19 April 2018.

84 Ministry of Foreign Affairs of the Republic of Kazakhstan, 'Chairman and judges to Astana International Financial Centre Court take oath', 7 December 2017.

85 *Dawn*, 'Bonhomie marks opening of TAPI gas pipeline', 24 February 2018.

86 Eurasianet, 'Reports: Pakistan pushes through accelerated plan for TAPI', 2 May 2018.

87 *Pashtun Times*, 'Taliban announce stout support for TAPI gas pipeline project', 23 February 2018.

88 Anisa Shaheed, 'Taliban Discussing Peace Offer, says Former Member', *ToloNews*, 11 April 2018.

89 See for example *UzDaily,* Представители Узбекистана провели рабочие встречи с движением 'Талибан', 18 June 2018.

90 Associated Press, 'NATO Backs Afghan Leader's Offer of Talks With the Taliban', 27 April 2018.

91 Department of Defense, 'Department of Defense Press Briefing by General Nicholson via teleconference from Kabul, Afghanistan', 22 August 2018.

92 US Department of State, Office of Inspector General, Operation Freedom's Sentinel: Report to the United States Congress, 1 January 2018–31 March 2018 (2018).

93 Bob Woodward, *Fear: Trump in the White House* (London, 2018), p. 221.

94 See, for example, Reuters, 'Taliban fighters seize district in northern Afghanistan', 4 May 2018.

95 US Geological Survey, 'Preliminary Assessment of Non-Fuel Mineral Resources of Afghanistan, 2007' (October 2007).

96 Global Witness, *War in the Treasury of the People. Afghanistan, lapis lazuli and the battle for mineral wealth* (May 2016)

97 Global Witness, *Talc: The Everyday Mineral Funding Afghan Insurgents. How talc from Afghanistan's opaque and poorly regulated mining sector is helping fuel the Islamic State and Taliban* (May 2018).

98 Uran Botobekov, 'ISIS Uses Central Asians for Suicide Missions', *The Diplomat,* 1 December 2016; Edward Lemon, *Pathways to Violent Extremism: evidence for Tajik recruits to Islamic State* (2018).

99 Mohammed. Elshimi, Raffaello Pantucci, Sarah Lain and Nadine Salman, *Understanding the Factors Contributing to Radicalisation Among Central Asian Labour Migrants in Russia,* Royal United Services Institute for Defence and Security Studies, Occasional Papers (2018).

100 Fikret Dolukhanov, 'Uzbekistan, Tajikistan to hold joint military drills for first time', *Trend News Agency,* 18 April 2018. TASS, 'Россия и Узбекистан дали старт совместному антитеррористическому учению', 4 October 2017; Fakhir Rizvi, 'China, Pakistan, Afghanistan, Tajikistan to conduct joint Counter-terrorism Exercise', *Urdu Point,* 26 April 2018.

101 Indian Defence Ministry spokesman, quoted in *Hindustan Times,* 'India, Kazakhstan armies begin joint military exercises in Himchal Pradesh', 2 November 2017.

102 TASS, 'Более трех тысяч военных примут участие в учениях ШОС 'Мирная миссия – 2018' на Урале', 4 June 2018.

103 Dipanjan Roy Chaudhury, 'First joint military drills for India and Pakistan courtesy SCO', *Economic Times,* 9 June 2018.

104 PressTV, 'Iran, Pakistan to share border or peace, friendship: Pakistani Army', 29 December 2017; Mehr News Agency, 'Iran, Pakistan determined to boost border security', 12 March 2018. For the summoning of the Iranian ambassador to Pakistan, Al-Jazeera, 'Iran threatens to hit "terror safe havens" in Pakistan', 9 May 2017.

105 *Financial Tribune*, 'Iran Welcomes Gas Swap Deals with Turkmenistan', 3 April 2018; *Iran Daily*, 'Turkmenistan, Iran, to take gas dispute to intl. arbitration', 5 December 2017.

106 AKIPress, 'Turkmenistan lodges lawsuit against Iran in International Court of Arbitration', 17 August 2018.

107 *Ozodlik*, 'Бердымухамедов вызвал к себе руководство компании, строившей ашхабадский аэропорт из-за дефекта здания', 13 January 2017.

108 Bruce Pannier, 'Good News for Uzbekistan Is Not Good News for Turkmenistan', *Qishloq Ovozi*, 25 April 2018; Radio Azatlyk, 'В Туркменистане дорожают лекарства, ощущается дефицит', 27 July 2018.

109 IMF, *Opening Up in the Caucasus and Central Asia. Policy Frameworks to Support Regional and Global Integration*, July 2018.

110 Jason Holland, 'Turkmenistan opens US$2.25 billion airport with 1,100sq m of duty free and retail space', *The Moodie Davitt Report*, 14 October 2016.

111 *Озодлик*, 'Бердымухамедов вызвал к себе руководство компании, строившей ашхабадский аэропорт из-за дефекта здания', 13 January 2017.

112 Альтернативные новости Туркменистана, 'Ниже уровня толчка. В Гумдаге полиция занялась туалетами и мусорными свалками', 21 May 2018.

113 Attracta Mooney, 'Kazakh sovereign wealth fund is latest victim of oil price fall', *Financial Times*, 8 January 2016.

114 Edward Robinson, 'Bank's $4 Billion Fraud Allegations Return to London Courtroom', Bloomberg, 20 November 2017.

115 Max Seddon, Lionel Barber and Kathrin Hille, 'Elvira Nabiullina shuts down Russia's banking "banditry"', *Financial Times*, 19 October 2016.

116 *BNE Intellinews*, 'Taliban pledge protection as construction starts on Afghan part of TAPI pipeline', 26 February 2018.

117 Bruce Pannier, 'Why Didn't Turkmen, Uzbek Leaders Mention "Line D" To China?', *Qishloq Ovozi*, 27 April 2018.

118 RadioFreeEurope, 'Tajik Muslim Leader Declares Boxing, Other Sports Forbidden', 1 June 2018.

119 Eurasianet, 'Tajikistan slaps restrictions on imports from Uzbekistan', 6 July 2018.

120 Mullorachab Yusyfi, 'Тақозо аз додситонӣ: 'Қарори вазорати маорифро бекор кунед', Radio Ozodi, 26 June 2018.

121 Radio Azatlyk, 'Туркменистан: не достигшие тридцатилетия мужчины не будут допущены к зарубежным поездкам', 16 April 2018.

122 *New Fronts, Brave Voices. Press Freedom in South Asia 2016–2017*, IFJ Press Freedom Report for South Asia (2016–2017); *Daily Times*, 'Another journalist targeted', 23 June 2018; Raju Gopalakrishnan, 'Indian journalists say they are intimidated, ostracised if they criticise Modi and the BJP', Reuters, 26 April 2018.

123 Reuters, 'Kazakh police detain dozens at anti-government rally', 9 May 2018; Joanna Lillis, 'Is Kazakhstan's political opposition creeping back?' *Eurasianet*, 24 May 2018.

124 Artemy Kalinovsky, 'Central Asia's Precarious Path to Development', *Foreign Affairs*, 2 August 2018.

125 *Eurasianet*, 'Internet grinds to a near-halt in Tajikistan', 6 August 2018.

126 Catherine Putz, 'From Bad to Worse: Press Freedom in Eurasia Continues to Decline', *The Diplomat*, 26 April 2018.

127 For the difficulties of balancing competing views of Central Asia, see, for example, Paul Goble, 'A Year in Review: More Problems, More Reforms, More Cooperation for Central Asia in 2017', *Eurasia Daily Monitor* 15.4 (2018).

128 International Monetary Fund, Islamic Republic of Iran, IMF Country Report 18/93 (2018)

129 *Times of Israel*, 'Iran currency hits record low, crashing through 50,000 rial to the US dollar', 28 March 2018.

130 BBC News, 'Six charts that explain the Iran protests', 4 January 2018.

131 See, for example, Karim Sadjadpour, 'The Battle for Iran', *The Atlantic*, 31 December 2017; Najmeh Bozorgmehr, 'Iran's disillusioned youth spare no one in display of anger', *Financial Times*, 2 January 2018.

132 President Trump tweet, 1 January 2018.

133 Brent D. Griffiths, 'Giuliani: Trump is "committed to" regime change in Iran', *Politico*, 5 May 2018.

134 'Full text of speech by Rudy Giuliani at Grand Gathering 2018', Iran Probe, 5 July 2018.

135 White House, 'Remarks by President Trump on the Joint Comprehensive Plan of Action', 8 May 2018.

136 International Atomic Energy Agency, 'Verification and monitoring in the Islamic Republic of Iran in light of United Nations Security Council resolution 2231 (2015)', 22 February 2018.

137 Tasnim News, 'IRGC Warns US of Consequences of Military Action', 24 May 2018.

138 White House, Remarks by LTG H. R. McMaster at the United States Holocaust Memorial Museum Simon-Skjodt Center – 'Syria, Is the Worst Yet to Come?', 15 March 2018.

139 Jeffrey Goldberg, 'Saudi Crown Prince: Iran's Supreme Leader "Makes Hitler Look Good"', *The Atlantic*, 2 April 2018.

140 BBC News, 'Iran hits back over Saudi's prince's "Hitler" comment', 24 November 2017.

141 *Al Arabiya*, 'Mohammad bin Salman's full interview', 3 May 2017.

142 *Middle East Eye*, 'Iran warns Saudi Arabia after prince's "battle" comments", 8 May 2017.

143 *Haaretz*, 'After Crown Prince Recognizes Israel's Right to Exist, Saudi King Reiterates Support for Palestinians', 4 April 2018.

144 Raf Sanchez, 'Saudi Arabia "doesn't care" about the Palestinians as long as it can make a deal with Israel against Iran, says former Netanyahu advisor', *Daily Telegraph*, 25 November 2017.

145 *Daily Sabah*, 'Israel welcomes Saudi mufti's pro-Israel remarks, invites him to visit the country', 14 November 2017.

146 Anshel Pfeffer, 'Israeli minister confirms "secret" Saudi talks', *The Times*, 21 November 2017.

147 'Arab nations slam Israel's "racist, discriminatory" Jewish nation-state law', *Times of Israel*, 21 July 2018; 'High Court said to advise El Al to drop suit over Saudi route to India', *Times of Israel*, 22 July 2018.

THE ROADS TO BEIJING

1 Xinhua, Speech by Xi Jinping, 'Promote People-to-People Friendship and Create a Better Future', 7 September 2013.

2 Richard A. Boucher, 'US Policy in Central Asia: Balancing Priorities (Part II)', Statement to the House International Relations Subcommittee on the Middle East and Central Asia, 26 April 2006.

3 *People's Daily*, 'US scheming for 'Great Central Asia' strategy', 4 August 2006; for S. Frederick Starr's paper, 'A Partnership for Central Asia', *Foreign Affairs* July/August 2005.

4 US State Department, 'Remarks on India and the United States: A Vision for the 21st Century', 20 July 2011.

5 China.org.cn, 'Decision of the Central Committee of the Communist Party of China on Some Major Issues Concerning Comprehensively Deepening the Reform', Article 26, Section VII, 12 November 2013.

6 State Council Information Office, 'Six major economic corridors form the "Belt and Road" framework. China Development Bank invests $890bn', 2 May 2015.

7 Export-Import Bank of China, press release, 'Bank plays a policy-based financial role to support the construction of "One Belt and One Road"', 14 January 2014.

8 China International Trade Institute, *Industrial Cooperation between Countries along the Belt and Road* (August, 2015).

9 HSBC, 'Reshaping the Future World Economy', 11 May 2017.

10 Xinhua, 'Full text of President Xi Jinping's speech at opening of Belt and Road forum', 14 May 2017.

11 Rani Sankar Bosu, 'BRI will bring China and ASEAN closer', China. org.cn, 22 May 2017.

12 Xinhua, 'President Xi says to build Belt and Road into road for peace, prosperity', 14 May 2017.

13 Youtube, 'What's wrong with the world? What can we do?', https://www.youtube.com/watch?v=RkkGb14zIVY

14 Xinhua, 'Full text of President Xi Jinping's speech at opening of Belt and Road forum', 14 May 2017.

15 James Kynge, 'How the Silk Road plans will be financed', *Financial Times*, 9 May 2016.

16 For China's experiences in the 1980s and 90s, see Gewirtz, *Unlikely Partners*, op. cit.

17 Jamil Anderlini, 'Interview: 'We say, if you want to get rich, build roads first', *Financial Times*, 25 September 2018.

18 Jonathan E. Hillman, 'How Big Is China's Belt and Road?', Center for Strategic and International Studies, 3 April 2018.

19 Frankopan, *Silk Roads*, passim.

20 *Press TV*, 'Iran opens new trade link under new Silk Road plan', 26 June 2018.

21 Turkmenistan Segodnya, 'В Туркменабате тожественно открыт монумент «Шёлковый путь,' 8 April 2018.

22 Rigina Madzhitova, 'Уникальный проект, или как 12 ворот Ташкента превратят город в сердце Великого шелкового пути', Podrobno.uz, 5 September 2018.

23 Jonathan Hillman, 'A Chinese world order', *Washington Post*, 23 July 2018.

24 For example, Sajjad Hussain, 'China's CPEC investment in Pakistan reach $62 billion', *Livemint*, 12 April 2017; Arif Rafiq, 'China's $62 Billion Bet on Pakistan', *Foreign Affairs*, 25 October 2017;

25 Dr Shahid Rashid, executive director to the Center of Excellence for CPEC, quoted in *The News International*, 'CPEC contribution to cross $100bn by 2030', 9 February 2018.

26 Khaleeq Kiani, 'If all goes well, 10 CPEC projects may be completed', *Dawn*, 1 January 2018.

27 Mehtab Haider, 'China may be involved in running Karachi–Peshawar railway', *The News*, 5 February 2018.

28 *Tribune*, 'Cement sales touch record high at 4.2 million tons in October', 4 November 2017.

29 Eva Grey, 'China turns Malaysia's East Coast Rail Link into reality', *Railway Technology*, 1 October 2017.

30 Xinhua, 'Laotians expect Laos–China railway to bring tangible benefits', 4 February 2018.

31 For a survey of current major BRI infrastructure projects, see *International Financing Review Asia. Asian Development Bank Special Report: Coming up Fast* (April 2018).

32 'China to establish court for OBOR disputes', *Asia Times*, 25 January 2018.

33 Saptarshi Ray, 'China to tunnel beneath Himalayas for Nepal railway link', *The Times*, 23 June 2018.

34 Anil Giri, 'China looks at Nepal as potential gateway to South Asia, expands footprints in market', *Hindustan Times*, 19 October 2017.

35 Turloch Mooney, 'New Asia–Europe rail services added amid weak ocean rates', *Journal of Commerce*, 31 May 2016.

36 An additional ten containers were unloaded at Duisberg, *Railway Gazette*, 'First China to UK rail freight service arrives in London', 18 January 2017.

37 Dirk Visser, 'Snapshot: The World's Ultra-Large Container Ship Fleet', *The Maritime Executive*, 2 June 2018.

38 Quoted in the *Economist*, 'Western firms are coining it along China's One Belt, One Road', 3 August 2017.

39 Goldman Sachs, 'The Rise of China's New Consumer Class' at http://www.goldmansachs.com/our-thinking/macroeconomic-insights/growth-of-china/chinese-consumer/

40 Zhidong Li, Kokichi Ito and Ryoichi Komiyama, *Energy Demand and Supply Outlook in China for 2030 and A Northeast Asian Energy Community – The automobile strategy and nuclear power strategy of China* (2018).

41 Robin Mills, 'China's Big Play for Middle East Oil', Bloomberg, 10 May 2017; Elena Mazneva, Stephen Bierman and Javier Blas, 'China Deepens Oil Ties With Russia in $9 Billion Rosneft Deal',

Bloomberg, 8 September 2017; Anthony Dipaola and Aibing Guo, 'China's CNPC pays $1.18 billion for concessions in Abu Dhabi', *World Oil*, 21 March 2018.

42 US Energy Information Administration, 'China surpassed the United States as the world's largest crude oil importer in 2017', 5 February 2017.

43 Reuters, 'Kazakhstan to produce nuclear fuel for China', 26 May 2017.

44 Fred Gale, James Hansen and Michael Jewison, *China's Growing Demand for Agricultural Imports*, US Department of Agriculture, (2014), pp. 11–12.

45 China Water Risk, 'North China Plain Groundwater', statement, 26 February 2013.

46 *South China Morning Post*, 'Air quality worsening in China's Yangtze River Delta in 2018, figures show', 23 May 2018.

47 Li Gao, 'Greening Chinese Patent Law to Incentivize Green Technology Innovation in China', in Yahong Li, *The Role of Patents in China's Industrial Innovation* (Cambridge, 2017), pp. 79–105.

48 See, for example, Xinhua, 'President vows vast battle with pollution', 19 May 2018.

49 International Monetary Fund, Press release 18/200, 'IMF Staff Completes 2018 Article IV Mission to China', 29 May 2018.

50 Yan Chunlin, 'Visible and invisible hand in creating and reducing overcapacity', in Scott Kennedy (ed.), *State and Market in Contemporary China: Toward the 13ᵗʰ Five-Year Plan* (Lanham, 2016), pp. 30–32; Peter Ferdinand, 'Westward ho – The China dream and "one belt, one road": Chinese foreign policy under Xi Jinping', *International Affairs* 92.4 (2016), pp. 941–57.

51 Andrei Kirillov, 'В Казахстане регулярно говорят о некачественном ремонте дорог', *Kapital*, 26 June 2014.

52 Asian Development Bank, *Meeting Asia's Infrastructure Needs* (2017).

53 ICE, PeopleResearch on India's Consumer Economy, 360° survey 2016.

54 Tom Hancock, 'US fast food chains chase growth in small-town China', *Financial Times*, 18 October 2017; Salvatore Babones, 'China's middle class is pulling up the ladder behind slowly', *Foreign Policy*, 1 February 2018.

55 Tom Hancock and Wang Xueqiao, 'China's smaller cities compete to increase population', *Financial Times*, 20 July 2018.

56 Zhao Lei, 'Xinjiang's GDP growth beats the national average', *China Daily*, 20 October 2017; Frank Tang, 'Xinjiang halts all government

projects as crackdown on debt gets serious', *South China Morning Post*, 4 April 2018.

57 Joseph Hope, 'Returning Uighur Fighter and China's National Security Dilemma', *China Brief* 18(13), 25 July 2018.

58 Emily Feng, 'Crackdown in Xinjiang: Where have all the people gone?' *Financial Times*, 5 August 2018.

59 Nectar Gan, 'Ban on beards and veils – China's Xinjiang passes law to curb 'religious extremism', *South China Morning Post*, 30 March 2017.

60 The *Economist*, 'China has turned Xinjiang into a police state like no other', 3 May 2018; Stephanie Nebehay, 'UN says it has credible reports that China holds million Uighurs in secret camps', Reuters, 10 August 2018. For re-education camps, see Radio Free Asia, 'Around 120,000 Uyghurs Detained For Political Re-Education in Xinjiang's Kashgar Prefecture', 22 January 2018.

61 Feng, 'Crackdown in Xinjiang', op. cit.

62 Human Rights Watch, *'Eradicating Ideological Viruses.' China's Campaign of Repression against Xinjiang's Muslims* (London, 2018).

63 Weida Li, 'Beijing responds to Xinjiang policy criticism, blames "anti-China forces"', *GB Times*, 14 August 2018.

64 Associated Press, 'China to UN panel: No arbitrary detention in Uighur region', 13 August 2018.

65 Radio Free Asia, 'Xinjiang Political "Re-Education Camps" Treat Uyghurs "Infected by Religious Extremism"', CCP Youth League, 8 August 2018.

66 Xinhua, 'President Xi vows intense pressure on terrorism', 27 June 2014.

67 Reuters, 'China stages another mass anti-terror rally in Xinjiang', 19 February 2017.

68 Adrian Zenz and James Liebold, 'Chen Quanguo: The Strongman Behind Beijing's Securitization Strategy in Tibet and Xinjiang', *China Brief* 17(12), 21 September 2017.

69 Abdullo Ashurov, 'Аз донишҷӯёни тоҷик дар Чин хостанд, рӯза нагиранд', *Radioi Ozodi*, 9 June 2018.

70 Nurtai Lakhanuly, 'Это было как в аду'. Рассказы побывавших в китайских лагеря,' *Radio Azattyk*, 23 May 2018. Also see here Bruce Pannier, 'China's New Security Concern – The Kazakhs', *Qishloq Ovozi*, 8 August 2017.

71 Xinhua, 'Xi calls for building "great wall of iron" for Xinjiang's stability', 10 March 2017.

72 Congressional-Executive Commission on China, 'Chairs Urge Ambassador Branstad to Prioritize Mass Detention of Uyghurs,

Including Family Members of Radio Free Asia Employees', 3 April 2018.

73 See, for example, Franz J. Marty, 'The curious case of Chinese troops on Afghan soil', *Central Asia-Caucasus Analyst*, 3 February 2017.

74 Paul Goble, 'What Is China's Military Doing on the Afghan–Tajik Border?', *Eurasia Daily Monitor* 15(20), 8 February 2018.

75 Farhan Bokhari, Kiran Stacey and Emily Feng, 'China courted Afghan Taliban in secret meetings', *Financial Times*, 8 August 2018.

76 Reuters, 'Pakistan scrambles to protect China's "Silk Road" pioneers', 11 June 2017.

77 Permanent Court of Arbitration, 'The South China Sea Arbitration (The Republic of Philippines v. The People's Republic of China)', 12 July 2016 at https://www.pcacases.com/web/view/7

78 Richard A. Bitzinger, 'China's Plan to Conquer the South China Sea Is Now Clear', *The National Interest*, 10 May 2018.

79 Vu Huang, 'Vietnam asks China to end bombers drills in Paracels', *VnExpress*, 31 May 2018.

80 Manuel Mogato, 'Philippines takes "appropriate action" over Chinese bomber in disputed South China Sea', Reuters, 21 May 2018.

81 US Department of Defense, 'Remarks by Secretary Hagel at plenary session at International Institute for Strategic Studies Shangri-La Dialogue', 31 May 2014.

82 Ankit Panda, 'How Much Trade Transits the South China Sea? Not $5.3 Trillion a Year', *The Diplomat*, 7 August 2017.

83 *China Power*, 'How much trade transits the South China Sea?' 2 August 2017.

84 *Tanker Shipping & Trade*, 'China looks beyond the Middle East for its crude oil fix', 29 August 2017.

85 See, for example, Ian Storey, 'China's "Malacca Dilemma"', *China Brief* 6(8), 12 April 2006.

86 *Japan Times*, 'China–Japan maritime crisis would undermine "Belt and Road" initiative: PLA document', 23 September 2018.

87 *Japan Times*, 'Japan developing supersonic glide bombs to defend Senkaku Islands', 25 September 2018.

88 Jeffrey Wasserstrom, *Global Shanghai, 1850–2010: A History in Fragments* (London, 2009), p. 1.

89 For example, James A. Millward, 'Is China a colonial power?' *New York Times*, 4 May 2018.

90 Keith Johnson, 'Why is China Buying Up Europe's Ports?', *Foreign Policy*, 2 February 2018.

91 *Seatrade Maritime News*, 'Cosco reveals $620m Piraeus development plan', 29 January 2018.

92 For OOCL see Costas Paris, 'China's Cosco Agrees to Buy Shipping Rival OOCL', *Wall Street Journal*, 8 July 2017.

93 Janet Eom, '"China Inc." Becomes China the Builder in Africa', *The Diplomat*, 29 September 2016.

94 David Dollar, 'China's engagement with Africa. From Natural Resources to Human Resources', *John L. Thornton Center at Brookings* (2016).

95 Xinhua, 'Full text of Chinese President Xi Jinping's speech at opening ceremony of 2018 FOCAC Beijing summit', 4 September 2018.

96 Yusuf Alli, 'Obasanjo urges African leaders to ensure peace', *The Nation*, 28 June 2018.

97 Rogerio Jelmayer, 'Chinese investment, loans to LatAm staying high', *BN Americas*, 25 June 2018.

98 *TeleSur*, 'China Approves US$5Bn Loan For Venezuelan Oil Development', 3 July 2018. For inflation in Venezuela, Reuters, 'Venezuela's hyperinflation soars to 24,572 percent', 12 June 2018.

99 *América Economica*, 'Venezuela recibirá US$250M del Banco de Desarrollo de China para impulsar producción de crudo', 4 July 2018.

100 Haley Zaremba, 'Maduro looks to China for a bailout', OilPrice.com, 23 September 2018.

101 Ministry of Foreign Affairs of the People's Republic of China, 'China's Policy Paper on Latin America and the Caribbean (full text)', 5 November 2008. Carlos Torres and Randy Woods, 'China is Boosting Ties in Latin America. Trump Should Be Worried', Bloomberg, 3 January 2018.

102 *People's Daily*, 习近平致信祝贺中国—拉美和加勒比国家共同体论坛第二届部长级会议开幕, 23 January 2018.

103 Digital Belt and Road Program (DBAR), *Science Plan. An International Science Program for the Sustainable Development of the Belt and Road Region Using Big Earth Data* (2017), p. 2.

104 Hillman, 'How Big Is China's Belt and Road?', op. cit..

105 See, for example, Fernando Ascensão et al, 'Environmental challenges for the Belt and Road Initiative', *Nature Sustainability* 1 (2018), pp. 206–9.

106 Leo Timm, 'The Authoritarian Model Behind China's "One Belt, One Road"', *Epoch Times*, 21 May 2018.

107 Jonathan E. Hillman, 'China's Belt and Road is Full Of Holes', Center for Strategic and International Studies, 4 September 2018.

108 Joseph S. Nye, 'Xi Jinping's Marco Polo Strategy', Project Syndicate, 12 June 2017; Sarah McGregor, 'China Boosts Its US Treasuries Holdings by Most in Six Months', Bloomberg, 18 April 2018.

109 James Kynge, 'How the Silk Road plans will be financed', *Financial Times*, 9 May 2016.

110 Testimony by Jonathan Hillman, Statement Before the US–China Economic and Security Review Commission, 25 January 2018.

111 Quoted by Mark Magnier and Chun Han Wang, 'China's Silk Road Initiative Sows European Discomfort', *Wall Street Journal*, 15 May 2017.

112 US Department of State, 'Remarks – Secretary of State Rex Tillerson On US–Africa Relations: A New Framework', 6 March 2018.

113 Embassy of the People's Republic of China in the Republic of Zimbabwe, 'All-weather Friendship between China and Zimbabwe Beats the Slander', 26 May 2016.

114 For Mugabe's fortune, see Wikileaks, 'Assets of President Mugabe and Senior Goz and ruling party leaders', 29 August 2001. For Grace Mugabe's Ph.D., *News24*, 'Grace Mugabe's PhD the greatest academic fraud in history: academics', 3 February 2018. For China's role, Simon Tisdall, 'Zimbabwe: was Mugabe's fall as a result of China flexing its muscle?', *Guardian*, 21 November 2017.

115 Xinhua, 'Xi announces 10 major programs to boost China–Africa cooperation in coming 3 years', 4 December 2015.

116 Victoria Breeze and Nathan Moore, 'China has overtaken the US and UK as the top destination for anglophone African students', 30 June 2017.

117 James Carey, 'Tired of US "Aid" (Exploitation), Africa and Global South Look to China', *Mint Press News*, 18 January 2018.

118 Howard French, 'From Quarantine to Appeasement', *Foreign Policy*, 20 May 2015.

119 Colum Lynch, 'Genocide Under Our Watch', *Foreign Policy*, 18 April 2015.

120 Amitav Acharya, 'Asia after the liberal international order', *East Asia Quarterly* 10.2 (2018).

121 David Pilling and Adrienne Klasa, 'Kenya president urges rebalance of China–Africa trade', *Financial Times*, 14 May 2017.

122 *Business Day*, Kenya's Nairobi–Mombasa highway faces delays as legislators fret over debt', 12 April 2018.

123 David G. Landry, 'The Risks and Rewards of Resource-for-Infrastructure deals; Lessons from the Congo's Sicomines Agreement', *China Africa Research Initiative*, Working Paper 16 (May 2018)

124 David G. Landry, 'The Belt and Road Bubble is starting to burst', *Foreign Policy*, 27 June 2018.

125 Center for Global Development, *Examining the Debt Implications of the Belt and Road Initiative from a Policy Perspective*, CGD Policy Paper 121 (2018).

126 Charles Clover, 'IMF's Lagarde warns China on "Belt and Road" debt', *Financial Times*, 12 April 2018.

127 Alexander Sodiqov, 'Tajikistan Cedes Disputed Land to China', *Eurasia Daily Monitor*, 24 January 2011.

128 Jeffrey Reeves, *Chinese Foreign Relations with Weak Peripheral States. Assymetrical economic power and Insecurity* (London, 2016), pp. 78ff.

129 John Hurley, Scott Morris and Gailyn Portelance, 'Examining the Debt Implications of the Belt and Road Initiative from a Policy Perspective', *Center for Global Development Policy Paper* 121 (March 2018), p. 17; also IMF, 'Lao People's Democratic Republic. 2017 Article IV Consultation', March 2018.

130 Joaquim José Reis, 'Mais de metade da dívida ao estrangeiro é à China, a quem cada angolano já deve 754 USD', *Expansão*, 11 May 2018. For Angola's per capita income, see https://data.worldbank.org/ country/Angola

131 Tatyana Kudryavtseva, 'State debt of Kyrgyzstan reaches $703 per each resident', 24.kg, 11 April 2018; World Bank, GDP per capita (current US$), Kyrgyzstan.

132 Nurjamal Djanibekova, 'Kyrgyzstan: Power plant blame game threatens political showdown', *Eurasianet*, 18 May 2018.

133 P. K. Vasudeva, 'Sri Lanka's Handing Over Hambantota Port to China has Enormous Ramifications', *Indian Defense Review*, 30 January 2018.

134 *Gulf News*, 'No more flights from Sri Lanka's second airport', 6 June 2018.

135 *NewsIn.Asia*, 'Mattala airport in south Sri Lanka may help India strengthen links with ASEAN', 17 August 2017.

136 *Times of India*, 'Arun Jaitley's remark on "One Belt, One Road" shows unease in ties with China', 8 May 2017.

137 Ministry of External Affairs, India, 'Official spokesperson's response to query on participation of India in OBOR/BRI Forum', 13 May 2017.

138 Indrani Bagchi, 'India slams China's One Belt One Road initiative, says it violates sovereignty', *Times of India*, 14 May 2017.

139 Zhong Nan, 'World loves belt and braces approach', *China Daily*, 15 May 2017.

140 Zhang Xin, 'Indian Ambassador to China optimistic about future of bilateral relations', *Global Times*, 25 January 2018.

141 Liaqat Ali (et al.), 'The potential socio-economic impact of China Pakistan Economic Corridor', *Asian Development Policy Review* 5.4 (2017), pp. 191–8.

142 Ankit Panda, 'Geography's Curse: India's Vulnerable "Chicken's Neck"', *The Diplomat*, 8 November 2013.

143 *India Today*, 'Full-scale India–China war likely soon, Washington will back New Delhi: Meghnad Desai', 5 August 2017.

144 *The Hindu*, 'Army prepared for a two and a half front war: General Rawat', 8 June 2017.

145 See Frankopan, *Silk Roads*, pp. 294ff and above all Christopher Clark, *The Sleepwalkers: How Europe Went to War in 1914* (London, 2012).

146 *First Post*, 'Pakistan seals $5 billion deal to buy eight Chinese attack submarines', 31 August 2016.

147 Christopher Clary and Ankit Panda, 'Safer at Sea? Pakistan's Sea-Based Deterrent and Nuclear Weapons Security', *Washington Quarterly* 40(3) (2017), pp. 149–68.

148 Asian News International, 'Chinese navy ships in Gwadar, a concern: Indian Navy Chief', 1 December 2017.

149 Yuji Kuronuma, 'Maldives lifts state of emergency, defusing China–India tensions', *Nikkei Asian Review*, March 23 2018.

150 Manu Pubby, 'No confrontation or warning shots at Chinese warships near Maldives: Indian Navy', *The Print*, 28 March 2018.

151 Brahma Chellaney, 'India's Choice in the Maldives', *Project Syndicate*, 19 February 2018.

152 Ai Jun, 'Unauthorized military intervention in Malé must be stopped', *Global Times*, 12 February 2018.

153 Saurav Jha, 'Successful Pre-Induction Trial of India's Agni-V Intercontinental Ballistic Missile Takes It Closer to Deployment', *Delhi Defence Review*, 18 January 2018

154 Yin Han, 'India naval exercises inflame tensions with China, expand potential conflict from land to sea: observers', *Global Times*, 26 February 2018.

155 *The Economist*, 'Australia is edgy about China's growing presence on its doorstep', 20 April 2018.

156 Catherine Graue and Stephen Dziedzic, 'Federal Minister Concetta Fierravanti-Wells accuses China of funding "roads that go nowhere"', ABC News, 10 January 2018.

157 David Wroe, 'Australia takes over Solomon Islands internet cable amid spies' concerns about China', *Sydney Morning Herald*, 25

January 2018; prime minister of Australia, media release, 'Australia and France sign future submarine inter-governmental agreement', 20 December 2016.

158 ABC, 'New Ait Force spy drones to monitor South China Sea, fleet of six planes to cost $7bn', 26 June 2018.

159 Government of New Zealand, *Strategic Defence Policy Statement 2018* (2018).

160 Rod McGurk and Nick Perry, 'Pacific nations plan new security pact as Chinese aid grows', *Associated Press*, 6 July 2018.

161 A reduction of the French force by a third was eventually agreed: *La Croix*, 'La France réduit ses effectifs sur sa base de Djibouti', 27 July 2015.

162 *Middle East Monitor*, 'Djibouti welcomes Saudi Arabia plan to build a military base', 28 November 2017,

163 Michel Oduor, 'Erdoğan opens largest Turkish embassy during visit to Somalia', 4 June 2016.

164 *Horn Observer*, 'Turkey Government to Construct a Modern Military Training Base for Somali Army', 18 February 2018.

165 *Japan Times*, 'Japan to expand SDF base in tiny but strategically important Djibouti', 19 November 2017.

166 *Stratfor*, 'The UAE joins an exclusive club', 8 December 2016.

167 Adel Abdul Rahim and Ahmed Yusuf, 'Sudan, Qatar ink $4B deal to develop Suakin seaport', 26 March 2018.

168 *Qaran News*, 'Russia offers to build military base in Zeila in exchange for Somaliland recognition', 2 April 2018.

169 Katrina Manson, 'Jostling for Djibouti', *Financial Times*, 1 April 2016.

170 United States Africa Command, Transcript, 'Gen. Thomas D. Waldhauser at HASC Hearing on National Security Challenges and US Military Activities in Africa; US Africa Commander's 2018 Posture testimony to the House Armed Services Committee', 6 March 2018.

171 Simeon Kerr and John Aglionby, 'DP World accuses Djibouti of illegally seizing container terminal', *Financial Times*, 23 February 2018; IMF, 'Djibouti. Staff Report for the 2016 Article IV Consultation – Debt Sustainability Analysis', 6 February 2017.

172 For the purpose of the base, Wang Xu, 'Beijing confirms military support facilities in Djibouti', *China Daily*, 27 November 2015; for construction, *Stratfor*, 'Looking Over China's Latest Great Wall', 27 June 2017.

173 Dennis J. Blasko, 'The 2015 Chinese Defense White Paper on Strategy in Perspective: Maritime Missions Require a Change in the PLA Mindset', *China Brief* 15(12), 19 June 2015.

174 Yang Sheng, 'More support bases to be built to assist PLA Navy: analyst', *Global Times*, 12 February 2012.

175 World Bank, 'The World Bank in Sao Tome and Principe. Overview', 8 April 2016.

176 Visão, 'Empresa chinese vai construer porto de águas profundas em São Tomé e Príncipe', 13 October 2015.

177 Xinhua, 'Chinese FM meets São Tomé and Prìncipe counterpart', 17 January 2018.

178 Leng Shumei, 'São Tomé and Prìncipe breaks ties with Taiwan', 21 December 2016.

179 *Panamá América*, 'Empresa China invertirá $900 millones en Colón', 23 May 2016.

180 BBC News, 'Panama cuts ties with Taiwan in favour of China', 13 June 2017.

181 CDN, 'Gobierno RD rompe relaciones diplomáticas con Taiwan y establece relaciones con China', 30 April 2018.

182 Xinhua, 'El Salvador establishes diplomatic ties with China', 21 August 2018.

183 Bollettino Sala Stampa della Santa Sede, 'Comunicato circa la firma di un Accordo Provvisorio tra la Santa Sede e la Repubblica Popolare Cinese sulla nomina dei Vescovi', 22 September 2018; *Focus Taiwan*, 'Vatican–China accord unlikely to be political: ROC ambassador', 18 September 2018.

184 The *Economist*, 'Donald Trump's phone call with Taiwan's president spreads alarm', 3 December 2016.

185 Jeff Mason, Stephen J. Adler and Steve Holland, 'Exclusive: Trump spurns Taiwan president's suggestion of another phone call', Reuters, 28 April 2017.

186 White House, 'Statement from the Press Secretary on China's Political Correctness', 5 May 2018.

187 David Bandurski, 'Yan Xuetong on the bipolar state of our world', *China Media Project*, 26 June 2018.

188 Ibid.

189 State Department, 'US Chiefs of Mission to the Dominican Republic, El Salvador, and Panama Called Back for Consultations', 7 September 2018.

190 White House, 'Statement from the Press Secretary on El Salvador', 23 August 2018.

191 Office of Senator Marco Rubio, 'Rubio, Gardner, Colleagues Introduce Legislation Requiring US Strategy to Help Strengthen Taiwan's Diplomatic Standing', 5 September 2018.

192 United States Trade Representative, 2017 Report to Congress on China's WTO Compliance, January 2018.

193 Commission on the Theft of American Intellectual Property, 'Update to the IP Commission Report. The Theft of American Intellectual Property: Reassessments of the Challenge and United States Policy', February 2017.

194 Robert Sutter, 'China-Russia Relations. Strategic Implications and US Policy Options', National Bureau of Asian Research, September 2018.

195 Department of Defense, 'Remarks by Secretary Mattis at the US Naval War College Commencement, Newport, Rhode Island', 15 June 2018.

196 Department of Defense, 'Press Briefing by Pentagon Chief Joint Spokesperson Dana W. White and Joint Staff Director Lt. Gen Kenneth F. McKenzie Jr. in the Pentagon Briefing Room', 31 May 2018,

197 Office of the Secretary of Defense, *Military and Security Developments Involving the People's Republic of China 2018, Annual Report to Congress* (2018).

198 US Senate, Armed Services Committee, 'Advance Policy Questions for Admiral Philip Davidson', 17 April 2018.

199 Ben Guarino, 'The Navy called USS *Zumwalt* a warship Batman would drive. But at $800,000 per round, its ammo is too pricey to fire', *Washington Post*, 8 November 2016.

200 Arthur Dominic Villasanta, 'China Says "No" to USS *Zumwalt* Patrols Off Eastern North Korea near China', *Chinatopix*, 7 February 2017.

201 *Navy Times*, 'Navy's *Zumwalt* back underway after Panama Canal breakdown', 1 December 2016.

202 John M. Donnelly, 'Zombie *Zumwalt*: The Ship Program That Never Dies', *Roll Call*, 21 May 2018.

203 Christopher Cavas, 'China among invitees to major US exercise', *Defense News*, 29 May 2017.

204 US Department of Defense, 'Remarks by Secretary Mattis at Plenary Session of the 2018 Shangri-La Dialogue', 2 June 2018.

205 Jiang Shigong, 'Philosophy and History: Interpreting the "Xi Jinping Era" through Xi's Report to the Nineteenth National Congress of the CCP', translated by David Ownby, *Open Times* (2018); for a commentary, David Ownby and Timothy Creek, 'Jiang Shigong, On Philosophy and History', Australian Centre on China in the World, *The China Story*, 11 May 2018.

206 Jiang Shigong, 'Philosophy and History' op. cit.

THE ROADS TO RIVALRY

1   Ellen Sheng, 'The Five Biggest Chinese Investments in the US in
    2016', *Forbes*, 21 December 2016.

2   Tom Kington, 'Mosque-Building Bin Ladens Buy Marble Once Used
    for Churches', *Daily Beast*, 4 August 2014.

3   Michele Nash-Hoff, 'Should We Allow the Chinese to Buy Any
    Company They Want?', *Industry Week*, 9 January 2018.

4   Dylan Byers, 'Pacific Exclusive: Warner talks tough on big tech', CNN
    Tech, Pacific Newsletter, 27 April 2018.

5   Michael LaForgia and Gabriel J. X. Dance, 'Facebook Gave Data
    Access to Chinese Firm Flagged by US Intelligence', *New York Times*,
    5 June 2018.

6   House of Representatives, Energy and Commerce Committee, Press
    Release, 'Walden and Pallone on Facebook's Data-Sharing Partnerships
    with Chinese Companies', 6 June 2018.

7   Ali Breland, 'Facebook reveals data-sharing partnerships, ties to
    Chinese firms in 700-page document dump', *The Hill*, 30 June 2018.

8   Casey Newton, 'Google's ambitions for China could trigger a crisis
    inside the company', *The Verge*, 18 August 2018.

9   Kate Conger, 'Google Removes "Don't Be Evil" Clause from Its Code
    of Conduct', *Gizmodo*, 18 May 2018.

10 *Good Morning America*, Interview, ABC, 3 November 2015.

11 Trump, Staten Island speech, 'Trump: I'm So Happy China Is Upset;
    "They Have Waged Economic War Against Us"', Transcript on Real
    Clear Politics, 17 April 2016.

12 The *Economist*, 'The Economist interviews Donald Trump', 3
    September 2015.

13 B. Milanović, *Global Inequality: a new approach for the age of
    globalization* (Cambridge, MA, 2016), p. 20.

14 Woodward, *Fear*, pp. 272–3.

15 Shawn Donnan, 'Is there political method in Donald Trump's trade
    madness', *Financial Times*, 23 March 2018.

16 Lingling Wei and Yoko Kubota, 'Trump Weights Tariffs on $100
    Billion More of Chinese Goods', *Wall Street Journal*, 5 April 2018

17 For the text of the letter to the president, see https://fonteva-customer-
    media.s3.amazonaws.com/00D61000000dOrPEAU/psDunXQF_
    RILA%20301%20Letter.pdf

18 Scott Horsley, 'Trump Orders Stiff Tariffs on China, In Hopes Of
    Cutting Trade Gap by $50 Billion', *NPR*, 22 March 2018.

19 BlackRock Investment Institute, *Global Investment Outlook Q2 1018* (April 2018).

20 For example, Ana Swanson, 'Trump Proposes Re-joining Trans-Pacific Partnership', *New York Times*, 12 April 2018.

21 White House, 'Peter Navarro: "Donald Trump Is Standing Up For American Interests"', 9 April 2018.

22 Sarah Zheng, 'How China hit Donald Trump's supporters where it hurts as tariffs target Republican Party's heartlands', *South China Morning Post*, 5 April 2018.

23 Nathaniel Meyersohn, 'Walmart is where the trade war comes home', *CNN Money*, 19 September 2018.

24 Woodward, *Fear*, pp. 135–6.

25 Eli Meixler, 'President Trump Is "Very Thankful" for Xi Jinping's Conciliatory Talk on Trade', *Time*, 11 April 2018.

26 White House, 'Joint Statement of the United States and China Regarding Trade Consultations', 19 May 2018.

27 David Lawder, 'US–China trade row threatens global confidence: IMF's Lagarde', Reuters, 19 April 2018.

28 Ashley Parker, Seung Min Kim and Philip Rucker, 'Trump chooses impulse over strategy as crises mount', *Washington Post*, 12 April 2018.

29 Bob Woodward, *Fear: Trump in the white House* (New York, 2018).

30 Mark Lander and Ana Swanson, 'Chances of China Trade Win Undercut by Trump Team Infighting', *New York Times*, 21 May 2018.

31 *The National Interest*, 'The Interview: Henry Kissinger', 19 August 2015.

32 *National Security Strategy of the United States of America* (2017).

33 *Summary of the 2018 National Defense Strategy of the United of America. Sharpening the American Military's Competitive Edge* (2018).

34 CNN Transcripts, 'Intelligence Chiefs Take Questions from Senate Intelligence Committee', 13 February 2018.

35 Paul Heer, 'Understanding the Challenge from China', *The Asan Forum*, 3 April 2018; Evan Feigenbaum, 'Reluctant Stakeholder: Why China's Highly Strategic Brand of Revisionism is More Challenging Than Washington Thinks', *Carnegie Endowment*, 27 April 2018.

36 John Micklethwait, Margaret Talev, Jennifer Jacobs, 'Trump threatens to pull US out of WTO if it doesn't "shape up"', Bloomberg, 30 August 2018.

37 BBC News, 'US quits UN Human Rights Council', 20 June 2018.

38 Ministry of Foreign Affairs, Russian Federation, 'Вступительное слово и.о. Министра иностранных дел России С.В.Лаврова в ходе

переговоров с Министром иностранных дел Ирана М.Д.Зарифом, Москва, 14 мая 2018 года', 14 May 2018.

39 Brent D. Griffiths, 'Giuliani: Trump is "committed to regime change in Iran", *Politico*, 5 May 2018.

40 TASS, 'Зариф: США, а не Иран играют деструктивную роль в Сирии', 28 April 2018. ·

41 PressTV, 'Rouhani warns of US unilateralism threat in address to SCO summit', 10 June 2018.

42 President of Russia, Transcript, 'Пленарное заседание Петербургского международного экономического форума', 25 May, 2018.

43 Chris Giles, 'IMF chief warns trade war could rip apart global economy', *Financial Times*, 11 April 2018.

44 Donald Trump tweets, 26 July 2018.

45 Samuel Smith, 'Mike Pence Spoke With Pastor Andrew Brunson, Threatens Turkey With Sanctions If Not Released', *Christian Post*, 26 July 2018.

46 *Hürriyet Daily News*, 'Turkish Lira hits record low after US says reviewing duty-free access', 6 August 2018.

47 Alyza Sebenius and Toluse Olorunnipa, 'Trump calls Turkey a "problem", says detained pastor isn't spy', Bloomberg, 17 August 2018; Maximillian Hess, 'Turkish lira casts pall over Caucasus and Central Asia', *Eurasianet*, 21 August 2018.

48 Mike Bird, 'Sinking Turkish lira, Indian rupee fuel fears of contagion', *Wall Street Journal*, 14 August 2018.

49 Permanent Mission of the People's Republic of China to the UN, 'Foreign Ministry Spokesperson Hua Chunying's Regular Press Conference', 16 July 2018.

50 Francis Elliott, 'Trump turns up heat as G7 splits over Russia', *The Times*, 9 June 2018.

51 Guy Chazan, 'Germany to miss NATO defence spending pledge', *Financial Times*, 27 April 2018.

52 Paul Taylor, 'Trump's Next Target: NATO', *Politico*, 14 June 2018.

53 Gabrila Galindo, 'Trump: EU was "set up to take advantage"of US', *Politico*, 28 June 2018.

54 Fox News, 'Transcript. President Trump: Supreme Court nominees will move quickly if I choose right person', 1 July 2018.

55 Cristina Maza, 'Donald Trump threw Starburst candies at Angela Merkel, said "Don't say I never give you anything"', *Newsweek*, 20 June 2018.

56 Jennifer Hansler, 'Merkel responds to Trump: "I have witnessed Germany under Soviet control"', 11 July 2018.

57 Spencer Ackerman, 'US Officials "at a Fucking Loss" Over Latest Russia Sellout', 18 July 2018; BBC News, 'Trump rejects proposal for Russia to interrogate US citizens', 19 July 2018.

58 Susan Rice tweet, 18 July 2018.

59 Donald Trump tweet, 10 June 2018.

60 BBC News, 'G7 summit: UK PM Theresa May backs Trudeau after Trump attacks', 11 June 2018.

61 Josh Dawsey, 'Trump derides protections for immigrants from "shithole" countries,' *Washington Post*, 12 January 2018.

62 Daniel Estrin, 'New cuts in medical aid to Palestinians by Trump administration', NPR, 7 September 2018.

63 Ainara Tiefenthäler and Natalie Reneau, 'Swastikas, Shields and Flags: Branding Hate in Charlottesville', 15 August 2017; Allison Kaplan Sommer, 'From Swastikas to David Duke; Nazism and anti-Semitism Take Centre Stage at Charlottesville Rally', *Haaretz*, 13 August 2017; *Washington Post*, 'Deconstructing the symbols and slogans spotted in Charlottesville', 18 August 2017.

64 Rosie Grey, 'Trump Defends White-Nationalist Protesters: "Some Very Fine People on Both Sides"', *The Atlantic*, 15 August 2017.

65 Sasha Abramsky, 'Trump Is Now Openly Supporting Fascists', *The Nation*, 30 November 2017.

66 Jeffrey Goldberg, 'A Senior White House Official Defined the Trump Doctrine: "We're America, Bitch"', *The Atlantic*, 11 June 2018.

67 Ibid.

68 Bien Perez, 'Apple's China sales grow for second straight quarter on strong iPhone demand', *South China Morning Post*, 2 February 2018.

69 Peter Eavis, 'How Trump's Tariffs Tripped up Alcoa', *New York Times*, 19 July 2018.

70 Daniel Ren, 'Half of US firms in China foresee acute pain from new tariffs as trade war escalates, AmCham survey finds', *South China Morning Post*, 12 September 2018.

71 David Welch, 'GM Falls Victim to Trump's Trade War as Metal Prices Sink Profit', Bloomberg, 25 July 2018.

72 Boeing Statement, 'Boeing Raises Forecast for New Airplane Demand in China', 6 September 2017.

73 Scott Cendrowski, 'Inside China's Global Spending Spree', *Fortune*, 12 December 2016; Keith Bradsher, 'US Firms Want In on China's Global "One Belt, One Road" Spending', *New York Times*, 14 May 2017.

74 US Department of the Treasury, 'Treasury Sanctions Russian Cyber Actors for Interference with the 2016 US Elections and Malicious Cyber-Attacks', 15 March 2018.

75 Henry Sanderson, 'Metal prices surge after US sanctions on Rusal', *Financial Times*, 19 April 2018; Henry Sanderson, 'Alumina price hits all-time high as US sanctions hit Irish refinery', *Financial Times*, 18 April 2018.

76 Heather Long, 'Foreign suppliers are flooding the US aluminium market', *Washington Post*, 1 March 2018.

77 Julian Barnes and Matthew Rosenberg, 'Kremlin sources go quiet, leaving CIA in the dark about Putin's plans for midterms, *New York Times*, 24 August 2018.

78 'Iran tells Trump to stop tweeting about oil prices', Associated Press, 5 July 2018.

79 Owen Matthews, 'U.S. Gives Russia "Unexpected Present" With Iran Sanctions and Oil Price Surge', *Newsweek*, 30 May 2018.

80 US Senate, Committee on Armed Services, *Political and Security Situation in Afghanistan*, 3 October 2017.

81 Peter Frankopan, 'These Days All Roads Lead to Beijing', *New Perspectives Quarterly* (2017).

82 Henny Sender and Kiran Stacey, 'China takes "project of the century" to Pakistan', *Financial Times*, 17 May 2017.

83 Centre for Strategic and International Studies, 'Defining Our Relationship with India for the Next Century: An Address by Secretary of State Rex Tillerson', 18 October 2017.

84 'HASC Hearing on National Security Challenges', 6 March 2018, op. cit.

85 Deb Riechmann, 'CIA: China is waging a "quiet kind of cold war" against US', Associated Press, 21 July 2018.

86 *Indian Express*, 'Donald Trump's quotes on India: Narendra Modi is a great man, I am a fan of Hindus', 16 October 2016.

87 White House, 'Vice President Mike Pence Editorial: "Donald Trump's New American Strategy for Afghanistan Will Undo Past Failures"', 21 August 2017.

88 US Senate, *Political and Security Situation in Afghanistan*, 3 October 2017.

89 Andrew J. Pierre, *The Global Politics of Arms Sales* (Princeton, 1982), pp. 221–2.

90 Richard Staar, *Foreign Policies of the Soviet Union* (Stanford, 1991), p. 250.

91 Stockholm International Peace Research Institute, 'Asia and the Middle East lead rising trend in arms imports, US exports grow significantly, says SIPRI', 12 March 2018.

92 Saurav Jha, 'The India–Russia–US Energy Triangle', *The Diplomat*, 12 July 2018.

93 US Senate, 'Political and Security Situation in Afghanistan', 3 October 2017.

94 US State Department, 'Briefing on the Indo-Pacific Strategy', 2 April 2018.

95 US Pacific Command, 'Raisina Dialogue Remarks: Let's Be Ambitious Together', 2 March 2016.

96 Greg Torode, Jess Macy Yu, 'Taiwan courts security ties with bigger friends as Beijing snatches allies', Reuters, 14 September 2018.

97 Dipanjan Roy Chaudhury, 'Old friends better than two new friends: PM Modi to Putin', *Economic Times*, 16 October 2016.

98 *Business Standard*, 'No joint patrols with foreign navies for India: Manohar Parrikar', 26 July 2016.

99 *News18*, 'We're the Piggy Bank Everybody Likes to Rob: Trump Targets India at G-7 Over 100% Tariff', 11 June 2018.

100 Indrani Bagchi, 'Amid trade war, India offers to buy 1,000 planes, more oil from US', *Times of India*, 23 June 2018; Neha Dasgupta, Nidhi Verma, 'India, top buyers of US almonds, hits back with higher duties', Reuters, 21 June 2016.

101 Sujan Dutta, 'India, US sign landmark miltiary communications secrecy pact at historic meeting', *The Print*, 6 September 2018.

102 *Times of India*, 'I'm first Indian PM you came out of Beijing to receive: PM Narendra Modi to Xi Jinping in Wuhan', 27 April 2018.

103 Ankit Panda, 'How Far Can Sin-India Joint Economic Cooperation in Afghanistan Go?', *The Diplomat*, 1 May 2018.

104 *India Today*, 'India, China ink 2 MoUs on sharing of Brahmaputra river data and supply of non-Basmati rice', 9 June 2018; *The Hindu*, 'India, China militaries to set up hotline after Wuhan meeting', 2 May 2018.

105 Brent D. Griffith, 'Giuliani: Trump is "committed to" regime change in Iran', *Politico*, 5 May 2018.

106 'Full text of speech by Rudy Giuliani at Grand Gathering 2018', Iran Probe, 5 July 2018.

107 White House, 'Remarks by President Trump on the Joint Comprehensive Plan of Action', 8 May 2018.

108 State Department, 'After the Deal: A New Iran Strategy', 21 May 2018.

109 Kenneth Katzman, *Iran Sanctions*, Congressional Research Service, 29 June 2018, p. 60.

110 Asa Fitch and Aresu Eqbali, 'Iran's Rial at Historic Low as US Sanctions Loom', *Wall Street Journal*, 30 July 2018; Thomas Erdbrink, 'Protests Pop Up Across Iran, Fueled by Daily Dissastisfaction', *New York Times*, 4 August 2018.

111 *Asharq al-Awsat*, 'Iran arrests 67 people amid approval for special corruption courts', 13 August 2018; Bozorgmehr Sharafedin, 'Iran parliament censures Rouhani in sign pragmatists losing sway', Reuters, 28 August 2018.

112 Agence France-Presse, 'Iran urges UN court to halt "economic strangulation" by US', 27 August 2018.

113 Paris Today, 'US lawyer: ICJ "lacks prima facie jurisdiction to hear Iran's claims"', 28 August 2018.

114 US Department of State, 'After the Deal: A New Iran Strategy', 21 May 2018.

115 Reuters, 'Destroying Iran deal would have unforeseeable consequences, China's Li warns', 9 July 2018.

116 Imran Khan, 'The US, electricity and Iran: What's behind the Iraq protests', Al-Jazeera, 21 July 2018.

117 Rohollah Faghihi, 'How Trump is uniting Rouhani and Iran's Revolutionary Guards', *Al-Monitor*, 9 July 2018.

118 *Kommersant*, 'Иран не та страна, на которую можно давить', 18 July 2018.

119 El'nar Bainazarov, 'Из Севастополя — в Тегеран и Дамаск', *Izvestiya*, 21 August 2018.

120 Gordon Duff, 'Iran Promises Trump "The Mother of All Wars"', *New Eastern Outlook*, 29 July 2018.

121 IRNA, 'Pakistani media widely covers President Rouhani's remarks', 23 July 2018.

122 Donald Trump tweet, 23 July 2018.

123 Amanda Macias, 'No walkback this time: National security advisor John Bolton doubles down on Trump's Iran threat', CNBC, 23 July 2018.

124 Tasnim News, سرلشکر سلیمانی خطاب به ترامپ: شما تا امروز چه ن July 2018.

125 *Times of India*, 'Countries that continue to deal with Iran could face US sanctions, warns John Bolton', 13 May 2018.

126 Yashwant Raj, 'US wants India to stop Iran oil imports by November 4, no waiver on sanctions', 27 June 2018.

127 Office of the Supreme Leader, Iran, 'Ayatollah Khamenei: Let Muslims lead fight on terror', 24 May 2016.

128 'India commits huge investment in Chabahar', *India Today*, 23 May 2016.

129 Ritesh Kumar Singh, 'India Pushes for Stronger Eurasian Linkages', *Brink News*, 29 July 2018.

130 F. M. Shakil, 'Chabahar Port lures Afghan traffic away from Karachi', *Asia Times*, 2 February 2018.

131 BNE Intellinews, 'US to tolerate India's Iran trade corridor but demands end to oil imports', 28 June 2018.

132 Atul Aneja, 'India, Uzbekistan to route their trade through Chabahar', *The Hindu*, 10 June 2018.

133 Reuters, 'Turkey says will not cut off trade ties to Iran at behest of others', 29 June 2018.

134 Islamic Republic News Agency, 'Turkey to continue to trade with Iran: Minister of Economy', 11 May 2018.

135 Vahap Munyar, 'Turkey "won't take step back against US: Erdoğan"', *Hürriet Daily News*, 29 July 2018.

136 Rufiz Hafizoglu, 'Turkey does not intend to stop relations with Iran for sake of US – Erdoğan', *Trend*, 25 July 2018.

137 Sam Borden, 'Nike withdraws Iran World Cup squad's supply of boots due to sanctions', *ESPN*, 11 June 2018.

138 Reuters, 'Total marks return with South Pars gas deal', 3 July 2017.

139 Steven Mufson and Damian Paletta, 'Boeing, Airbus to lose $39 billion in contracts because of Trump sanctions on Iran', *Washington Post*, 9 May 2018.

140 Reuters, 'China says will maintain normal ties with Iran', 21 June 2018.

141 Peter Siegenthaler and Dahai Shao, 'Swiss firms pushed to put Tehran dreams on hold', Swissinfo.ch, 14 June 2018.

142 United States Securities and Exchange Commission, 'Exxon Mobil Corporation Form 10-K', 28 February 2018.

143 Henry Foy, 'Exxon says to withdraw from Russia JVs with Rosneft', *Financial Times*, 1 March 2018,

144 *Die Welt*, 'Neuer US-Botschafter Grenell sorgt in Berlin für Ärger', 9 May 2018.

145 *Frankfurter Allgemeine*, 'Wie hart Amerikas Forderung deutsche Unternehmen trifft', 11 May 2018.

146 *Der Spiegel*, 'Altmaier nennt Schutz deutscher Firmen vor US-Sanktionen schwierig', 11 May 2018.

147 Hans von der Burchard, 'EU to block Trump's Iran sanctions by activating old law', *Politico*, 17 May 2018.

148 Emmanuel Macron tweet, 9 June 2018.

149 Roberta Rampton, 'Any agreement with North Korea will be "spur of the moment" – Trump', Reuters, 9 June 2018.

150 Armin Arefi, 'Strobe Talbott: "Trump, c'est l'Amérique toute seule"', 28 June 2018.

THE ROADS TO THE FUTURE

1 Barbara Stephenson, 'Time to Ask Why. President's Views', American Foreign Service Association, December 2017.

2 Bill Faries and Mira Rojanasakul, 'At Trump's State Department, Eight of Ten Top Jobs Are Empty', Bloomberg, 2 February 2018; Robbie Gramer, 'Mapped: 38 US Ambassadorships remain empty', *Foreign Policy*, 9 April 2018.

3 James Hohmann, 'The Daily 202: Trump has no nominees for 245 important jobs, including an ambassador to South Korea', *Washington Post*, 12 January 2018.

4 Jonathan Stempel, 'Saudi Arabia must face US lawsuits over September 11 attacks', Reuters, 28 March 2018.

5 Bruce Riedel, 'Saudi defense spending soars, but not to America's benefit', *Al Monitor*, 13 May 2018.

6 White House, 'Remarks by President Trump and Crown Prince Mohammed Bin Salman of the Kingdom of Saudi Arabia Before Bilateral Meeting', 20 March 2018.

7 Ibid.

8 US State Department, 'Remarks with Saudi Foreign Minister Adel al-Jubeir', 29 April 2018.

9 White House, 'Remarks by President Trump and Crown Prince Mohammed, op. cit.'

10 Tim Marcin, 'Donald Trump pitched "beautiful" weapons to Qatar, then suggested country supports 'radical ideology', *Newsweek*, 6 June 2017.

11 *The National*, 'Saudi official hints at Qatar-canal announcement', 1 September 2018.

12 Reuters, 'Iran sends planes of food to Qatar amid concerns of shortages', 11 June 2017.

13 Lawrence Delevingne, Nathan Layne, Karen Freifeld, 'Inside Qatar's charm offensive to win over Washington', Reuters, 5 July 2018.

14 White House, 'Remarks by President Trump and Crown Prince Mohammed, op. cit.'

15 Ivan Safronov and Tatiana Edovina, '"Триумф" для монарха. От первого визита в Россию короля Саудовской Аравии ждут ракетного контракта', *Kommersant*, 5 October 2017.

16 Marc Bennetts, 'Putin: Syria war is priceless for testing weapons', *The Times*, 8 June 2018.

17 Richard Mably and Yara Bayoumy, 'Exclusive – OPEC, Russia consider 10- to 20-year oil alliance: Saudi Crown Prince', Reuters, 27 March 2018.

18 TASS, 'Путин и Эрдоган наметили пути развития сотрудничества России и Турции', 4 April 2018.

19 Carlotta Gail and Andrew Higgins, 'Turkey Signs Russian Missile Deal, Pivoting From NATO', *New York Times*, 12 September 2017.

20 Xinhua, 'Turkey inks deal to buy S-400 missile', 25 July 2017.

21 *Hürriyet Daily News*, 'Ankara, Moscow seal historic S-400 missile deal', 29 December 2017.

22 Reuters, 'US's Pompeo presses Turkey on S-400 missiles purchase from Russia', 27 April 2018.

23 TASS, 'СМИ: Турция рассматривает возможность приобретения истребителей Су-57 вместо F-35', 29 May 2018.

24 *Hürriyet Daily News*, 'Turkish, Chinese army officials to meet soon', 28 July 2018.

25 Ministry of Foreign Affairs of the People's Republic of China, 'Xi, Erdgogan agree to enhance China–Turkey cooperation', 27 July 2018.

26 *Global Times*, 'Look at China–Turkey ties objectively', 20 August 2018.

27 Joe Gould, 'Top 3 takeaways from Mattis on Capitol Hill', *Defense News*, 26 April 2018.

28 TASS, 'Зариф: США, а не Иран играют деструктивную роль в Сирии', 29 April 2018.

29 TASS, 'Россия, Турция и Иран договорились стимулировать переговоры по новой сирийской конституции', 29 April 2018.

30 *Hürriyet Daily News*, 'Russia, Turkey, Iran stress unity at Syria talks', 28 April 2018.

31 Mark Galeotti, 'The international army games are decadent and depraved', *Foreign Policy*, 24 August 2018.

32 Robert Hutton, 'Russia Using KGB Tactics to Wage War on West, UK Lawmaker Says', Bloomberg, 4 June 2018.

33 House of Commons Foreign Affairs Committee, 'Moscow's Gold: Russian Corruption in the UK', 15 May 2018.

34 *The Tower*, 'New Turkish Reports, Statements Trigger Scrutiny of New-Ottoman Foreign Policy', 25 April 2013.

35 Diyar Guldogan, 'Turkish Republic continuation of Ottoman Empire', Anadolu Agency, 10 February 2018.

36 Dilly Hussain, 'Turkish TV's new-found love for all things Ottoman', *Middle East Eye*, 29 September 2017.

37 For the Ottoman revival, Nick Danforth, 'Turkey's New Maps are Reclaiming the Ottoman Empire', *Foreign Policy*, 23 October 2016. For responses to the US, Dorian Jones. 'Turkey's Erdoğan Vows Not to Bow to US Threats', *Voice of America*, 29 July 2018.

38 Ministry of External Affairs India, 'Official Spokesperson's response to query on participation of India in OBOR/BRI Forum', 13 May 2017.

39 Xinhua, 'Full text of President Xi Jinping's speech at opening of Belt and Road forum', 14 May 2017.

40 Department of Transport, UK, '£20 million Leeds station entrance opens up access to city's development', 4 January 2016.

41 Archbishop of Canterbury, 'An address to the Assembly of the Conference of European Churches', Novi Sad, Serbia, 3 June 2018.

42 European Council, 'Remarks by President Donald Tusk before the G7 summit in Ise-Shima, Japan', 26 May 2016.

43 Theresa Fallon, 'The EU, the South China Sea, and China's successful wedge strategy', *Asia Maritime Transparency Initiative*, 13 October 2016.

44 Prime Minister of Hungary, 'Viktor Orbán's speech at the conference "China-CEE Political Parties Dialogue"', 8 October 2016.

45 Macedonian Information Agency, 'EU failure in Balkans is a call to China and Russia, President Ivanov tells UK's Telegraph', 5 November 2017.

46 Mark Galeotti, 'Do the Western Balkans face a coming Russian storm?', European Council on Foreign Relations, 4 April 2018.

47 Ryan Heath and Andrew Gray, 'Beware Chinese Trojan horses in the Balkans, EU warns', *Politico*, 27 July 2018.

48 Lucrezia Poggetti, 'One China – One Europe? German Foreign Minister's Remarks Irk Beijing', *The Diplomat*, 9 September 2017.

49 Ministry of Foreign Affairs of the People's Republic of China, 'Foreign Ministry Spokesperson Hua Chunying's Regular Press Conference', 31 August 2017.

50 Federal Foreign Office of Germany, 'Speech by Foreign Minister Sigmar Gabriel at the Munich Security Conference', 17 February 2018.

51 Federal Foreign Office of Germany, Speech by Minister for Foreign Affairs, Heiko Maas at the National Graduate Institute for Policy Studies in Tokyo, Japan, 25 July 2018.

52 Associated Press, 'Chinese premier praises EU, says free trade must be upheld', 7 July 2018.

53 Wang Yi, 'China and Arab states draw up a blueprint for cooperation in the new era', *Gulf News*, 8 July 2018.

54 Gu Liping, 'China sees Saudi Arabia as important partner in Belt and Road construction: Chinese FM', *China News Service*, 22 May 2018.

55 Chen Aizhu, 'China's CNPC ready to take over Iran project if Total leaves: sources', Reuters, 11 May 2017.

56 Peter Frankopan, 'How long can China stay out of Middle East politics?', 27 September 2017.

57 Agence-Presse France, 'China to provide $20bn in loans for Arab states' economic development', 10 July 2018.

58 *The New Arab*, 'Chinese leader pledges billions of dollars for Arab "revival"', 10 July 2018.

59 Ministry of Foreign Affairs of PRC, 'The Ministry of Foreign Affairs Holds a Briefing for Chinese and Foreign Media on President Xi Jinping's Attendance at the Opening Ceremony of the 8th CASCF Ministerial Meeting', 6 July 2018.

60 Shibley Telhami, 'Why is Trump undoing decades of US policy on Jerusalem?', Brookings Institution, 5 December 2017.

61 US State Department, Remarks on 'America's Indo-Pacific Economic Vision', 30 July 2018.

62 Donald Trump tweet, 1 January 2018.

63 Philip Rucker and Robert Costa, '"It's a hard problem": Inside Trump's decision to send troops to Afghanistan', *Washington Post*, 21 August 2017.

64 Saeed Shah, 'Pakistan Foreign Minister Says US Has Undermined Countries' Ties', *Wall Street Journal*, 5 January 2018.

65 Anwar Iqbal, 'America suspends entire security aid to Pakistan', *Dawn*, 5 January 2018.

66 Reuters, 'US's Pompeo warns against IMF bailout for Pakistan that aids China', 30 July 2018.

67 Farhan Bokhari and Kiran Stacey, 'Pakistan hits back at US resistance to IMF bailout', *Financial Times*, 31 July 2018.

68 Wang Cong, 'New govt to expand ties with China: officials', *Global Times*, 31 July 2018.

69 Shahbaz Rana, 'China agrees to give $2b loan to Pakistan', *Express Tribune*, 28 July 2018.

70 *First Post*, 'India's missile deal with Russia, trade with Iran despite US sanctions may create unease in New Delhi–Washington ties', 29 May 2018.

71 Samuel Ramani, 'Russia and Pakistan: a durable anti-American alliance in South Asia', *The Diplomat*, 21 April 2018; Zafar Bhutta,

'Pakistan, Russia set to sign $10b offshore pipeline deal next week', *Express Tribune*, 3 June 2018.

72 Marie Solis, 'Children will be separate from parents at border if crossing illegally, Jeff Sessions says in immigration crackdown', *Newsweek*, 7 May 2018; Franco Ordoñez, 'Exclusive; Trump looking to erect tent cities to house unaccompanied children', McClatchy Bureau DC, 12 June 2018.

73 Katy Vine, 'What's Really Happening When Asylum-Seeking Families Are Separated?', *Texas Monthly*, 15 June 2018.

74 Sonia Moghe, Nick Valencia and Holly Yan, 'DNA tests are in the works for separated migrant children and parents', CNN Politics, 5 July 2018; Matt Smith and Aura Bogado, 'Immigrant children forcibly injected with drugs, lawsuit claims', *Reveal*, 20 June 2018.

75 Heather Timmons, 'Chart: Trump's new tariffs punish America's closest allies', *Quartz*, 31 May 2018.

76 Leigh Thomas and Pascale Denis, 'France says Europe united against US tariffs as Germany eyes negotiation', 8 July 2018.

77 *National Security Strategy of the United States of America* (2017).

78 US Treasury statement, 'Treasury Designates Russian Oligarchs, Officials, and Entities in Response to Worldwide Malign Activity', 6 April 2018.

79 Dan Merica, 'Trump declares "nobody has been tougher on Russia" in meeting with Baltic leaders', CNN Politics, 3 April 2018.

80 Nicholas Trickett, 'Russia's Unhappy Energy Marriage with China', *The Diplomat*, 28 March 2018.

81 Galina Starinskaya, 'Россия увеличит экспорт нефти в Китай', *Vedemosti*, 12 January 2018.

82 Ravi Prasad, 'Can the Belt and Road Initiative offer New Hope for China's rust belt?', *The Diplomat*, 28 June 2018.

83 Reuters, 'China says Syrian strikes violate international law, urges dialogue', 14 April 2018.

84 Associated Press, 'China's defense chief calls his Moscow trip a signal to the US', 3 April 2018.

85 Xinhua, 'Chinese president says relations with Russia at "best time in history"', 3 July 2017.

86 Bill Gertz, 'Chinese military joining Russians, for nuclear war games, Wasington Fre Beacon, 24 August 2018.

87 Asawin Suebsaeng, Andrew Desiderio, Sam Stein and Bethany Allen-Ebrahimian, 'Henry Kissinger Pushed Trump to Work With Russia to Box in China', *Daily Beast*, 25 July 2018.

88 Robert Sutter, *China-Russia Relations. Strategic Implications and US Policy Options*, National Bureau of Asian Research, September 2018.

89 US State Department, Remarks on 'America's Indo-Pacific Economic Vision', 30 July 2018.

90 Amy Brittin, Ashley Parker and Anu Narayanswamy, 'Jared Kushner and Ivanka Trumo made at least $82 million in outside income last year while serving in the White House, filings show', *Washington Post*, 11 June 2018.

91 Qingdao Declaration, 10 June 2018.

92 Catherine Putz, 'Sauytbay Trial in Kazakhstan Puts Astana in a Bind with China', *The Diplomat*, 27 July 2018.

93 Oleg Yegorov, 'Russian intelligence saved Erdoğan from overthrow – media reports', Russia Beyond the Headlines, 21 July 2016.

94 International Crisis Group 'Russia and Turkey in the Black Sea and South Caucasus', Report No. 250, 28 June 2018.

95 Sam Jones and Kathrin Hille, 'Russia's military ambitions make waves in the Black Sea', *Financial Times*, 13 May 2016.

96 Kira Latukhina, 'Путин рассказал про 'вежливых людей' в Крыму', *Rossiiskaya Gazeta*, 15 March 2015.

97 Radio Free Europe, 'Erdogan pledges support for Ukraine's territorial integrity during Kyiv visit', 10 October 2017.

98 Order of the President of the Republic of Kazakhstan, 'Об утверждении Военной доктрины Республики Казахстан', Zakon.kz, 29 September 2017.

99 US Department of State, 'The United States and Kazakhstan – An Economic Partnership for the 21st century', 16 January 2018.

100 Kommersant, 'Москва выговорилась в адрес союзников', 11 June 2018.

101 *RIA Novosti*, 'Кайрат Абдрахманов: речь не идет о размещении военных баз США на Каспии', 11 August 2018.

102 Tatiana Ivanshchenko, 'Сибиряки считают, что теряют Байкал', *Regum*, 27 February 2018.

103 Charles Clover and Archie Zhang, 'China land grab on Lake Baikal raises Russian ire', *Financial Times*, 4 January 2018.

104 Catherine Putz, 'Protests in Kazakhstan Over Land Code Changes', *The Diplomat*, 27 April 2016.

105 Saeed Kamali Dehghan, 'Iran threatens to block Strait of Hormuz over US oil sanctions', 5 July 2018.

106 Allan Jacob, 'US says it's ready to protect shipping in the Gulf after Iran threat', 1 September 2018.

107 US Central Command, 'Theater Counter Mine and Maritime Security Exercise', 10 September 2018.

108 The Tower, 'Experts: Iran Advancing Nuclear Program with Help of North Korea', 1 March 2017; The Tower, 'Pentagon Looks at New Evidence of Military Cooperation beween Iran and North Korea', 5 May 2017.

109 For the amount of oil and liquids passing through the Strait of Hormuz, US Energy Information Administration, 'World Oil Transit Chokepoints', 25 July 2017. For UK dependence on oil and gas imports from this region, Office for National Statistics, 'UK energy: how much, what type and where from?', 15 August 2016.

110 Rick Roack, 'The oil route that could be behind the escalating Trump–Iran threats, explained', 24 July 2018.

111 Jonathan Fulton, 'China's power in the Middle East is rising', *Washington Post*, 9 August 2018.

112 Reuters, 'China chides Iran over threat to block oil exports through Strait of Hormuz', 6 July 2018.

113 *Vesti*, 'МИД Китая призвал 'Роснефть' уважать суверенитет КНР', 17 May 2018.

114 Tass, 'Сухопутные войска РФ получили бригадный комплект комплекса "Искандер-М",' 8 June 2017.

115 Guy Plopsky, 'Why is Russia Aiming Missiles at China?', *The Diplomat*, 12 July 2017.

116 Laura He, 'HNA sells property and logistics assets to Chinese tycoon Sun Hongbin for US$305 million', 12 March 2018; Don Weiland, 'Default reignites questions over China groups' state backing', 7 June 2018; Elvira Pollina, 'Elliott launches action to take control of AC Milan – source', Reuters, 9 July 2018.

117 Zhou Xiaochuan, '守住不发生系统性金融风险的底线', http://www.pbc.gov.cn/goutongjiaoliu/113456/113469/3410388/index.html

118 Stefania Palma, 'Malaysia suspends $22bn China-backed projects', *Financial Times*, 5 July 2018; Kuunghee Park, 'Malaysia finally scraps $ 3billion China-backed pipeline plans', Bloomberg, 10 September 2018.

119 Jeremy Page and Saeed Shah, 'China's Global Building Spree Runs Into Trouble in Pakistan', 22 July 2018.

120 Jamil Anderlini, Henny Sender and Farhan Bokhari, 'Pakistan rethinks its role in Xi's Belt and Road plan', *Financial Times*, 9 September 2018.

121 Stephen Dziedzic, 'Tonga urges Pacific nations to press China to forgive debts as Beijing defends its approach', ABC, 16 August 2018.

122 Jon Emont and Myo Myo, 'Chinese-funded port gives Myanmar a sinking feeling', *Wall Street Journal*, 15 August 2018.

123 James Kynge, 'China's Belt and Road difficulties are proliferating across the world', *Financial Times*, 9 July 2018.

124 Sarah Zheng, 'China embarks on belt and road publicity blitz after Malaysia says no to debt-heavy infrastructure projects', *South China Morning Post*, 26 August 2018.

125 Xinhua, 'Xi pledges to bring benefits to people through Belt and Road Initiative', 27 August 2018.

126 Xinhua, 'Full text of Chinese President Xi Jinping's speech at opening ceremony of 2018 FOCAC Beijing summit', 4 September 2018.

127 Yonas Abiye, 'Chinese government to restructure Ethiopia's debt', *The Reporter*, 8 September 2018.

128 Christian Shepherd, Ben Blanchard, 'China's Xi offers another $60bn to Africa, but says no to "vanity" projects', Reuters, 3 September 2018.

129 Bank of England, 'From the Middle Kingdom to the United Kingdom: spillovers from China', *Quarterly Bulletin* Q2 (2018), op. cit.

130 David Lawder and Elias Glenn, 'Trump says US tariffs could be applied to Chinese goods worth $500 billion', Reuters, 5 July 2018.

131 Bank of England, 'From the Middle Kingdom to the United Kingdom.' op. cit.

132 BBC News, 'Boris Johnson's resignation letter and May's reply in full', 9 July 2018.

133 Tasnim News Agency, 'Iran, Kazakhstan plan trade in own currencies', 12 August 2018.

134 Heiko Maas, 'Wir lassen nicht zu, dass die USA über unsere Köpfe hinweg handeln', *Handelsblatt*, 21 August 2018.

135 Christina Larsen, 'China's massive investment in artificial intelligence has an insidious downside', *Science*, 8 February 2018.

136 Xinhua, 'Beijing to build technology park for developing artificial intelligence', 3 January 2018; *The Economist*, 'China talks of building a "digital silk road"', 31 May 2018.

137 CB Insights, *Top AI Trends To Watch in 2018* (2018).

138 Embassy of the People's Republic of China in the United Kingdom of Great Britain and Northern Ireland, 'Xi Jinping Urges Breaking New Ground in Major Country Diplomacy with Chinese Characteristics', 23 June 2018.

139 Stephen Chen, 'Artificial Intelligene, immune to fear or favour, is helping to make China's foreign policy', *South China Morning Post*, 30 July 2018.

140 Jamie Fullerton, 'China's new CH-5 Rainbow drone leaves US Reaper "in the dust"', *The Times* 18 July 2017.

141 Jeremy Page and Paul Sonne, 'Unable to Buy US Military Drones, Allies Place Orders With China', *Wall Street Journal*, 17 July 2017.

142 Bill Gertz, 'China in race to overtake the US in AI warfare', *Asia Times*, 30 May 2018.

143 George Allison, 'The speech delivered by the Chief of the Defence Staff at the Air Power Conference', *UK Defence Journal*, 13 July 2018.

144 Stephen Chen, 'New Chinese military drone for overseas buyers "to rival" US's MQ-9 Reaper', *South China Morning Post*, 17 July 2017.

145 Boris Egorov, 'Rise of the Machines: A look at Russia's latest combat robots', 8 June 2017.

146 Robert Mendick, Ben Farmer and Roland Oliphant, 'UK military intelligence issues warning over Russian supertank threat', *Daily Telegraph*, 6 November 2016.

147 Anastasia Sviridova, 'Специалисты обсудили успехи и недостатки в сегменте отечественной робототехники', *Krasnaya Zvezda*, 4 June 2018.

148 Dave Majumdar, 'The Air Force's Worst Nightmare: Russia and China Could Kill Stealth Fighters', *The National Interest*, 28 June 2018.

149 Zachary Keck, 'China's DF-26 "Carrier-Killer" Missile Could Stop the Navy in Its Track (without Firing a Shot)', *The National Interest*, 20 April 2018.

150 Aanchal Bansal, 'India's first manned space mission to send three persons', *Economic Times*, 29 August 2018.

151 Stephen Clark, 'China sets new national record for most launches in a year', *Spaceflight Now*, 27 August 2018; Ernesto Londoño, 'China on the march in Latin America with new space station in Argentina', *Financial Review*, 2 August 2018.

152 White House, 'Remarks by President Trump at a Meeting with the National Space Council and Signing of Space Policy Directive-3', 18 June 2018.

153 Shawn Donnan, 'US strikes deal with ZTE to lift ban', 7 June 2018.

154 Charles Clover, 'China-Russia rocket talks sparks US disquiet over growing links', *Financial Times*, 17 January 2018.

155 Patti Domm, 'US could target 10 Chinese industries, including new energy vehicles, biopharma', CNBC, 22 March 2018.

156 John Grady, 'Pentagon Research Chief Nominee: China, Russia Racing to Develop Next Generation Weapon Technology', United States Naval Institute, 11 May 2018.

157 Shane Harris, 'The CIA is returning its central focus to nation-state rivals, director says', *Washington Post*, 24 September 2018.

158 *China–Russia Relations*, p.5.

159 Bandurski, 'Yan Xuetong on the Bipolar state of our world, op.cit.'

160 Edward Luce, 'Henry Kissinger: "We are in a very, very grave period"', 20 July 2018.

161 Xinhua, 'Reform, opening up break new ground for China: article', 13 August 2018.

162 Clare Foges, 'Our timid leaders can learn from strongmen', *The Times*, 23 July 2018.

163 State Council Information Office, 'Full text: Xi Jinping's keynote speech at the World Economic Forum', 6 April 2017.

164 Reuters, 'Trump says tariffs could be applied to Chinese goods', 5 July 2018.

165 Frankopan, *Silk Roads*, xv.

166 Minnie Chan, 'China's army infiltrated by "peace disease" after years without a war, says its official newspaper', *South China Morning Post*, 3 July 2018.

167 US Department of Defense, *Military and Security Developments Involving the People's Republic of China* 2018, op. cit.

168 Jessica Donati. 'US signals it could sanction China over Iran oil imports', *Wall Street Journal*, 16 August 2018.

169 Rachel Adams-Heard and Nick Wadhams, 'China rejects US request to cut Iran oil imports', Bloomberg, 3 August 2018; Xinhua, 'Reform, opening up break new ground for China: article', 13 August 2018, op. cit.

170 Jia Xiudong, 'Deep understanding of the trade war allows China more composure', *People's Daily*, 10 August 2018.

171 Reuters, 'China paper warns it won't play defense on trade as Trump lauds tariffs', 17 September 2018.

172 Cheng Li, 'How China's Middle Class Views the Trade War', *Foreign Affairs*, 10 September 2018.

173 '許章潤, '我們當下的恐懼與期待'at https://theinitium.com/article/20180724-opinion-xuzhangrun-fear-hope/

174 Xinhua, 'Xi Jinping Thought on Socialism with Chinese Characteristics for a New Era', 17 March 2018.

175 Julian Gewirtz, 'Xi Jinping Thought Is Facing a Harsh Reality Check', *Foreign Policy*, 15 August 2018.

176 Jihad Azour, 'How to Spend a $210 Billion Oil Windfall', Bloomberg, 18 June 2018.

177 Andrew Entous, 'Israeli, Saudi and Emirati officials privately pushed for Trump to strike a "grand bargain" with Putin', *New Yorker*, 8 July 2018.

178 Bureau of Democracy, Human Rights and Labor, *Country Reports on Human Rights Practices for 2017* (2018), p. i.

Acknowledgements

Most books include a section of acknowledgements so the author can thank those who have helped them bring their book to life. Over the past few years I have made lots of new friends, been introduced to many interesting and helpful contacts and been able to rely on a generous network of commentators who work on some or all of the regions, peoples and topics that I am interested in. There are a small handful of friends and colleagues who have read some or all of what I have written here, several of whom prefer to be anonymous. I am grateful to those who have helped this project in one way or another – I hope you know who you are.

As always, I owe a debt of thanks to Catherine Clarke and her team at Felicity Bryan, and to my editor Michael Fishwick and all at Bloomsbury for giving me the support I wanted and needed to get this book written. I am thankful to Sarah Ruddick for her patience and guidance, and to Richard Collins for his eye for detail. Emma Ewbank has produced another cover that is simply magnificent.

My family have had to put up with me writing away at all hours when I've been at home, but also in between dashes to the airport and trips abroad in what has been a very busy last couple of years. I could not have done this without you, Jess, Katarina, Flora, Francis and Luke: thank you.

I also could not have done this without my parents, who taught me to walk, to read, to write and to think. They have been a source of love, laughter and encouragement for nearly five decades. They have always been there for me when I have needed them, and also when I have not.

My father fell seriously ill when I was writing this book. He was my role model; a man of profound courage, modesty and intelligence. Since I was a small boy, he encouraged me to read, to think and to focus on my studies. I spoke with him almost every single day for decades, often about history and also about the past, present and future of the Silk Roads.

He was not just a father to me, but also my hero and my friend. He was endlessly patient and selfless; he did anything and everything for me (and indeed for many others), and never asked for anything in return. He was a model of generosity, kindness and love.

His loss, just before this book was published, has been heartbreaking for me and my family. The very last time I saw him, I gave him the first copy of this book. He beamed at me and told me he could not wait to read it. I do not mind that he did not have the chance to do so; it is so painful though not to be able to see him and talk with him about it. This book is dedicated to my beloved father – whom I miss very much indeed.

ACKNOWLEDGEMENTS

I am extremely grateful to Sir Tim Rice and the Walt Disney Company for giving me permission to quote from the lyrics of 'A Whole New World' from Aladdin – a song about the past of the Silk Roads that foretells their future.

The Provost and Fellows of Worcester College and my many colleagues at Oxford have been extremely supportive and provide one of the most exhilarating environments for a scholar anywhere in the world. I am grateful for their encouragement and the home they provide.

I reserve a special place, though, for one friend in particular. Mark Whittow was one of the finest historians of his generation. He was an extraordinarily gifted scholar and a magnificent friend not only to me but to everyone who worked with, was taught by or met him in Oxford. Mark was a source of never-ending good humour and kindness, but, more importantly, he was an inspiration to me – first as my doctoral examiner many years ago, then as a senior colleague I looked up to and then as a collaborator. Mark's loss in an accident just before Christmas 2017 was devastating for Oxford, where to the delight of us all he had just been elected provost of Oriel College. He was so proud that I'd written *The Silk Roads* and that it had been so visible, and continued to encourage me not to fear stepping outside the academic world to talk to more general audiences from time to time. Mark would have said that writing a follow-up called *The New Silk Roads* was 'a giggle and a hoot'. I've had to remind myself of that a few times while writing this volume. I owe Mark a debt of gratitude that I can now never repay. But thank you, Mark, for all you did for me over the course of nearly thirty years.

Last but not least, I must thank those who read *The Silk Roads* when it came out. I have been amazed and delighted by the response to a history book that is not the shortest book that has ever been written, and thrilled that so many people wanted to look at the past from a different perspective. I hope this slim volume comes as a reward for those who carried the heavier original around with them.

I am especially grateful to those who recommended *The Silk Roads* to their friends, families and even to complete strangers. That, of course, is the finest testimony a book can have. I hope all who read this book enjoy it as much and again encourage others to read it. History matters for a reason. It helps explain why we are who we are and can teach useful lessons to help avoid making the same mistakes as in the past.

In that sense, I am delighted that this new edition appears at the same time as a new version of *The Silk Roads*, which is aimed at a younger audience. Those of school age grow up quickly (more quickly than ever, we are told in the press), but this is the world they will inherit and need to be able to make sense of. Reading is one way to help the next generation learn and think, but discussing the past is invaluable, too. I hope that both books help bring people together. Understanding history is not just interesting; it is also important.

Peter Frankopan

Oxford, September 2018

Index

A Note on the Author

Peter Frankopan is Professor of Global History at Oxford University where he is also Senior Research Fellow at Worcester College, Oxford, and Director at the Centre for Byzantine Research. He was Schiff Scholar at Jesus College, Cambridge, and Senior Scholar at Corpus Christi College, Oxford. He has been Stanley J. Seeger Fellow at Princeton, Scaliger Visiting Professor at Leiden and Presidential Scholar at the Getty Center in Los Angeles. His revised translation of *The Alexiad* by Anna Komnene was published by Penguin Classics in 2009. He is the author of *The First Crusade: The Call from the East* (2012) and *The Silk Roads: A New History of the World* (2015).

A Note on the Type

The text of this book is set in Adobe Garamond. It is one of several versions of Garamond based on the designs of Claude Garamond. It is thought that Garamond based his font on Bembo, cut in 1495 by Francesco Griffo in collaboration with the Italian printer Aldus Manutius. Garamond types were first used in books printed in Paris around 1532. Many of the present-day versions of this type are based on the *Typi Academiae* of Jean Jannon, cut in Sedan in 1615.

Claude Garamond was born in Paris in 1480. He learned how to cut type from his father and by the age of fifteen he was able to fashion steel punches the size of a pica with great precision. At the age of sixty he was commissioned by King Francis I to design a Greek alphabet, and for this he was given the honourable title of royal type founder. He died in 1561.

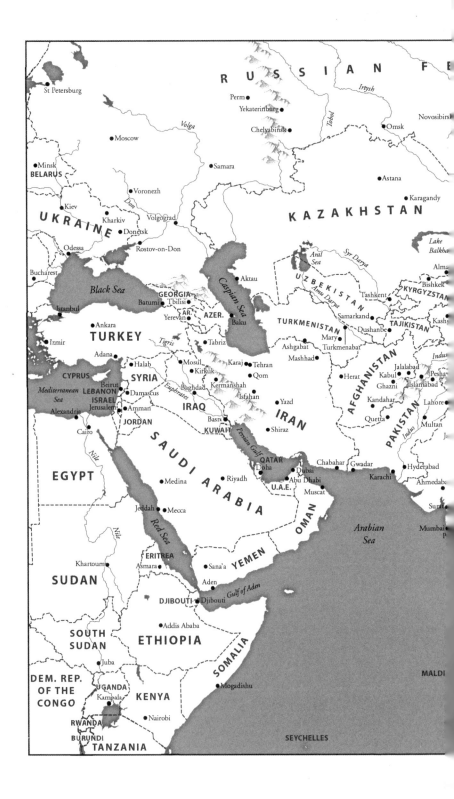